SOCIALISM AND WAR

F. A. HAYEK

THE COLLECTED WORKS OF

F. A. Hayek

SOCIALISM AND WAR

Essays, Documents, Reviews

F. A. HAYEK

Edited by Bruce Caldwell

Liberty Fund

INDIANAPOLIS

This book is published by Liberty Fund, Inc., a foundation established to encourage study of the ideal of a society of free and responsible individuals.

The cuneiform inscription that serves as our logo and as the design motif for our endpapers is the earliest-known written appearance of the word "freedom" (*amagi*), or "liberty." It is taken from a clay document written about 2300 B.C. in the Sumerian city-state of Lagash.

Socialism and War is volume 10 of The Collected Works of F. A. Hayek, published by The University of Chicago Press.

This Liberty Fund paperback edition of *Socialism and War* is published by arrangement with The University of Chicago Press and Taylor & Francis Books, Ltd., a member of the Taylor & Francis Group.

P   1   2   3   4   5   6   7   8   9   10

Library of Congress Cataloging-in-Publication Data

Hayek, Friedrich A. von (Friedrich August), 1899–1992.
Socialism and war: essays, documents, reviews/F. A. Hayek; edited by Bruce Caldwell.
p.   cm.—(The collected works of F. A. Hayek; v. 10)
Includes bibliographical references and indexes.
ISBN 978-0-86597-743-3 (pbk.: alk. paper)
1. War and socialism.   2. Economics.   I. Caldwell, Bruce, 1952—   II. Title.
HX545.H39   2009
335—dc22   2008028281

Liberty Fund, Inc.
8335 Allison Pointe Trail, Suite 300
Indianapolis, Indiana 46250-1684

Cover design by Erin Kirk New, Watkinsville, Georgia
Printed and bound by Thomson-Shore, Inc., Dexter, Michigan

THE COLLECTED WORKS OF F. A. HAYEK

Founding Editor: W. W. Bartley III
General Editor: Stephen Kresge
Associate Editor: Peter G. Klein
Assistant Editor: Gene Opton
Editor of the Spanish edition: Jesús Huerta de Soto

Published with the support of

The Hoover Institution on War, Revolution and Peace,
Stanford University

Anglo American and De Beers Chairman's Fund, Johannesburg

Cato Institute, Washington, D.C.

The Centre for Independent Studies, Sydney

Chung-Hua Institution for Economic Research, Taipei

Engenharia Comércio e Indústria S/A, Rio de Janeiro

Escuela Superior de Economia y Administración de Empresas
(ESEAD), Buenos Aires

The Heritage Foundation

The Institute for Humane Studies, George Mason University

Instituto Liberal, Rio de Janeiro

Charles G. Koch Charitable Foundation, Wichita

The Carl Menger Institute, Vienna

The Morris Foundation, Little Rock

Verband der Osterreichischen Banken und Bankiers, Vienna

The Wincott Foundation, London

The Bartley Institute, Oakland

To the memory of my mother, Maryann Caldwell, who died January 12, 1997, aged seventy-eight; the center of our family, her influence lives on in every member of it.

CONTENTS

PART III. *Planning, Freedom, and the Politics of Socialism*

EDITORIAL FOREWORD

The cry for control of economic means, for social planning and political direction of individual activity, is always loudest at moments of crisis when apparent limits of resources restrict the ambitions or compulsions of a nation. F. A. Hayek's heroic achievement is the consistent argument that these are the very times when liberty is most necessary. Advocacy of a free market comes easily to those who believe in an ever more abundant future; while those who can paint the vanishing point of dwindling resources have no trouble drawing plans for preferential use. Hayek demonstrated that it is precisely when there is great demand for a limited supply of given resources that knowledge of individual circumstances is crucial to determining the value of possible choices. Even in the midst of war, he has argued, it is more efficient to let individuals use the mechanism of a market to produce what is demanded than to impose controls upon them from a central plan that must be deficient in knowledge of individual capabilities.

The significance, so Hayek maintained, of the marginalist revolution in economic theory, and particularly the contribution of Carl Menger, came from the demonstration that economic value was to be found not merely in "man's relation to a particular thing or a class of things but the position of the thing in the whole means-end structure—the whole scheme by which men decide how to allocate the resources at their disposal among their different endeavours." The pursuit of war, on the other hand, is believed to require altogether different means, since the end—victory— is so compelling that it must be attained at whatever cost.

Even when the guns fall silent, the argument persists. The victors can point to the success of their plans, the losers to the failure to properly execute their plans: given any compelling objective, so it is claimed, an efficient means-end structure can be planned. Thus the compulsions of war are extended to such improbable domains as trade, drugs, and even gender, using some utilitarian calculus to determine the odds for casualties. War, it was said, is politics by other means. The logic of the argument for economic planning was believed to be beyond challenge. Hayek successfully made the challenge. He argued, and the failure of planned economies has demonstrated, that economics is neither politics nor engineering by other means.

Socialism and War, volume 10 of *The Collected Works of F. A. Hayek,* brings together Hayek's seminal contribution to the 'socialist calculation' debate with related essays and reviews from the crucible of the late 1930s and early 1940s. There are striking parallels between the period following the First World War and the present period of confusion after the undeclared end of the Cold War. There is one great difference: then it was capitalism that was apparently discredited, now it is socialism. We know now that in the first instance appearance was not reality; will the same prove true of socialism?

I would like to express my considerable appreciation to Bruce Caldwell for his clear and perceptive re-creation of the context of the original debate and of its continuing significance. We are grateful to Gene Opton for her careful preparation of the manuscript, and to Leif Wenar for his timely bibliographical assistance. Penelope Kaiserlian and Margaret Mahan of the University of Chicago Press and Alan Jarvis of Routledge have tactfully blended enthusiasm with patience to see this volume into print. *The Banker,* Blackwell Publishers for the *Economic Journal* and *Economica, Contemporary Review,* Macmillan Magazines Ltd. for *Nature,* Routledge, *The Spectator,* and the *University of Chicago Law Review* have kindly granted permission to reprint various of the essays and reviews here included. To the original sponsors of the Collected Works of F. A. Hayek project may we once again express our gratitude.

Stephen Kresge
Big Sur, California

INTRODUCTION

An odd pairing it seems at first, the conjoining of 'socialism' with 'war'. It would not have seemed so, though, for Friedrich A. Hayek. His most famous book, *The Road to Serfdom,*[1] was written during the Second World War and dedicated "To the socialists of all parties" in an attempt to cool the growing passion for state planning emerging at that time in Britain. Nor would Hayek's mentor, Ludwig von Mises, have found the association strange. Mises's first paper on socialism, which appeared in 1920, was a response to the view that the extensive economic planning undertaken during the First World War could and should be continued in peacetime. The seismic social upheavals produced by the two world wars (and, not incidentally, by the Depression that separated them) provided both opportunity and impetus for a variety of socialist experiments, from Soviet and Chinese Communism to National Socialism to an assortment of social democracies. In the twentieth century, socialism and war have been frequent cohabitants.

The papers and reviews collected in this volume document the lonely battle against socialism carried on by F. A. Hayek throughout the 1930s and 1940s. The materials, in roughly chronological order, cover three areas. First in order are his debates with the market socialists, which were carried on chiefly in British academic journals in the 1930s. Next come Hayek's responses to the onset of war, most of which appeared in short articles in weeklies and in book reviews. The third section contains a series of his papers examining the relationship between economic planning and freedom. Many of the reviews of the literature on capitalism and on the varieties of socialism that Hayek wrote during this crucial period are gathered in an Appendix to this volume.

The purpose of this introduction is to provide background for the materials collected here. The discussions that Mises participated in a genera-

---

[1]F. A. Hayek, *The Road to Serfdom* (London: Routledge and Kegan Paul; Chicago: University of Chicago Press, 1944; 50th Anniversary Edition, with a New Introduction by Milton Friedman, University of Chicago Press, 1994).

tion earlier provided the groundwork for Hayek's contributions to the market socialism debates, so we will examine them first. While the seeds of what would become Hayek's 'knowledge-based' critique of socialism are present in essays published in 1935, it was only after his exchange with Oskar Lange that they reached their mature form. Among Hayek's wartime contributions collected in the next section, special emphasis is given to Hayek's reaction to, and further development of, John Maynard Keynes's proposals in *How to Pay for the War.*[2] If his new emphasis on knowledge forever changed the way that Hayek viewed economics, an equally important part of his 1930s transformation was his move away from economics proper and towards social theory. Hayek's 1944 book *The Road to Serfdom* constitutes the most widely known evidence of this change of direction. But work on that book had begun by the late 1930s, and his progress can be traced in the papers gathered in part 3. As will be shown in the final part of the introduction, Hayek's path was much influenced by his desire to refute the claims of his opponents—in this instance virtually all of the British intelligentsia and in particular those who believed that the rational scientific planning of society provides the only means for ensuring the preservation of freedom.

1. German Language Debates on Socialism

Until the turn of the century, Continental Marxism was closely identified with German Social Democracy. Its statement of principles was the Gotha Program of 1875, in which various of Marx's doctrines were combined with the more moderate ideas of one of his chief rivals, Ferdinand Lassalle (much to the consternation of Marx himself). In 1891 the Erfurt Program, with Karl Kautsky the principal architect, superseded the Gotha Program. It marked a return to the more revolutionary, and hence more purely Marxian, socialist vision. The consensus was not to last long. At the end of the decade, Eduard Bernstein published *Die Voraussetzungen des Sozialismus.*[3] Influenced by his experience with the English Fabian socialists, Bernstein questioned Marx's theoretical edifice, as well as a number of his predictions, and touted an evolutionary rather than revolutionary path to the socialist future. Bernstein's vision directly contradicted that of Kautsky; the first revisionist controversy had begun. The second

---

[2]J. M. Keynes, *How to Pay for the War,* reprinted in *Essays in Persuasion,* vol. 9 (1972) of *The Collected Writings of John Maynard Keynes,* Austin Robinson and Donald Moggridge, eds, 30 vols (London: Macmillan, for the Royal Economic Society, 1971–89), pp. 367–439.

[3]Eduard Bernstein, *Die Voraussetzungen des Sozialismus und die Aufgaben der Sozialdemokratie* (Stuttgart: Dietz, 1899), translated as *Evolutionary Socialism: A Criticism and an Affirmation* (New York: Huebsch, 1909; reprinted, New York: Schocken, 1961).

would come two decades later when Lenin split from Kautsky. This resulted in the great schism between Soviet-style Communism (with its ultimate dedication to revolution and extensive central planning) and German-style Social Democracy (which was more gradualist, and whose proponents tended to endorse variants of market socialism). The many divisions within Marxism meant that anyone who chose to criticize 'socialism' confronted a Hydra rather than a monolith. To be effective, the argument against socialism had to be a general one.

Another type of Marxist thought emerged at the turn of the century, this one from within the Austro-Hungarian Empire. Austro-Marxists retained a theoretical adherence to Marx's writings and, influenced by the physicist Ernst Mach,[4] were taken with the idea that Marxism constituted a truly 'scientific' approach to the study of social phenomena.[5]

The third volume of Marx's *Das Kapital* appeared in 1894, eleven years after its author's death. Advocates hoped that the final book would resolve certain key problems with the labour theory of value that were evident in the earlier volumes. In 1896, the Austrian economist Eugen von Böhm-Bawerk offered a comprehensive assessment of Marx's system and concentrated on the Marxian theory of value.[6] The title of the English translation, *Karl Marx and the Close of His System,* arguably carries a double meaning. The original German reads, "The *Completion* of the Marxian System", indicating that Böhm-Bawerk's essay was simply meant as a response to Marx's now finally completed trilogy. But Böhm- Bawerk's closing sentence, in which Marx is compared to Hegel, makes evident his intent to bring on the collapse of the Marxian edifice: "The specific theoretical work of each was a most ingeniously conceived structure, built up by a fabulous power of combination, of innumerable storeys of thought,

---

[4]For Hayek's view of Mach's influence, see his essay "Ernst Mach (1838–1916) and the Social Sciences in Vienna", reprinted as chapter 7 of *The Fortunes of Liberalism,* ed. Peter Klein, which constitutes vol. 4 (1992) of *The Collected Works of F. A. Hayek* (Chicago: University of Chicago Press, and London: Routledge), pp. 172–175. Compare his remarks in *Hayek on Hayek,* Stephen Kresge and Leif Wenar, eds (Chicago: University of Chicago Press, and London: Routledge, 1994), p. 47.

[5]The attempt by Viennese groups like the Austro-Marxists (as well as the psychoanalysts) to claim the mantle of science for their systems provoked Karl Popper to try to provide a criterion to demarcate science from pseudo-science; see his "Intellectual Autobiography", in vol. 1 of *The Philosophy of Karl Popper,* ed. Paul Schilpp (LaSalle, Ill.: Open Court, 1974), pp. 23–33.

[6]Eugen von Böhm-Bawerk, "Zum Abschluss des Marxschen Systems", in *Staatswissenschaftliche Arbeiten: Festgaben für Karl Knies,* ed. Otto von Boenigk (Berlin: Haering, 1896), translated as *Karl Marx and the Close of His System* (London: Fisher Unwin, 1898) and reprinted in *Karl Marx and the Close of His System and Böhm-Bawerk's Criticism of Marx,* ed. Paul Sweezy (New York: Kelley, 1949; reprinted, 1975).

held together by a marvelous mental grasp, but—a house of cards".[7] The most important reply to Böhm-Bawerk's critique came in 1904 from Rudolf Hilferding, a leader of the Austro-Marxists, in the first issue of the Marxist periodical *Marx-Studien,* which he co-edited with Max Adler.[8]

At about the same time that Hilferding's article appeared, Böhm-Bawerk returned to teach at the University of Vienna, after many years of government service (including three periods as Finance Minister). For the next decade he conducted a seminar in economics, a gathering that remains noteworthy in the history of economics. Participants included Böhm-Bawerk's young critic Rudolf Hilferding, who published *Das Finanz-kapital* in 1910, perhaps the most important work in Marxian economic theory in the twentieth century;[9] Otto Bauer, political theorist of the Austro-Marxists who, at the conclusion of the First World War, became the leader of the Austrian Social Democrats; Emil Lederer, who became the first Dean of the Graduate Faculty of Political and Social Science at the New School for Social Research; the brilliant young economist Joseph Schumpeter;[10] the sociologist Otto Neurath, who became one of the leading members of the Vienna Circle of Logical Positivists in the 1920s; and finally Ludwig von Mises, who, though trained in the style of the historical school economists, embraced the doctrines of his teacher and in 1912

---

[7]Böhm-Bawerk, *Karl Marx and the Close of His System,* op. cit., p. 118.

[8]Rudolf Hilferding, "Böhm-Bawerk's Marx-Kritik", *Marx-Studien,* vol. 1, 1904, pp. 1–61, translated as *Böhm-Bawerk's Criticism of Marx,* reprinted in *Karl Marx and the Close of His System and Böhm-Bawerk's Criticism of Marx,* op. cit., pp. 121–196.

[9]Rudolf Hilferding, *Das Finanzkapital* (Vienna: I. Brand, 1910); translated as *Finance Capital* (London: Routledge and Kegan Paul, 1980). M. C. Howard and J. E. King, in their *A History of Marxian Economics, Volume I 1883–1929* (Princeton: Princeton University Press, 1989), p. 100, judge *Finance Capital* "the most influential text in the entire history of Marxian political economy, only excepting *Capital* itself".

[10]Schumpeter's early works included *Das Wesen und der Hauptinhalt der Theoretischen Nationalökonomie* (Leipzig: Duncker & Humblot, 1908); *Theorie der wirtschaftlichen Entwicklung* (Leipzig: Duncker & Humblot, 1912), translated by Redvers Opie as *The Theory of Economic Development* (Cambridge, Mass.: Harvard University Press, 1934; reprinted, New York: Oxford University Press, 1961); and *Epochen der Dogmen- und Methodengeschichte, Grundriss der Sozialökonomik,* vol. 1, part 1, first ed. (Tübingen: J. C. B. Mohr, 1914), translated by R. Aris as *Economic Doctrine and Method, An Historical Sketch* (New York: Oxford University Press, 1954). The first contained a variety of methodological insights as well as praise for the Walrasian variant of marginal analysis; Schumpeter would in his *History of Economic Analysis* (New York: Oxford University Press, 1954), p. 827, call Walras "the greatest of all economists", a remark sufficient in itself to remove him from the pantheon of Austrian School economists. His second book contained a theory of capitalist development, and the last book foreshadowed his lifelong interest in the history of ideas. For Hayek's assessment of Schumpter, see chapter 5 of *The Fortunes of Liberalism,* op. cit., pp. 160–165.

published his classic contribution to monetary theory, *Theorie des Geldes und der Umlaufsmittel.*[11]

Mises reminisced in his memoirs about the first semester's meetings of Böhm-Bawerk's seminar. His respect for other members of the seminar, even those with whom he sharply disagreed, is evident.

> As the subject matter of the first seminar Böhm-Bawerk chose the fundamentals of the theory of value. From his Marxian position, Otto Bauer sought to dissect the subjectivism of the Austrian value theory. With the other members of the seminar in the background, the discussion between Bauer and Böhm-Bawerk filled the whole winter semester. Bauer's intellect was very impressive; he was a worthy opponent of the great master whose critique had mortally wounded Marxian economics.[12]

But while he praised Böhm-Bawerk and his rivals, Mises excoriated one member of the group.

> Böhm-Bawerk was a brilliant seminar leader. He did not think of himself as a teacher, but as a chairman who occasionally participated in the discussion. Unfortunately, the extraordinary freedom to speak which he granted to every member was occasionally abused by thoughtless talkers. Especially disturbing was the nonsense which Otto Neurath presented with fanatical fervor.[13]

Otto Neurath, who was born in Vienna in 1882, received his doctorate in Berlin, then returned to Vienna to teach at the Neue Wiener Handelsakademie. In 1909 he began publishing articles on the subject of 'war economy', that is, how to run an economy under conditions of modern

[11]Ludwig von Mises, *Theorie des Geldes und der Umlaufsmittel* (Munich and Leipzig: Duncker & Humblot, 1912), 2nd edition translated by H. E. Batson as *The Theory of Money and Credit* (London: Cape, 1934; reprinted, Indianapolis, Ind.: LibertyClassics, 1981). Hayek said of the seminar, "There is no doubt that the foundations of Mises's characteristic ideas on socialism were laid then. . . ."; see his Foreword to Ludwig von Mises, *Socialism: An Economic and Sociological Analysis,* reprinted in chapter 4 of *The Fortunes of Liberalism,* op. cit., pp. 136–143.

[12]Ludwig von Mises, *Notes and Recollections* (South Holland, Ill.: Libertarian Press, 1978), pp. 39–40.

[13]*Ibid.,* p. 40.

warfare. He argued that the continued use of a peacetime market economy would hinder the pursuit of military objectives, that only with centralized control could a successful war effort be mounted. Otto Neurath thus was one of the first to link socialism explicitly with war.

His efforts continued at the end of the First World War.[14] By then his theses were, first, that the experience of the war had demonstrated that the efficient central planning of a complex economy was feasible, and, second, that a concern for justice dictated that such planning should be continued now that the fighting had stopped. Neurath envisioned the full socialization of the economy. A 'central office for measurement in kind' would be set up that would run the economy as if it were one giant enterprise. Planning and administration authorities would make extensive use of statistics to guide them in their decision-making.

Perhaps most controversially, Neurath believed that money would be unnecessary in the new planned order. Calculation regarding the appropriate inputs and outputs of goods would be handled in physical terms. For the determination of societal needs, various statistics measuring demographic and social variables would be employed. In Neurath's opinion, the real needs of society could not be measured in money terms. The monetary system was uncontrolled and disorderly. Any attempt to employ monetary calculations within a planned society would render impossible scientific economic management, which had to be conducted in terms of 'real' physical quantities.

In 1919 Neurath served as the President of the Central Planning Office of the short-lived Bavarian Soviet Republic. Returning to Austria, he became in 1924 the Director of the Social and Economic Museum, one of the showplaces of the 'Red Vienna'[15] of the 1920s. Visitors to the museum observed Neurath's ISOTYPE system (the International System of Typographical Picture Education), a collection of images meant to represent economic and social conditions. He also participated in the Vienna Circle, where he advocated physicalism, the doctrine that all scientific statements must make a reference to phenomena that are observable and,

---

[14]See Otto Neurath, *Durch die Kriegswirtschaft zur Naturalwirtschaft* (Munich: Georg D. W. Callwey, 1919), which collects a number of his articles. The table of contents and selected articles are translated and appear as chapter 5 of Otto Neurath, *Empiricism and Sociology*, Marie Neurath and Robert S. Cohen, eds (Dordrecht, Holland: D. Reidel, 1973). The title is translated there as "Through War Economy to Economy in Kind". *Naturalwirtschaft* can also be translated as 'barter economy' or 'natural economy'.

[15]Though they took part in two coalition governments directly after the war ended, the Austrian Social Democratic Party fell from power nationally in June 1920. After that, their stronghold was in large urban centers, and Vienna became the centerpiece for various socialist experiments, hence the epithet.

when feasible, quantifiable.[16] Neurath fled Vienna in 1934, ultimately settling in Oxford, where he died in December 1945.

Neurath's apparently disparate projects were actually all of a piece. His insistence that non-monetary statistics be used to manage a planned economy led naturally to the development of ISOTYPE. The ISOTYPE system, in which signs represent social reality, was itself a practical analog to the Logical Positivist assertion that scientific theories are nothing more than formal systems of signs, rules for their manipulation, and 'correspondence rules' which link up the signs to elements of phenomenal reality. Neurath's physicalism was wholly compatible with the view that statistical information on physical quantities of goods and on 'life dispositions' are all that is needed to scientifically manage a complex economy. It was also a good antidote to the 'metaphysical' view that a monetary order expresses through prices such subjective 'entities' as 'utility' and 'value'.

According to Hayek, it was Neurath's book that "provoked" Ludwig von Mises to initiate the socialist calculation debate.[17] Mises wrote about socialism in a book published in 1919, and though Neurath is not mentioned by name, there is no mistaking his ideas, nor Mises's reaction to them: "Right at the beginning of the war a catchword turned up whose unfortunate consequences cannot be completely overlooked even today: the verbal fetish 'war economy'."[18] Mises argued that 'war socialism', widely credited for helping the war effort, in fact hindered it; that while "statism sought to avoid the inevitable collapse, it only hastened it."[19]

Mises's main contribution to the calculation debate came in a journal article published the next year. He took as a starting premise that under socialism all 'production-goods' (factors of production) are owned by the state, and that as such there is no market for them. But this has substantial consequences:

> . . . because no production-good will ever become the object of exchange, it will be impossible to determine its monetary value. Money could never fill in a socialist state the role it fills in a competitive society

[16]For more on the doctrines of the Vienna Circle, see Bruce Caldwell, *Beyond Positivism: Economic Methodology in the Twentieth Century* (London: Allen and Unwin, 1982; reprinted, London: Routledge, 1994), chapter 1.

[17]F. A. Hayek, Foreword to Mises, *Socialism*, in *The Fortunes of Liberalism*, op. cit., p. 139.

[18]Ludwig von Mises, *Nation, Staat und Wirtschaft: Beiträge zur Politik und Geschichte der Zeit* (Vienna: Manz'sche Verlags und Universitäts-Buchhandlung, 1919), translated by Leland Yeager as *Nation, State and Economy: Contributions to the Politics and History of Our Time* (New York and London: New York University Press, 1983), p. 140.

[19]*Ibid.*, p. 147.

in determining the value of production-goods. Calculation in terms of money will here be impossible.[20]

Mises's reasoning was straightforward. In a market economy, entrepreneurs choose from among innumerable possible combinations of factors of production in an attempt to find the combination that minimizes their expected costs. They do this in an attempt to maximize their profits, which is the difference between revenues and costs. This self-interested search for the best combination helps to guide resources to their highest-valued uses, an outcome beneficial to society as a whole. Because of the multiplicity of production-goods and the fact that production takes place through time (during which all manner of changes on both the demand and the supply side of the market might occur), the task is not an easy one. Entrepreneurs are aided in their deliberations by the money prices attached to the factors which reflect their relative scarcity. But in the socialist state no such prices would exist. Socialist managers would not have recourse to price signals to tell them which factors are relatively scarce and which relatively plentiful; they would be left "groping in the dark". The results were plain to see: "Where there is no free market, there is no pricing mechanism; without a pricing mechanism, there is no economic calculation."[21]

The contrast between two views could hardly be greater. Neurath argued that the use of money undermined the rational management of a planned economy. Mises, the monetary theorist, argued that in the absence of market-generated money prices to direct the allocation of resources, the rational planning of production (by which he meant, planning that attempts to avoid wasting resources) in a complex economy is impossible. Mises's article also makes clear that the two apparently unrelated subjects under discussion (monetary theory and socialism) are in fact intimately linked. He spends a number of pages examining the limitations of money as a tool for measuring value, noting that its own value need not be stable, and that many aspects of life are not subject to monetary calculation. Only when the value of money is itself stable will prices accurately reflect relative scarcities and thereby help to guide production. For Mises, sound money and freely adjusting relative prices go hand in hand in making a private enterprise system work. Neurath wanted to do

[20]Ludwig von Mises, "Die Wirtschaftsrechnung im sozialistischen Gemeinwessen", *Archiv für Sozialwissenschaft*, vol. 47, 1920, pp. 86–121, translated by S. Adler as "Economic Calculation in the Socialist Commonwealth", in *Collectivist Economic Planning*, ed. Friedrich A. Hayek (London: Routledge and Sons, 1935; reprinted, Clifton, N. J.: Kelley, 1975), p. 92.

[21]*Ibid.*, p. 11.

away with all of it and justified his views by invoking principles of scientific management.

Mises's article bears close reading. His statement that "No single man can master all the possibilities of production, innumerable as they are, so as to be in a position to make straightway evident judgements of value without the aid of some system of computation"[22] is suggestive of Hayek's later arguments about the dispersion of knowledge. In a like manner, his brief paragraph stating that calculation would be unnecessary in the 'static state' foreshadows Hayek's argument that his opponents are blinded by an unhealthy preoccupation with the conditions of static equilibrium.[23] Finally, in the section entitled "Responsibility and Initiative in Communal Concerns", Mises discusses a number of incentive problems that exist under socialism, most of them due to the absence of private property.[24]

It is not surprising that in the debate with Neurath, Ludwig von Mises very quickly won the day; most socialists of the time agreed with him that Neurath's scheme of a moneyless planned economy was fundamentally flawed.[25] This was doubtless in part due to the clear and horrifying evidence provided by Soviet policies during the period of 'War Communism' from May, 1918, through the end of 1920.[26] But Neurath was not the only person calling for planning based on the wartime model. Had that

[22]*Ibid.*, p. 102.

[23]*Ibid.*, pp. 109–110. This is not to say that the positions of Mises and Hayek are identical. Indeed, a debate has arisen recently among Austrian scholars as to whether one of the positions (either Mises's "calculation based on property rights" critique or Hayek's "knowledge-based" one) should be viewed as more fundamental. See Joseph T. Salerno, "Ludwig von Mises as Social Rationalist", *The Review of Austrian Economics*, vol. 4, 1990, pp. 26–54, and Leland Yeager, "Mises and Hayek on Calculation and Knowledge", *The Review of Austrian Economics*, vol. 7, 1994, pp. 91–107.

[24]*Ibid.*, pp. 116–122.

[25]Thus, for example, Helene Bauer, Otto Bauer's wife, attacked Neurath by citing Marxist literature; Otto Leichter proposed that calculations in a centralized economy be made in terms of labour-hours. See Günther Chaloupek, "The Austrian Debate on Economic Calculation in a Socialist Society", *History of Political Economy*, vol. 22, no. 4, Winter 1990, especially pp. 662–670.

[26]Policies enacted during the period of 'State Capitalism' (which directly preceded the 'War Communism' episode) were explicitly drawn from German *Kriegwirtschaft* models. Peter Boettke, in *The Political Economy of Soviet Socialism: The Formative Years, 1918–1928* (Boston: Kluwer, 1990), p. 106, notes that, for Lenin, "the Soviet dictatorship of the proletariat provides the political basis for social transformation, while the German war-planning machine provides the economic basis". Under War Communism the first steps towards the abolition of money were instituted. For more on this, see Eugène Zaleski, *Planning for Economic Growth in the Soviet Union, 1918–1932* (Chapel Hill, N. C.: University of North Carolina Press, 1971), pp. 13–24.

been the case, Mises would probably not have felt the necessity of writing a whole book devoted to the refutation of socialism.[27]

Socialization schemes were in fact being proposed everywhere, and not just by socialists. One of the most widely respected voices was that of the German industrialist Walther Rathenau. During the war he was instrumental in setting up a new division at the Ministry of War, the KRA (*Kriegsrohstoffabteilung*), or Raw Materials Section, which made raw materials procurement secure for much of the duration. The KRA became for many social democrats the model of what could be accomplished through efficient central planning. Rathenau, a successful industrialist and a man of action, was also an urbane intellect. He wrote an influential pamphlet published in 1918 in which the variety of goods available under capitalism was portrayed as indicative of the system's great wastefulness.[28] Rathenau argued that far greater amounts of standardized goods could be produced (thereby ensuring plenty for all) if centrally controlled mass production techniques developed during the war were utilized. Given his role in the war, Walther Rathenau was a hero to the German-speaking people in a period when precious few heroes were to be found.[29] That he was bourgeois rather than socialist, and one who spoke from experience, added further to his credibility. This progressive Jewish internationalist was assassinated by right-wing thugs soon after becoming Foreign Minister. Instead of playing a leading role in the Weimar Republic, he ended up a harbinger of the world that was to come.

2. Hayek and the Socialist Calculation Debate

F. A. Hayek, born in Vienna in 1899, was too young to have attended Böhm-Bawerk's seminar and knew him only as an occasional guest at the home of his grandparents. After war service, Hayek entered the University of Vienna, receiving degrees in 1921 and 1923. While working on his second doctoral degree he came to know Ludwig von Mises, with whom he worked in a temporary government office. At the time, Mises was known principally as a monetary theorist and a champion of sound money. Within the year, Mises's massive tome on socialism had appeared. As Hayek says in a preface to a later edition, the book "gradually but

---

[27]Ludwig von Mises, *Die Gemeinwirtschaft: Untersuchungen über den Sozialismus* (Jena: Gustav Fischer, 1922), 2nd edition translated by J. Kahane as *Socialism: An Economic and Sociological Analysis* (London: Cape, 1936; reprinted, Indianapolis, Ind.: Liberty*Classics*, 1981). Mises criticizes socialism from a number of different perspectives in the book.

[28]Walter Rathenau, *Die neue Wirtschaft* (Berlin: S. Fischer, 1918).

[29]Hayek mentions the pamphlets of Rathenau and of Karl Renner as providing his first exposure to economic and social analysis; see F. A. Hayek, *Hayek on Hayek*, op. cit., p. 47.

fundamentally altered the outlook of many of the young idealists returning to their university studies after World War I".[30]

Hayek wrote nothing about socialism during the 1920s. He worked mainly on monetary theory, developing his own version of the Austrian theory of the trade cycle, one that drew upon the earlier writings of the Swedish economist Knut Wicksell as well as those of Mises. On the basis of this work, Hayek was invited by Lionel Robbins to deliver a series of lectures at the London School of Economics (LSE) in the spring of 1931. By the next year he had been appointed to the Tooke Chair of Economic Science and Statistics at the LSE, a position he would hold (except for a semester at the University of Arkansas) until he moved to the University of Chicago in 1950.[31] Hayek's immediate task was to challenge the rival cycle theory of John Maynard Keynes, which the latter had presented in *A Treatise on Money*, published late in 1930.[32]

Although England provided a physical sanctuary for socialist revolutionaries like Marx and Engels, Marxist doctrine found few supporters there, even among members of socialist societies such as the Fabian Society. The Fabian Society began in 1884 as a small discussion group and counted among its founders Sidney Webb, George Bernard Shaw, and Graham Wallas. The Fabians debated the merits of Marxian analysis at some of the earliest meetings. But most were dissatisfied, and soon thereafter the economists Philip Wicksteed and F. Y. Edgeworth were invited to explain to the group the new marginalist analysis of Stanley Jevons. The Fabians ultimately accepted the marginalist theory of value and attempted to work out a socialist program based on marginalist principles. In addition to this difference over theoretical issues, an adherence to parliamentary democracy, to 'socialism of the ballot box', also separated British socialists from Marxists. Fabians finally believed in 'the inevitability of gradualness', in an evolutionary rather than revolutionary transformation of society: their name, after all, was taken from the Roman general Fabius Maximus, "Cunctator", famed for his holding tactics.

The political equivalent in Britain of the various Continental Social Democratic parties was the Labour party. Officially formed in 1906, it was little more than a lobbying group in the prewar years; indeed, the

---

[30]F. A. Hayek, Foreword to Mises, *Socialism*, in *The Fortunes of Liberalism*, op. cit., p. 136.

[31]For more on Hayek in the 1920s and 1930s, see F. A. Hayek, *Hayek on Hayek*, op. cit., pp. 64–98; "The Economics of the 1920s as Seen from Vienna", in *The Fortunes of Liberalism*, op. cit., pp. 19–38; "The Economics of the 1930s as Seen from London", in *Contra Keynes and Cambridge: Essays and Correspondence*, ed. Bruce Caldwell, vol. 9 1995) of *The Collected Works of F. A. Hayek*, op. cit., pp. 49–63 and the Introduction.

[32]J. M. Keynes, *A Treatise on Money* [1930], reprinted as vols 5 and 6 (1971) of *The Collected Writings of John Maynard Keynes*, op. cit.

other two major parties (the Conservatives and the Liberals) themselves passed a substantial amount of social legislation in the first decade as they vied against each other for the workers' votes. After the First World War there were some electoral successes, as minority Labour governments formed under the leadership of Ramsay MacDonald in 1923 and again in 1929.

A major question facing the party during the interwar period was how to bring together a coherent program that would reflect the views of its various constituencies. Intellectual groups like the Fabians wanted to replace markets with an efficient administrative bureaucracy composed of experts, while the trade unions had the improvement of the lot of workers as their principal goal. Guild Socialists, whose intellectual leaders included G. D. H. Cole and R. H. Tawney, wanted to found a new society in which there existed worker control of industry and collective ownership of the means of production. Finally, many who were drawn to socialism had no clearly articulated vision of the future, but were driven more by a deeply held resentment of the British class structure and the economic inequities that accompanied it.

The postwar economy in Britain was moribund, a situation not unfavourable to the growth of radical thought. Throughout the 1920s the unemployment rate hovered in the 10 per cent range. Labour unrest grew, culminating in a general strike in 1926. It was during this period that the Liberal economist John Maynard Keynes began to formulate his own set of remedies for rescuing the British economy, remedies that would in the next decade come to be considered necessary palliatives for the saving of capitalism itself. Keynes's was a minority view; neither the Labour nor the Conservative parties would deviate from the 'sound finance' doctrines of the 'Treasury view'. Only the Liberal party accepted the interventionist heresies of Keynes and Lloyd George, and for this they were repudiated in the 1929 general elections.

The Great Depression caused the unemployment rate to rise even higher and allowed socialists to add to their arguments against capitalism. Socialists had always considered the market system unjust. Now it appeared to be inefficient and unstable as well. The English socialist Barbara Wootton observed in 1934 a "shift of contemporary interest from the wickedness to the stupidity of our economic organization", and noted with some incredulity that even G. D. H. Cole was now writing "not so much of wrongs as of muddles".[33] The time seemed right for a search for alternatives.

In the late 1920s and early 1930s articles began to appear in English-language economics journals arguing that rational calculation under so-

---

[33]Barbara Wootton, *Plan or No Plan* (London: V. Gollancz, 1934), pp. 104–105.

cialism was at least theoretically possible. Particularly important was a 1933 article by H. D. Dickinson.[34] Dickinson cited a paper originally published in 1908 by the Italian economist Enrico Barone in support of the notion that any economy, whether socialist or capitalist, can be represented mathematically by a system of equations, an approach made famous by the founders of the Lausanne School, Léon Walras and Vilfredo Pareto. Within a capitalist system the equations are "solved" by the market. Within a socialist system they are solved by the planning authorities. On a theoretical level, Dickinson concluded, there is no difference between the two systems. This was the first step in any successful defense of socialism on economic grounds.[35] The next would be to show that the socialist state is able to avoid the distributional inequities and cyclical disturbances that apparently plague a free market system.

Hayek's first contribution to the English-language debate was his inaugural address at the LSE, "The Trend of Economic Thinking", delivered in March 1933 and published two months later in *Economica*.[36] Hayek did not bring up the topic of calculation; as is usually the case with such talks, his themes were broader. The question he set out to answer was: Why did contemporary public opinion on economic issues differ so dramatically from that held by professional economists like himself? Hayek answered that the cleavage had originated some seventy years earlier, when historicalist criticisms of the (admittedly crude) theories of the classical economists were broadened into a general attack on the use of theory in the social sciences. This questioning of the validity of theory had had a number of adverse effects. The most consequential of these was a decline in understanding of how the market mechanism works: Too few realized any longer that "we are a part of a 'higher' organized system which, without our knowledge, and long before we tried to understand it, solved problems the existence of which we did not even recognize, but which we should have had to solve in much the same way if we had tried to run it deliberately".[37] By failing to understand how the market solves these

[34]H. D. Dickinson, "Price Formation in a Socialist Economy", *Economic Journal,* vol. 43, June 1933, pp. 237–250. He also argued that, were the prices not correct, a trial and error process of adjustment could be used to obtain the right ones.

[35]Not all on the left were pleased with Dickinson's claims. For example, the Marxist academic Maurice Dobb in his article "Economic Theory and the Problem of a Socialist Economy", *Economic Journal,* vol. 43, December 1933, pp. 588–598, denied that socialist and capitalist economies were governed by the same principles.

[36]F. A. Hayek, "The Trend of Economic Thinking", which is chapter 1 of *The Trend of Economic Thinking,* W. W. Bartley and Stephen Kresge, eds, vol. 3 (1991) of *The Collected Works of F. A. Hayek,* op. cit., pp. 17–34. Many themes in this address re-emerge in Hayek's later work; for more on this, see Bruce Caldwell, "Hayek's 'The Trend of Economic Thinking'", *Review of Austrian Economics,* vol. 2, 1987, pp. 175–178.

[37]F. A. Hayek, "The Trend of Economic Thinking", op. cit., pp. 27–28.

problems, many had been led to conclude that only by deliberate planning would an economy be capable of functioning efficiently and justly. Near the end of his talk Hayek noted the linkage between planning and socialism:

> I have discussed planning here rather than its older brother socialism, not because I think that there is any difference between them (except for the greater consistency of the latter), but because most of the planners do not yet realize that they are socialists and that, therefore, what the economist has to say with regard to socialism applies also to them. In this sense, there are, of course, very few people left today who are not socialists. . . .[W]hatever we may think about particular problems, there can be no doubt that recent additions to knowledge in this respect have made the probability of a solution of our difficulties by planning appear less, rather than more, likely.[38]

Not long afterward, Hayek shared with his English-language audience the content of some of those recent additions to knowledge in the 1935 publication *Collectivist Economic Planning: Critical Studies on the Possibilities of Socialism*, which he edited.[39] The book contained translations of three articles, including an early (1907) article by the Dutch economist N. G. Pierson on "The Problem of Value in the Socialist Community", Mises's "Economic Calculation in the Socialist Commonwealth", and "Further Considerations on the Possibility of Adequate Calculation in a Socialist Community", a review by the German economist Georg Halm of the Continental literature since Mises. Hayek provided introductory and concluding essays to the book; these constitute the first and second chapters of this volume.

In the introductory essay, Hayek reiterates certain themes from the "Trends" essay, pointing out the origins and current ubiquity of the unfortunate notion that planning is necessary for a rational allocation of resources. He also notes how difficult it is to define 'socialism', and ultimately settles on "public ownership of the means of production" as its essential characteristic. The primary purpose of the chapter is to review the Continental debates, placing the writings of the proponents of various socialization schemes (among those mentioned are Kautsky, Neurath, Bauer, Lederer, and Rathenau) and those of their opponents in context. One of the opponents is Boris Brutzkus, a Russian economist who, writ-

---

[38]*Ibid.*, p. 32; p. 33.
[39]*Collectivist Economic Planning*, ed. F. A. Hayek, op. cit.

ing in the aftermath of the Revolution, independently came to substantially the same conclusions as Mises regarding calculation.[40]

Hayek's concluding essay, reprinted as chapter 2 of this volume, is titled, "The Present State of the Debate". Hayek first evaluates the 'Russian experiment', which he deems a failure, citing Brutzkus in support. He next moves to the 'mathematical solution' of Dickinson and others, in which the central planning board would, in essence, solve a giant system of equations for the relevant prices and quantities. About this Hayek states:

> Now it must be admitted that this is not an impossibility in the sense that it is logically contradictory. But to argue that a determination of prices by such a procedure being logically conceivable in any way invalidates the contention that it is not a possible solution only proves that the real nature of the problem has not been perceived.[41]

Hayek then enumerates a variety of obstacles that would hinder the implementation of the mathematical solution: the staggering amount of information that would need to be gathered; the immense difficulty of formulating the correct system of equations; the hundreds of thousands of equations that would then need to be solved, not just once but repeatedly; the inability of such a system to adapt to change. He notes that although the "theoretical abstractions used in the explanation of equilibrium include the assumption that a certain range of technical knowledge is 'given'", it is "absurd" to think that the necessary knowledge is anywhere already "'in existence' in this readymade form".[42] In making his case, Hayek also pointedly includes a translation of Barone's 1908 article as an appendix to *Collectivist Economic Planning*. Since socialists had begun to cite the article in support of their own arguments, Hayek thought it useful to provide Barone's own words on the matter:

> For the solution of the problem it is not enough that the Ministry of Production has arrived at tracing out for itself the system of equations

---

[40]Boris Brutzkus, *Economic Planning in Soviet Russia* (London: Routledge and Sons, 1935; reprinted, Westport, Conn.: Hyperion Press, 1981). As Hayek notes, Brutzkus's book appeared in 1935 as a kind of companion volume to *Collectivist Economic Planning*. Hayek's Foreword to Brutzkus appears as an addendum to chapter 1, this volume.

[41]F. A. Hayek, "The Present State of the Debate", this volume, p. 93.

[42]*Ibid.*, p. 95.

best adapted for obtaining the collective maximum. . . .It is necessary to solve the equations afterwards. And that is the problem.

Many of the writers who have criticized collectivism have hesitated to use as evidence the practical difficulties in establishing on paper the various equivalents; but it seems they have not perceived what really are the difficulties—or more frankly, the impossibility—of solving such equations a priori.[43]

Towards the end of his discussion of the mathematical solution, Hayek gives his opponents the benefit of the doubt, acknowledging that, appearances notwithstanding, what they must have had in mind was some sort of trial-and-error method rather than one that required the solving of a gigantic system of equations. But even this apparently simpler method would not do, since it still required that a regime of price-fixing

... be applied not to a few but to all commodities, finished or unfinished, and that it would have to bring about as frequent and as varied price changes as those which occur in a capitalistic society every day and every hour. . . . Almost every change of any single price would make changes of hundreds of other prices necessary and most of these other changes would by no means be proportional but would be affected by the different degrees of elasticity of demand, by the possibilities of substitution, and other changes in the method of production.[44]

In the latter half of his essay, Hayek provides a preliminary analysis of "pseudo-competition", or market socialism, the discussion of which in England was still "in a very embryonic stage".[45] Because no concrete proposals were yet on the table, Hayek had to imagine the forms of market organization that his opponents might envision. Before turning to that task, he notes that a key question in any such scheme is whether managers not disciplined by the prospects of profits and losses could be relied upon to serve "the common ends loyally and to the best of their capacity".[46] As they did for Mises, issues of incentives played an essential role in Hayek's initial critique of socialism.

[43]Enrico Barone, "The Ministry of Production in the Collectivist State", in *Collectivist Economic Planning*, op. cit., pp. 286–287.
[44]F. A. Hayek, "The Present State of the Debate", this volume, p. 97.
[45]*Ibid.*, p. 99.
[46]*Ibid.*, p. 101.

Hayek discusses two potential forms of market organization. The first, analyzed in Sections 6 through 9, is a world in which every industry is a monopoly. He raises a number of problems with this scheme, some of which draw on already existing theory. Some of the criticisms, though, are uniquely his own. One of the most innovative of these is found in his section on "The Criterion of Marginal Cost". Hayek asks:

> Does the instruction that they [the managers of a socialized industry] should aim at prices which will just cover their (marginal) cost really provide a clear criterion of action?
>
> It is in this connection that it almost seems as if perhaps excessive preoccupation with the conditions of a hypothetical state of stationary equilibrium has led modern economists in general, and especially those who propose this particular solution, to attribute to the notion of costs in general a much greater precision and definiteness than can be attached to any cost phenomenon in real life.[47]

Hayek goes on to say that in a world of constant change, "the value of most of the more durable instruments of production has little or no connection with the costs that have been incurred in their production but depends only on the services which they are expected to render in the future. . . ."[48] These services depend, of course, on the demand for the various sorts of products that the resources can be used to help to produce. The process of market competition itself reveals what the competing (and ever-changing) possible uses of the resources might be, and thereby what the true costs are (in terms of alternative uses) for their employment in a particular production process. One cannot duplicate the results of competition without competition itself being present: "To make a monopolist charge the price that would rule under competition, or a price that is equal to the necessary cost, is impossible, because the competitive or necessary cost is not known unless there is competition."[49]

Hayek next examines a market structure in which competition among firms within socialized industries would be permitted to exist. Though it might seem that there is little need for central direction in such a system, the appearance is misleading. The crucial question here is how to determine how much capital and other resources each firm should receive. In a free-market system the problem is solved when entrepreneurs bid for

---

[47]*Ibid.*, p. 105.
[48]*Ibid.*, 105–106.
[49]*Ibid.*, p. 107.

capital based on their individually formed expectations about profit opportunitites within their specific markets. They are guided in making their decisions by the carrot of potential profits and the stick of potential losses. Under a socialist regime, a central planner would be in charge of disbursing resources to the managers of the different enterprises. He would have to estimate where capital could be put to its most efficient use, where future demands might be expected to materialize and where they might diminish, which managers' past behaviours were to be rewarded and which punished, and so on. In his summary, Hayek emphasizes two problems with such a set-up. First, lines of responsibility for decision-making are blurred, creating all those difficulties that "arise in connection with freedom of initiative and the assessment of responsibility which are usually associated with bureaucracy".[50] (This is the question of 'incentives' again.) And second, "All this involves planning on the part of the central authority on much the same scale as if it were actually running the enterprise".[51] The most competitive form of market socialism would result in central planners having to take over the role of entrepreneurs.

Writing in 1935, unsure about which of his many opponents might respond (remember, they ran the gamut from the Marxist Dobb to the Barone-enthusiast Dickinson to those engaging in the still 'embryonic' discussion of 'pseudo-competition'), Hayek nonetheless tried to identify the essential economic arguments against socialism. Four that he identified stand out:

1) Hayek enumerates the many difficulties associated with "the mathematical solution", or any regime that relied on formulating and solving a system of thousands of equations. Should socialist authorities decide to employ a trial-and-error method instead, other problems would arise. The most important of these is the inability of any price-changing mechanism to replicate the automatic adjustments that occur in a free-market system in response to underlying changes in supply and demand.

2) Within the spectrum of possible market socialist ("pseudo-competitive") regimes, one possible arrangement is for industries to be monopolies, but with managers directed to price at marginal cost. Hayek points out that under such a set-up it would be difficult to know exactly what marginal costs were. In a competitive system market competition itself reveals this information; it would be absent in a world of monopolized industries.

3) In a market socialist regime in which firms within an industry compete, decisions concerning how much capital each firm should receive

[50]*Ibid.*, p. 112.
[51]*Ibid.*

18

would still have to be made by some central authority. But in order for this decision to be properly made, the planning authority would require complete information about each firm's and each industry's prospects. The planning authority would in essence need to take over the role played by the entrepreneur in a market system. Hayek simply states this as an (obviously undesirable) implication, but does not specify the nature of the problem that the result entails.

4) Finally, the absence of private ownership in the means of production creates all sorts of 'agency' or incentive problems for managers, who will shy away from making difficult decisions and who will tend towards risk-aversion in making their 'investment' decisions.

3. *Oskar Lange's* Economic Theory of Socialism

Market socialism was finally given a more complete articulation for the English-language audience in a flurry of articles appearing in British academic journals in 1936 and 1937. It is appropriate here to note the awkward position that a market-socialist system perforce occupies within the spectrum of possible economic regimes. Market socialists are obviously critics of capitalism. But their acknowledgement that perfectly competitive markets have certain desirable efficiency characteristics (albeit only under rather strict assumptions) must leave a Marxist like Maurice Dobb in a rather bad humour and economists like Hayek wondering why the market should be replaced by an elaborate scheme whose sole intent is simply to duplicate its workings. If markets work so well, why not just leave them alone?

A key claim of the market socialists is the denial that market structures under late capitalism resemble, in any meaningful way, perfect competition. According to this view, few competitive industries exist anymore, having been replaced by industrial giants, cartels, and monopolists. As such, contemporary capitalism *lacks* the beneficial efficiency characteristics of competition, while retaining all of its defects. With careful planning, market socialism can replicate the benefits of truly competitive markets, correct for remaining problems regarding efficiency, and all the while avoid capitalism's pernicious effects on distributive justice. This was at least the vision of hope that was offered by the market socialists to a world stuck in Depression and careening towards war.

The most famous blueprint for a market socialist system was laid out in a two-part article by a Polish economist and recent émigré to America, Oskar Lange.[52] The first footnote reference in Lange's article was to Hay-

[52]Oskar Lange, "On the Economic Theory of Socialism", *Review of Economic Studies*, vol. 4, October 1936, pp. 53–71, and February 1937, pp. 123–142. Reprinted with additions

ek's *Collectivist Economic Planning;* and his essay might fairly be viewed as an extended critical comment on Hayek's book. Since Lange's articles were believed by many to have refuted the Austrian[53] case, it is worthwhile to examine his arguments in detail.

Lange begins with the playful suggestion that a statue of Mises be erected in the great hall of the Central Planning Board, since his criticisms had forced socialists to tackle the question of how resources were to be allocated in the socialist state. Mises's arguments were, however, wrong. His mistake was to think that prices, which (as Lange agreed) are necessary for rational calculation, must be formed in markets. Since there is no market for capital goods in the socialist commonwealth, there are no prices for such goods. This is why Mises was able to conclude that rational calculation by producers is "impossible". But if one recognizes that prices are merely "terms on which alternatives are offered", and that their determination in markets is not essential, but rather a peculiarity of a particular institutional arrangement (capitalism), then Mises's argument collapses. Accounting prices could be supplied by the Central Planning Board, and these could be taken by socialist managers as parameters in their decision-making. It turns out that rational calculation under socialism is not impossible, after all.

Turning next to the contributions of Hayek and Lionel Robbins, Lange asserts that since they "do not deny the *theoretical* possibility of a rational allocation of resources in a socialist economy; they only doubt the possibility of a *practical* solution of the problem", they have "given up the essential point of Professor Mises's position and retreated to a second line of defense".[54] Hayek and Robbins cannot conceive of how a socialist commonwealth can be made to yield the same results as a competitive market system. By providing a demonstration, Lange will show that even the weaker Austrian claim regarding the practical feasibility of socialism is wrong.

Under market socialism there would exist both a free market for consumer goods (thus, at least for those resources to be used for the production of consumer goods, consumer sovereignty would apply) and a free market for labour (so that freedom of occupational choice would also exist). Because of public ownership of the means of production, there

---

and some changes in *On the Economic Theory of Socialism,* ed. Benjamin E. Lippincott (Minneapolis: University of Minnesota Press, 1938; reprinted, New York: McGraw Hill, 1956), pp. 57–143. Citations in the text will be to the Lippincott volume.

[53]The term "Austrian" as used in this context refers to Mises and Hayek, but also to Lionel Robbins and others who argued against socialism on economic grounds in the 1930s.

[54]Lange, in Lippincott, ed., op. cit., pp. 62, 63, emphasis in the original.

would be no market for non-labour productive resources like capital. Note that this arrangement, taken alone, would not eliminate income inequality. Because labour incomes would still be determined in markets, they would continue to differ across professions. Even so, since capital ownership is a principal source of income disparities, its elimination under market socialism would serve to reduce inequality. Furthermore, individual incomes would be supplemented by receipt of some share of the 'social dividend': each worker would receive a share of the amount that previously went to owners of capital. Later discussions included progressive taxation and the public provision of 'necessities' as additional means to bring about a more just distribution.

The sticking point for market socialism is the absence of profit maximizing firms and of a market (and hence of prices that reflect relative scarcities) for non-labour productive resources. Standard economic analysis can demonstrate that under certain conditions, within a regime of perfect competition, profit maximization ensures that each firm uses the optimal (least cost) combination of inputs, and that it uses them to produce the optimal amount (the amount at which product prices just cover the marginal costs of production) of output. Furthermore, freedom of entry and exit (itself presumed to exist under perfect competition) guarantees that industries are of optimal size. But if there are no market prices for non-productive resources, how can the managers of socialist firms decide what the least-cost combination of inputs is? And if they are not trying to maximize profits, by what mechanism can we guarantee that the managers will choose to produce the optimal amount of output?

Lange proposed that the Central Planning Board provide "prices" for all goods and factors of production. Managers of socialist firms would then be instructed to choose, on the basis of these "given" prices, the combination of inputs that minimizes their costs. Operationally, the rule they would follow is: Combine inputs so as to equalize the marginal productivity of each input that can be purchased for a given sum of money. To ensure that managers produced the right amount of output, they would be instructed to follow a second rule. Again assuming that the Planning Board has provided managers with the relevant set of prices, the rule states: Choose that level of output so that the price of the product just covers its marginal cost of production. Finally, planners in charge of industries would apply the same rule at the industry level, expanding or contracting them as necessary, and thereby replicating the beneficial effects of free entry and exit under competition.

Lange's proposal obviously begs a key question: What if the Central Planning Board fails to choose the correct prices? That is, what if their chosen "terms on which alternatives are offered" do not accurately reflect underlying relative scarcities, a problem that one might expect to occur, given that the prices are not formed in markets? Lange's solution was simplicity itself (and indeed, one that Dickinson had already mentioned): By following a straightforward trial-and-error procedure, one similar to that used in actual markets, planners would adjust prices up or down in those factor and product markets in which gluts or shortages existed. Crucially, planners would *not* have to solve thousands of equations, or perform the complex manipulations that Hayek and Robbins argued were the chief obstacles to a feasible market socialism. If a factor was underutilized, its price would be lowered. If there was a shortage of some good, its price would be raised. Could anything be more simple?

We may recall Hayek's observation that, in a market socialist regime in which industries were not monopolized, planners would still be required to perform the role of entrepreneurs. This did not pose a problem for Lange, who argued that

> ... the trial and error procedure would, or at least could, work much better in a socialist economy than it does in a competitive market. For the Central Planning Board has a much wider knowledge of what is going on in the whole economic system than any private entrepreneur can ever have, and, consequently, may be able to reach the right equilibrium prices by a *much shorter* series of successive trials than a competitive market actually does.[55]

What about Hayek's claims about the skewing of incentives under socialism? Lange acknowledges that "the argument which might be raised against socialism with regard to the efficiency of public officials as compared with private entrepreneurs as managers of production" is an important one.[56] He then offers two arguments in response. The first is to deny that such agency questions are a proper topic for economists to study: "The discussion of this argument belongs to the field of sociology rather than of economic theory and must therefore be dispensed with here."[57] Sensing perhaps that this might not satisfy, he adds that the real problem is one of *bureaucracy*. Bureaucratization, however, is a generic problem, one that afflicts both capitalism and socialism. The dominant market structures under late capitalism have little resemblance to perfect

[55]*Ibid.*, p. 89, emphasis in the original.
[56]*Ibid.*, p. 109.
[57]*Ibid.*

competition. Because of the absence of competition, the managers within a bureaucratic modern organization are likely to be just as inefficient as their counterparts under socialism. A corporate structural change, the separation of ownership from control, exacerbates this: The modern corporation is increasingly run by a professional managerial class whose members care more about their own welfare than about running an efficient firm. For Lange, bureaucracy is an admitted problem. But it is a problem of modern life, not one that is unique to socialism.[58]

Lange's article was soon reprinted, along with another by the American economist Fred M. Taylor, in a book edited by political scientist Benjamin Lippincott. In 1940 Hayek published an extensive critical review of the Lange-Taylor volume together with a review of a book by the original proponent of the "mathematical solution", H. D. Dickinson. If Lange's essay can be viewed as a comment on Hayek's *Collectivist Economic Planning,* Hayek's review, reprinted as chapter 3, this volume, may be viewed as his reply.[59]

Hayek complains with considerable justice that his arguments had not been accurately represented. If we read only Lange, we might well come away with the impression that Hayek's objections focused exclusively on the "mathematical solution"; that the only problems that he identified had to do with trying to formulate and solve a giant system of equations. To be sure, Hayek had pointed out the difficulties that would exist under such a regime. But he also had addressed the trial and error elements in Dickinson's proposal and had offered arguments against their feasibility. All of this was conveniently ignored by Lange.

Hayek still believed, of course, that any proposed trial and error solution could not work as well as a real market system. From Hayek's point of view, Lange's proposal revealed that he misunderstood how a market system actually functions. He adds a conjecture about the origins of Lange's errors:

[58]*Ibid.*, pp. 109–110, 120. As one might expect, to support his case Lange cites (on p. 120) Adolf Berle and Gardiner Means, *The Modern Corporation and Private Property* (New York: Macmillan, 1933; revised edition, New York: Harcourt, Brace and World, 1968), the classic study of the separation of ownership from control in the modern corporation and a forerunner of the modern principal-agent literature in economics. Lange's argument makes clear the crucial importance for market socialists of the claim that old-style atomistic competition is rare under late capitalism.

[59]F. A. Hayek, "Socialist Calculation: The Competitive 'Solution'", *Economica, N. S.,* vol. 7, May 1940, pp. 125–149; Lippincott, ed., op. cit.; H. D. Dickinson, *Economics of Socialism* (London: Oxford University Press, 1939). Dickinson's bibliography reveals that about a dozen books in support of planning or of socialism were published in England between 1935 and 1938. Hayek probably thought that these two were among the best of the lot.

. . .[I]t is difficult to suppress the suspicion that this particular proposal has been born out of an excessive preoccupation with problems of the pure theory of stationary equilibrium.[60]

When Hayek raises objections to "the pure theory of stationary equilibrium", he is emphasizing how a preoccupation with static equilibrium theory misleads planners about the true nature of the world. Hayek identifies a number of ways in which this occurs.

First, equilibrium theory concentrates on end-points, on a system that has achieved a state of rest. In solving for the equilibrium values of the system, certain data are assumed to be given, or constant. But the notion of a system moving towards some final end-point as determined by given data is radically at odds with the situation in the real world, "where constant change is the rule".[61] Parameters assumed to be given are in fact constantly changing; final equilibrium values are not final at all, but ever shifting. Concretely, in the real world, innumerable prices are changing every day, and every time a price changes, part of the 'given' data on which all other prices are set is also altered. This sets up innumerable further changes, which cause other parameters to alter, and so on, and so on. It is difficult to imagine any trial and error mechanism being able to duplicate such a process. Hayek wonders aloud "whether anyone should really be prepared to suggest that, within the domain of practical possibility, such a system will ever even distantly approach the efficiency of a system where the required changes are brought about by the spontaneous action of the persons immediately concerned".[62] He notes that neither author even clearly specifies how often prices are to be changed, a matter of no small consequence given the criticism outlined above. From Hayek's perspective, his opponents simply have failed to think through what they are saying.

Hayek points out other problems associated with an overemphasis on the static theory of competitive equilibrium. The theory of pure competition assumes homogeneous standardized products. But many goods, particularly capital goods, are built to order. Furthermore, static theory ignores that production takes place over time. Many decisions made by managers are of necessity forward-looking, and, as a result, existing prices are much less important to them than are anticipated future

[60]F. A. Hayek, p. 123.
[61]*Ibid.*
[62]*Ibid.*

prices.[63] Perhaps most important, market socialists fail to realize that the results of the market process cannot be separated from the actual process of competition.[64]

Hayek's criticisms, then, focus on the inadequacies of the existing theory. His adversaries might well respond: Theories are always abstractions from reality; why should any of this matter?

Hayek provides an example of the consequences of taking static theories too seriously in his discussion of Lange's cost minimization rule. The problem is a straightforward one: How, in the absence of price competition, will we know what the minimum costs are? Hayek's analysis includes a wonderful example of the role of the entrepreneur in the competitive process:

> In the discussion of this sort of problem, as in the discussion of so much of economic theory at the present time, the question is frequently treated as if the cost curves were objectively given facts. What is forgotten here is that the method which under given conditions is the cheapest is a thing which has to be discovered, and to be discovered anew sometimes almost from day to day, by the entrepreneur, and that, in spite of the strong inducement, it is by no means regularly the established entrepreneur, the man in charge of the existing plant, who will discover what is the best method. The force which in a competitive society brings about the reduction of price to the lowest cost at which the quantity saleable at that cost can be produced is the opportunity for anybody who knows a cheaper method to come in at his own risk and to attract customers by underbidding the other producers.[65]

Standard equilibrium theory assumes that an end-state is already reached, so that cost-minimizing input combinations are already known. This obscures the process by which they come to be known and may lead

---

[63]*Ibid.*, pp. 123–124.

[64]As Hayek would later put it, "competition is by its nature a dynamic process whose essential characteristics are assumed away by the assumptions of standard analysis" (F. A. Hayek, "The Meaning of Competition", in Hayek, ed., *Individualism and Economic Order* (Chicago: University of Chicago Press, 1948; Midway reprint, 1980), p. 94). This point was so crucial for the Austrians that they would ultimately argue that standard equilibrium theory should be replaced by a theory of the market process, one which underlines the importance of rivalrous market competition for obtaining the results that the static equilibrium model at best is only able to summarize.

[65]F. A. Hayek, "Socialist Calculation: The Competitive 'Solution'", op. cit., this volume, p. 130.

to the ultimate error: the belief that one can dispense with the very process (rivalrous market competition) that generates knowledge.[66]

There is another error concerning knowledge into which market socialists using standard equilibrium theory might easily fall. Recall that Hayek in 1935 had said that under competitive market socialism, planners in deciding how to allocate capital among firms would have to take on the role played in markets by entrepreneurs. Lange responded that that state of affairs might well improve on the workings of the free market. Entrepreneurs only have knowledge about a limited set of markets and prices. Since the Central Planning Board has access to more knowledge than do individual entrepreneurs, they could make better decisions, or so Lange argued.

In 1937 Hayek published "Economics and Knowledge",[67] an article that has more than a passing relevance for this discussion. He noted there that standard equilibrium theory assumes that all participants have access to the same, objectively correct, information. But in reality there is a division of knowledge. Knowledge as it actually exists in the world is dispersed; different people have access to different bits of it. The real question for the social sciences is how such dispersed knowledge might be put to use, how society might coordinate the knowledge that exists in many different minds and places. Equilibrium theory with its emphasis on end-states assumes that the process of coordination has *already* taken place. By doing so, it assumes away the most important question.

Citing his earlier article, Hayek argues that Lange has again been misled.

> As I have tried to show on another occasion, it is the main merit of real competition that through it use is made of knowledge divided among many persons which, if it were to be used in a centrally directed economy, would all have to enter the single plan. To assume that all this knowledge would be automatically in the possession of the planning authority seems to me to miss the main point.[68]

[66]As Hayek would later put it, competition may itself rightly be viewed as a "discovery procedure". F. A. Hayek, "Competition as a Discovery Procedure", in *New Studies in Philosophy, Politics, Economics, and the History of Ideas* (Chicago: University of Chicago Press, 1978), pp. 179–190.

[67]F. A. Hayek, "Economics and Knowledge", *Economica, N. S.*, vol. 4, February 1937, pp. 33–54; reprinted in F. A. Hayek, *Individualism and Economic Order*, op. cit., pp. 33–56. For the significance of this article in the further development of his thought, see Bruce Caldwell, "Hayek's Transformation", *History of Political Economy*, vol. 20, Winter 1988, pp. 513–541.

[68]Hayek, this volume, p. 134.

Tracing out the implications of the "dispersion of knowledge" became a major theme in Hayek's work. One can see additional development of it in a short piece (reprinted as chapter 4, this volume) that appeared in 1941.[69] There Hayek talks about what sorts of resources might be available at specific times and places and asserts that, "For what purposes and in what way particular resources are used with the greatest advantage can be intelligently decided only by the 'man on the spot'."[70] Hayek would later further develop the idea that much knowledge is localized, calling it "knowledge of the particular circumstances of time and place".[71] A further addition is that certain knowledge is tacit; it is "knowledge how" rather than "knowledge that". Such knowledge, Hayek would claim, cannot be easily passed on to others, even if one wanted to.

In his essays in *Collectivist Economic Planning* Hayek provided four opening arguments against a variety of socialist schemes. The first one, that no centrally imposed trial and error method could duplicate the workings of the market, was basically ignored by Lange, who shifted attention to Hayek's discussion of the mathematical solution. In his 1941 review Hayek reiterated and fleshed out the arguments against trial and error schemes. But it was his next two claims (that the competitive market process constitutes a discovery procedure, and that it assists the coordination of agents' plans in a world of dispersed knowledge) that ultimately emerged as Hayek's lasting and most original contributions. These arguments about markets and knowledge now constitute a central tenet of Austrian thought. Their refinement was a direct result of Hayek's battles with the market socialists.[72]

For many years it was the general consensus among economists that the debate over market socialism had ended in a draw. Lange's definition of prices as "terms on which alternatives are offered" seemed to many an adequate answer to Mises's insistence that prices be market-determined. It was further believed that Lange's trial and error procedure had

[69]F. A. Hayek, "The Economics of Planning", *The Liberal Review*, vol. 1, 1941, pp. 5–11, reprinted as chapter 4, this volume. This article has seen little circulation because *The Liberal Review*, although grandly described on its cover as the "Official Organ of the Oxford University Liberal Club", was little more than a mimeograph pamphlet. Note that the article contains the first outline of Hayek's well-known "tin example".

[70]*Ibid.*, p. 143.

[71]F. A. Hayek, "The Use of Knowledge in Society", in Hayek, *Individualism and Economic Order*, op. cit., p. 80.

[72]Hayek did not pursue his fourth argument against socialism, the claim (one that had also been made by Mises) that a socialist regime would be plagued by incentive problems. Interestingly, it is this claim that recent critics of market socialism, working within the 'economics of information' framework, tend to emphasize. For example, see Joseph Stiglitz, *Whither Socialism?* (Cambridge, Mass., and London: MIT Press, 1994).

demonstrated that calculation was feasible, since it did not require the formation and solution of a massive system of equations, which was assumed to have been the chief objection of Hayek and Robbins. On theoretical grounds, it appeared that socialism could not be distinguished from capitalism. The chief question then became: Which one is preferable?

Lange had taken up the desirability question in the latter half of his essay.[73] He argued there that market socialism was preferable to capitalism on four grounds:

1) Since the unequal income distribution under capitalism is itself inherently unjust, the mix of goods it creates does not maximize social welfare.

2) Free markets fail to account for the social costs and benefits of production (the externalities problem).

3) Since planners will be able to keep mistakes "localized", there will be less trouble with the business cycle under market socialism.

4) Under market socialism, the wastes of monopoly can be avoided.

In the postwar era, the debate over market socialism continued, but the socialist's opponents were neoclassical economists, not the Austrians. In one sense, Lange had won, since the neoclassicals more or less accepted the criticisms of capitalism enumerated above. The key question was what to do about them. By the 1950s and 1960s, the market socialists had lost this larger debate, at least within the economics profession, where the so-called 'neoclassical synthesis' emerged as the consensus view. In this theory, free markets are retained but supplemented by various forms of government intervention. There would be progressive income taxation and an assortment of transfer schemes to redress distributional injustices, increased attention to the provision of the public goods that free markets supposedly failed to produce, Pigovian subsidy and taxation responses to externalities, anti-trust policies to deal with problems associated with monopoly, and Keynesian fiscal and monetary policies to combat the business cycle. In this great debate, the minority view was not presented by Hayek, but by critics like Milton Friedman and George Stigler at the University of Chicago, or members of the Public Choice school. These maverick economists raised two objections to the standard view. First, they asserted that many so-called 'market' failures were actually caused by ill-conceived government policies. Next, they questioned on a variety of grounds the ability and desirability of government intervention to correct market failures that might exist, raising the spectre of

[73]Lange, in Lippincott, ed., op. cit., pp. 98ff.

cures that were worse than the original disease. Significantly, even though he was for a time on the faculty of the University of Chicago, Hayek was not really a participant in these discussions.[74]

How did all of this come about? The outcome is even stranger given that Hayek's opponents never really answered his knowledge-based critique of socialism. It turns out that few economists ever really seemed to have understood what Hayek was saying. To see why Hayek's argument was not answered, we must try to figure out why he was so poorly understood.

The first reason is something that Hayek himself identified when he derided economists' unhealthy preoccupation with static equilibrium theory. Lange's great accomplishment was to take mainstream economic theory and show how it could be applied to the case of a socialist economy. Paretian theory provides the logical foundation for Marshallian partial equilibrium analysis, and together they comprise the core of every modern undergraduate course in microeconomic theory as it has been taught since the 1930s. It is no small irony that Robbins, Hayek, and others at the London School of Economics were among those most responsible for the introduction of the Paretian approach to economists in Britain.[75] Both neoclassical economists and market socialists, then, were trained to model the economic system in the same way. For market socialists, Paretian theory provides them with the "marginal conditions" that the rules they impose on managers must approximate. For neoclassicals, it shows what an ideal perfectly competitive market system can accomplish and how deviation from this ideal might be corrected by the appropriate dose of government intervention. But whether one is a neoclassical or a market socialist, one's principal goal as an economist is the same: to make one's chosen system more efficient, using the marginal conditions provided by the Paretian system as the benchmark.

For Austrian economists, neoclassicals no less than market socialists

---

[74]Hayek's post was on the Committee on Social Thought at the University of Chicago, rather than the Economics Department. It should be noted, however, that portions of his book *The Constitution of Liberty* (Chicago: University of Chicago Press, and London: Routledge and Kegan Paul, 1960), written while he was at Chicago, show the influence of the "Chicago view" in economics.

[75]Thus Abba Lerner could quite correctly write in the preface of his book-length blueprint for market socialism, *The Economics of Control* (New York: Macmillan, 1944), p. viii: "It is almost impossible for me to say now exactly in what respects this work shows true originality. Most of it doubtless was absorbed from my teachers at the London School of Economics. To Professor Lionel C. Robbins, Professor Friedrich A. Hayek, Professor J. R. Hicks, and Professor D. H. Robertson I am indebted for my original training in handling the tools of economic analysis."

have been led astray by Paretian theory.[76] Hayek's ultimate endorsement of markets is not based on their alleged Pareto-efficiency characteristics. Rather, a system of free markets is one among a number of institutions that are vital for the creation and discovery of knowledge and for the coordination of agents' plans in a world in which knowledge is dispersed and error is possible. By assuming away these essential characteristics of the market process, the Paretian paradigm completely obscures the Austrian message. The rapid ascendance and subsequent dominance of the Paretian approach to welfare economics rendered the Austrian message (nearly literally) incomprehensible to economists, socialist and neoclassical alike.

The second reason why Hayek was not listened to is perhaps the most obvious one: His ideas were not in step with the prevailing opinion of his day, at least among the intelligentsia. The 1930s was a time when intellectuals could seriously posit socialism as representing a middle way between totalitarianism of the communist and fascist varieties on the one hand and laissez-faire capitalism on the other. Indeed, as the decade came to an end, Hayek began to believe that countering the statist views of progressive intellectuals, many of whom had claimed the authority of 'science' for their arguments, was the most important contribution that he could make. We will look at this development in Hayek's thought later in the introduction.

4. Hayek on the Economics of War

Many of the problems that wartime mobilization causes are identified in the following passage, written by one who had firsthand experience:

> When war broke out, however, the nations found that economic efficiency was a matter of life and death. The first shock forced governments and business interests to concoct immediately novel expedients to save credits from disruption. Presently all the large questions of war financing had to be faced—how much to borrow and how much to tax, how to adjust the burden of taxation, and how to manage the currency. Then it became clear that victory required drastic economic mobilization of all available resources to maintain military efficiency and civilian

---

[76]This is perhaps the appropriate place to point out that Hayek was by no means an unqualified opponent of general equilibrium theory. He spent much of the later 1930s trying to develop a dynamic intertemporal general equilibrium model of a capital-using monetary economy. It was *static* general equilibrium theory that Hayek felt was potentially misleading when used in the analysis of socialism.

morale. It was not merely a problem of getting money with which to buy goods, but a problem of organizing agriculture and industry, shipping and railways, of training labour and making inventions to procure the necessary amount of food, clothing, and munitions.

Economists in every belligerent country had a share in framing the many measures for mobilizing resources. They were called in as technical advisers for the most part, but some among them became responsible officials. Both executives and advisers were plunged into a situation where they had to think constructively about economic institutions. They did a vast amount of strenuous planning, and tried to change the institutions of their several nations even more radically than they succeeded in doing. . . .

One of the outstanding lessons of the war to all economists who had a share in planning was the indispensable necessity of carrying their analyses beyond the stage represented in orthodox treatises. It seldom sufficed to say that a given action would have consequences of a certain kind, that would have been easy—and trifling. The important thing was to find out at least in what order of magnitude these consequences should be reckoned. Continually grave decisions turned on the questions: How many? How much? How soon? Say that the limiting factor upon our military effectiveness in France was ships—ships to carry troops and munitions. Then we should put all the available tonnage under army control. And it was wasteful to recruit and train more soldiers or to make more materials within a given time than these available ships could carry. But how large a force would each thousand tons maintain in France and how many thousand tons were available for army use? The available tonnage depended partly on how soon the new shipyards could get their vessels finished, partly on how much tonnage we could acquire from neutrals, and partly on how much tonnage was needed to provision the Allies and to bring us necessary imports. What imports, then, were necessary? That again was a quantitative problem of almost infinite detail. We might cut down the output of tires for pleasure automobiles, for example, but we needed a great deal of rubber for military and for essential civilian uses. Just how much did we need, just how much was already in stock, just how much more crude rubber should be imported each month, and where could we get it with the shortest voyages? Such questions came up—literally by thousands—and they had to be answered in figures: figures drawn from official records if there were such, figures carefully estimated if there were no records, figures intelligently guessed at if there was no real basis for an estimate.

In the economic problems of peace this quantitative element is not less fundamental than it was in the problems of the war. Here, indeed, is one of the differentiating characteristics that set off the problems that crop up in real life from those that appear in books. The theorist discoursing at large may content himself with pointing out the kinds of causes and consequences to be considered; the practitioner dealing with specific cases must calculate the magnitudes involved. In proportion as economists face real problems they will strive to cast even their general theory into the quantitative mold.[77]

Mitchell identifies the problems of war financing, of rapid resource reallocation, and of the necessity for extensive quantitative planning in his reminiscence. The three problems are all interrelated. As mobilization begins, a massive amount of resources must be shifted from the production of consumption goods and of peacetime capital equipment to the production of war materials and capital. The government begins bidding resources away from the production of consumer goods and may even restrict by law the production of certain goods. This cutback in the production of consumption goods takes place at a time when workers' incomes are rising. If no countervailing measures are taken, the prices of many goods are bid up.

The ensuing inflation has a number of costs associated with it. It hurts those whose incomes do not keep pace, falling particularly hard on pensioners and others whose incomes are fixed in nominal terms. It triggers increased wage demands by workers whose real incomes are falling, thus setting up a vicious wage-price spiral: increased wage costs leading to higher prices, leading to increased wage demands, and so on. During wartime these distributional effects are particularly damaging, since they can distract attention from the war effort and weaken the nation's resolve. In addition, inflation reduces the value of outstanding debts, creating uncertainty among investors. This hinders the government's effort to finance some of its increased expenditure via borrowing.

For these reasons governments are often tempted to pursue another policy during wartime, the fixing of prices, which is usually justified on distributional grounds. But this policy has adverse consequences of its own. Since most prices get fixed at levels that are below equilibrium, shortages, queues, and rationing are the ultimate result. Even worse, the fixing of prices hinders the market from performing its allocative function. This makes central planning of the war effort all the more attractive.

[77]Wesley Clair Mitchell, "The Prospects of Economics", *The Backward Art of Spending Money*, New York and London: McGraw Hill, 1937, pp. 365–366, 376–377. The essay was first published in *The Trend of Economics*, edited by R. G. Tugwell (New York: F. S. Crofts, 1924). Hayek sat in on Mitchell's lectures on the history of economic thought when he visited the United States in the 1920s; see Hayek, *Hayek on Hayek*, op. cit., p. 66. Though Hayek might have agreed with Mitchell's diagnosis, they differed regarding remedies: It was in no small part the Tugwell volume to which Hayek was responding in his lecture, "The Trend of Economic Thinking". See note 36 above.

There was a final problem, one that Hayek recognized from the start. If the war brought about extensive central control of the economy, one could be quite sure that socialists would call for the continuation of that policy once peace had been restored. So in the case of British mobilization efforts at the beginning of the Second World War, the stakes were particularly high.

It was with these considerations in mind that Hayek made his first major contribution to the economics of war. It consisted of two articles published in *The Banker* just at the outset of the war, in September and October of 1939. They are reprinted as chapters 5 and 6 of this volume.[78] There were originally to have been more articles. In a letter to Tjalling Koopmans, Hayek later explained why only two appeared.

> There were intended to be quite a series but no more has been published than the two articles you have seen. The story is rather curious: When war actually broke out, *The Banker* decided that in view of the decisions already taken, they were no longer relevant! And though I probably still have somewhere fairly detailed notes at least for the third article, it was in fact never written out.[79]

The message of Hayek's first article is clear, simple, and uncompromising: In times of war no less than in peace, changing relative prices reveal changing conditions of scarcity and thereby provide important information. Whatever schemes might be adopted to assist the mobilization effort, the fixing of prices (and the rationing that typically accompanies such a policy) should be minimized. The authorities should, whenever possible, allow relative prices to do their work.

Hayek's second article applies the same principles to another "price", this one an intertemporal one, the interest rate. As Hayek notes in a pointed reference, John Maynard Keynes had been a prominent advocate of keeping interest rates low in the Depression, in the hopes that this would help stimulate the economy. Hayek had opposed this policy, arguing that the long-run effects would be further to disrupt the structure of production and thereby ultimately to exacerbate the business cycle.[80]

---

[78] F. A. Hayek, "Pricing versus Rationing", *The Banker,* September 1939, pp. 242–249, and "The Economy of Capital", *The Banker,* October 1939, pp. 38–42.

[79] Letter from F. A. Hayek to Tjalling Koopmans, August 6, 1956. In the Hayek collection, The Hoover Institution Archives, Stanford, Calif.

[80] The differences in their respective theories are highlighted in the editor's Introduction to *Contra Keynes and Cambridge: Essays and Correspondence,* ed. Bruce Caldwell, vol. 9 (1995) of *The Collected Works of F. A. Hayek,* op. cit. It is perhaps unsurprising that Keynes's first biographer, Roy Harrod, should identify the low interest rate policy followed by the British

These two articles contain Hayek's warnings about paths to avoid. They do not contain any positive proposals, and in particular there is no plan for avoiding the seemingly inevitable run-up in the prices of consumer goods. His positive contribution would not come until about a month later. Interestingly enough, it would consist of an addendum to a proposal made by his old nemesis, John Maynard Keynes.

Keynes's remarkable book *How to Pay for the War* began as a lecture delivered on October 20, 1939, before the Marshall Society, the undergraduate economics club at Cambridge. After he had discussed his ideas with a number of government officials, Keynes published a revised version of the proposal as two articles in *The Times,* on November 14 and 15.[81] To Hayek's delight, Keynes concurred that both inflation and rationing schemes (Keynes called the latter a "pseudo-remedy"[82]) should if at all possible be avoided during mobilization. Another possible strategy was to raise taxes. Keynes pointed out that if this alternative were chosen, the tax would have to extend to the working classes, for two reasons: First, the amounts needed were so large that a tax on the rich would not generate sufficient funds to finance the war; second, a tax on the rich would not sufficiently reduce current expenditure, so it would not help with the problem of excess demand for consumption goods.

In order to avoid the inflationary outcome, then, the present consumption levels of the working classes would have to be reduced. In an attempt to soften this unpopular but inevitable truth, Keynes came up with the novel idea of a 'deferred pay' or 'compulsory savings' provision.[83] A (progressively increasing) percentage of all incomes above some minimum level would be paid to the government, some of it in the form of taxes, the rest in the form of compulsory savings. The latter amount would be credited to each individual's account at his Post Office Savings Bank. This sum would earn interest of 2-1/2 per cent, but the individual would be blocked from use of the fund until after the war was over. Keynes envisioned that the funds would be unblocked in a series of installments and timed to counteract (in good Keynesian style) the first postwar slump.

---

and American governments during the war as one of Keynes's most important influences, and one that derived from his writings earlier in the 1930s. See Roy Harrod, *The Life of John Maynard Keynes* (New York: Harcourt Brace, 1951; reprinted, New York: Norton, 1982), pp. 492–493.

[81]J. M. Keynes, "Paying for the War", reprinted in *Activities 1939–1945: Internal War Finance,* ed. Donald Moggridge, vol. 22 (1978) of *The Collected Writings of John Maynard Keynes,* op. cit., pp. 41–51.

[82]*Ibid.,* p. 43.

[83]It is perhaps understandable that Keynes would not choose the phrase 'forced savings' to refer to this provision within his new proposal.

Hayek responded swiftly to Keynes's proposal. In an article published about two weeks later in *The Spectator* magazine, Hayek praised Keynes's ideas as "ingenious".[84] His only disagreement was to question the wisdom of using the release of the deposits as a tool of counter-cyclical fiscal policy. In its stead Hayek proposed his own novel idea: a capital levy on old wealth that would be used to create a giant holding company. Those who had deferred their consumption during the war would receive, instead of a cash claim against the government, equity in the industrial capital of the country. Hayek's scheme was a perfect complement to Keynes's. The latter had figured out how to reduce consumption during the war, and the former how ultimately to pay for it. Hayek's plan would, in short, turn workers into stockholders.[85]

Keynes's plan was not well received by the Labour party, the left press, or the unions; he would characterize the initial reaction of the Labour leaders as "frivolous and unthinking".[86] In an attempt to placate them, Keynes modified his proposal. In the book version, now called *How to Pay for the War* and published in February 1940, Keynes added a family allowance of £13 per year per child, an 'iron ration', or minimum ration of consumption goods made available at a low fixed price, and Hayek's capital levy provision.[87] Hayek's proposal was designed to prevent Keynes from using the distribution of the deferred pay as a tool of fiscal policy. With typical ingenuity, Keynes altered Hayek's proposal to meet his own ends, keeping the levy as a means of paying for the war, but using the receipts to finance his own preferred cash payments scheme. Hayek points this out in his review of *How to Pay for the War* in the *Economic Journal,* also reprinted in chapter 7, this volume.[88]

Unfortunately, Labour intransigence continued. Then everything was turned upside down, as 'the phony war' came to an abrupt conclusion. On May 10, 1940, Hitler's armies invaded Holland and Belgium. By the

[84]F. A. Hayek, "Mr. Keynes and War Costs", *The Spectator,* November 24, 1939, pp. 740–741, reprinted in chapter 7, this volume.

[85]A similar method has been used to distribute government-owned capital in the former East Bloc countries, most notably in the Czech Republic. Jack Birner has commented to the editor that Keynes's and Hayek's proposals reflect their respective theories of the cycle. 'Compulsory savings' causes consumption to be deferred. In order to meet future consumption demand, output would need to be increased in the future, which is only possible if there are investments. Hayek's proposal anticipates this problem, whereas Keynes's cash-claim scheme typically neglects these long-run capital-theoretic concerns.

[86]Reported on by D. E. Moggridge in *Activities 1939–1945: Internal War Finance,* op. cit., p. 82.

[87]J. M. Keynes, *How to Pay for the War,* op. cit., pp. 367–439.

[88]F. A. Hayek, "Book Review: John Maynard Keynes, *How to Pay for the War, Economic Journal,* vol. 50, June–September 1940, pp. 321–326.

end of the month both countries had surrendered; meanwhile British soldiers were desperately trying to escape from the beaches of Dunkirk. In June France sued for peace, and only Britain remained.

The moment for trying out such comprehensive and innovative proposals was over. Some of Keynes's recommendations eventually were enacted, including a modest deferred pay scheme that was added to the 1941 budget under the name of "postwar credits". But also enacted was a 100 per cent excess profits tax, a policy that Keynes had vehemently opposed in his proposals. His biographer Roy Harrod summed up Keynes's influence on the economics of war in Britain this way:

> . . . [I]t is difficult to hold that the main idea in *How to Pay for the War* was put into effect. He pointed out that there were only three logical solutions to the war problem, namely, his scheme, sufficient taxation, or inflation. Sufficient taxation was impractical, and he feared inflation. But he recognized there was also a pseudo-remedy, namely widespread rationing and price controls. . . . He thought that, with the prevailing outlook, this, rather than open inflation, was the most likely outcome of the lack of an orderly plan. And he dreaded it. He was appalled by the waste and the inefficiency of shortages and queues. His scheme was designed to avoid them. But, in the event, we had them![89]

Hayek made other contributions during this period. In the press he was a consistent advocate for a variety of forms of international cooperation, from the lowering of trade barriers among the allies to the formation of a federation of the Western democracies. He also called for increases in the flow of knowledge about Germany. In a letter dated September 9, 1939, Hayek wrote to the Director General of the Ministry of Information, noting that his "exceptional experience and somewhat special position might enable me to be of considerable help in connection with the organization of propaganda in Germany".[90] Despite providing as references such luminaries as Lord Josiah Stamp, A. M. Carr-Saunders (the Director of the London School of Economics), Sir William Beveridge, Ralph Hawtrey of the Treasury, and F. W. Ogilvie of the BBC, his offer apparently went unanswered.

---

[89]Roy Harrod, *The Life of John Maynard Keynes,* op. cit., p. 494.

[90]Letter, Hayek to the Director General of the Ministry of Information, September 9, 1939. In the Hayek collection, The Hoover Institution Archives, Stanford, Calif. There is no record of a reply in the Archives.

At the outbreak of the war the London School was evacuated to Cambridge, and with Keynes's help Hayek was able to find rooms at Kings College. This lasted until 1941, when Hayek and his family (the latter during the previous year had been put up in the Robbinses' country cottage) finally found a house in which to live in Cambridge, where they stayed until 1945. Hayek spent the duration of the war teaching, but also working on his 'war effort', *The Road to Serfdom*.

5. *Planning and Freedom: Mapping* The Road to Serfdom

In the penultimate section of his 1941 review, "Socialist Calculation: The Competitive 'Solution'", Hayek asks whether personal and political freedom can be preserved under a regime of extensive economic planning. This was a line of questioning that he had begun pursuing a few years earlier, and one he would follow with increasing urgency during the war years, finally producing *The Road to Serfdom* in 1944. In its preface, Hayek wrote that "The central argument of this book was first sketched in an article entitled 'Freedom and the Economic System', which appeared in the *Contemporary Review* for April, 1938, and was later reprinted in an enlarged form as one of the Public Policy Pamphlets edited by Professor H. D. Gideonse for the University of Chicago Press (1939)."[91] The two articles are reprinted as chapters 8 and 9 of this volume.[92]

Hayek explained the reason for his turn to these political concerns in an interview in 1978:

> A very special situation arose in England. . . . that people were seriously believing that National Socialism was a capitalist reaction against socialism. It's difficult to believe it now, but the main exponent whom I came across was Lord Beveridge. . . . I wrote a memorandum for Beveridge on this subject, then turned it into a journal article, and then used [my time during] the war to write out what was really a sort of advance popular version of what I had imagined would be the great book on the abuse and decline of reason. . . . It was adjusted to the moment and wholly aimed at the British socialist intelligentsia, who all seemed to have this

[91] F. A. Hayek, *The Road to Serfdom*, op. cit., p. xviii.

[92] F. A. Hayek, "Freedom and the Economic System", *Contemporary Review*, April 1938, pp. 434–442, reprinted as chapter 8, this volume, was reprinted in a slightly revised version under the title "What Price a Planned Economy", *American Affairs*, July 1945, pp. 178–181; *Freedom and the Economic System* (Chicago: University of Chicago Press, 1939), Public Policy Pamphlet no. 19 in the series edited by Harry D. Gideonse, reprinted as chapter 9, this volume.

idea that National Socialism was not socialism, just something contemptible.[93]

The argument against which Hayek fought existed on varying levels of sophistication. The vulgar version went something like this: Since communists and socialists are among the chief opponents of fascism (especially in countries where no viable liberal tradition has ever taken root), and since communists and socialists also oppose capitalism, then fascism must be a form of capitalism. The syllogism is invalid: Though both spinach and snakes may revolt me, this does not make my greens reptilian. But even were it not, the Communist Party betrayal of the Republican forces in Spain (documented by George Orwell in his 1938 book, *Homage to Catalonia*[94]) and the signing of the Molotov-Ribbentrop pact in 1939 provided incontrovertible evidence that the first premise was false.

A more robust version infers from the inability of the nascent liberal democracies on the Continent to contain fascism that liberal democracy is everywhere doomed to fall before the jackboot. This argument never made much headway in Britain, where experience spoke as eloquently in favour of the prospects of liberal democracy as it had against them on the Continent.

The most sophisticated account was doubtless that of the Hungarian émigré Karl Mannheim, who, having fled Frankfurt in 1933, soon gained an appointment as a Lecturer in Sociology at the London School of Economics. Mannheim's vision was a dark and depressing one. Reflecting on the recent experience of Germany, he concluded that the mass democracies of the Continent were lost, that all were headed towards totalitarianism. He held out some hope for England, but only if it would give up on liberal democracy and embrace a comprehensive system of planning. In Mannheim's apocalyptic analysis, the choice was no longer between laissez faire and planning, but between the good planning of the sort that he advocated and the horrific planning that would accompany totalitarianism.

In a lecture given at the London School of Economics and published in 1937, Mannheim also explained how capitalism had allowed fascism to take root. The sequence had the usual Mannheimian air of dismal inevitability. Monopoly capitalism leads naturally to sustained periods of mass unemployment. This creates a permanent state of collective insecurity among the population. Mass democratic society can be easily manipu-

---

[93]F. A. Hayek, *Hayek on Hayek*, op. cit., p. 102.
[94]George Orwell, *Homage to Catalonia* (London: Secker and Warburg, 1938).

lated by demagogues who play on the insecurity, providing scapegoats for the current problems and offering escape into symbols of past glories. There is a gradual breakdown of society, and totalitarian forms of government step in to fill the vacuum. The breakdown is further aided by capitalists, whose allegiances are few and fleeting, and who see new profit opportunities in every change of regime.[95]

Hayek does not mention Mannheim in his writings until the 1940s, perhaps because much of Mannheim's work on mass democracy and social structures was not translated until 1940 and so would be unfamiliar to his English audience. But by 1944 he is accorded a place of some prominence. Seeking to contrast his own views with those of the planners, Hayek cites Mannheim in the first chapter of *The Road to Serfdom*, stating, "The difference cannot be better illustrated than by the extreme position taken in a widely acclaimed book on whose program of so-called planning for freedom we shall have to comment yet more than once."[96] If *The Road to Serfdom* had its beginnings in an intellectual spat with Beveridge, its final form may owe more to the darkly brilliant sociological ruminations of Karl Mannheim.

At the outset of his 1938 paper, Hayek addressed Beveridge's opinions with a flurry of rhetorical questions:

> Are we certain that we know exactly where the danger to liberty lies? Was the rise of the fascist regimes really simply an intellectual reaction fomented by those whose privileges were abolished by social progress?[97]

He then states his principal thesis, the same one that he would develop in *The Road to Serfdom*.

> The main point is very simple. It is that the central economic planning, which is regarded as necessary to organize economic activity on more rational and efficient lines, presupposes a much more complete agreement on the relative importance of the different ends than actually exists, and that in consequence, in order to be able to plan, the planning

[95]Mannheim's lecture originally appeared as a chapter in *Peaceful Change: An International Problem*, ed. C. A. W. Manning (London: Macmillan, 1937). It later formed the basis for chapter 3 of Karl Mannheim, *Man and Society in an Age of Reconstruction: Studies in Modern Social Structure* (London: Kegan Paul and New York: Harcourt Brace, 1940).

[96]F. A. Hayek, *The Road to Serfdom*, op. cit., p. 21.

[97]Hayek, this volume, p. 182.

authority must impose upon the people that detailed code of values which is lacking.

... [A]greement that planning is necessary, together with the inability to agree on a particular plan, must tend to strengthen the demand that government, or some single person, should be given the power to act on their own responsibility. It becomes more and more the accepted belief that if one wants to get things done the responsible director of affairs must be freed from the fetters of democratic procedure.[98]

Under a system of free markets, each consumer makes his own choices. Under planning, at least some choices must be subject to the 'general will'. In making these choices, the planners will inevitably impose a code of values on the rest of the populace. Whatever choices are finally made, some members of the society will be made better off and some worse off. Since planners are political appointees who wish to retain power, they will seek ways to justify the choices that they have made. Those who support their choices will be rewarded, and those who oppose them will be sanctioned: "Planning becomes necessarily a planning in favour of some and against others."[99] In this way authoritarian government tends inevitably to expand beyond the economic and into the political domain. Liberty ends up being sacrificed, even under those forms of socialism that may have started out as democratic. Only if democracy is allied with the freedom of choice that inheres in a free market system will it have some hope of survival.

Democratic government worked successfully so long as, by a widely accepted creed, the functions of the State were limited to fields where real agreement among a majority could be achieved. The price we have to pay for a democratic system is the restriction of State action to those fields where agreement can be obtained; and it is the great merit of a liberal society that it reduces the necessity of agreement to a minimum compatible with the diversity of individual opinions which in a free society will exist.[100]

There is some value in seeing the 1938 and the 1939 versions of "Freedom and the Economic System" side by side. Though there is, of course, some duplication (parts of sections one, four, five, and six of the later

[98]*Ibid.*, pp. 182, 184.
[99]*Ibid.*, p. 185.
[100]*Ibid.*, p. 184.

version repeat some of the earlier text), new material is also evident. As befits a policy pamphlet, there are references to contemporary events and citations of the current popular literature. But there are also some substantial new ideas, three of which will be mentioned here.

First, there is an emphasis in Section 2 on the crucial importance of the rule of law in a liberal democratic society. Hayek introduces the idea by differentiating between the sort of planning that one experiences under socialism and the 'planning' that occurs under liberalism, namely, "the construction of a rational framework of general and permanent rules":

> We can 'plan' a system of general rules, equally applicable to all people and intended to be permanent (even if subject to revision with the growth of knowledge), which provides an institutional framework within which the decisions as to what to do and how to earn a living are left to the individuals. In other words, we can plan a system in which individual initiative is given the widest possible scope and the best opportunity to bring about effective coordination of individual effort.[101]

Later is his essay, Hayek notes that though the early liberals had understood the importance of these general rules, they had not carried their analyses far enough.

> [T]his task of creating a framework of law has by no means been carried through consistently by the early liberals. After vindicating on utilitarian grounds the general principles of private property and freedom of contract, they have stopped short of applying the same criterion of social expediency to the specific historic forms of the law of property and of contract. Yet it should have been obvious that the question of the exact content and the specific limitations of property rights, and how and when the state will enforce the fulfillment of contracts, require as much consideration on utilitarian grounds as the general principle.[102]

The rule of law would become a recurrent theme in Hayek's work. Hayek scholars should note, however, that (in 1939, anyway) he apparently had not developed an antipathy towards utilitarianism. Indeed, in his willingness to subject existing laws to a "criterion of social expediency", the

---

[101] F. A. Hayek, *Freedom and the Economic System*, op. cit. This volume, p. 194.
[102] *Ibid.*, p. 195.

author of "Freedom and the Economic System" sounds suspiciously like what the later Hayek might call a social constructivist (or, at the very least, a constitutional political economist)![103]

In a review of Hayek's pamphlet, the British socialist H. D. Dickinson agreed with Hayek's criticisms of his predecessors:

> [T]he liberal opponents of collectivism have not so far entered the field with a positive programme. Can they suggest any workable set of institutions in the realm of property, inheritance, contract, money, and business organization which will be compatible with private property and the free market and which will at the same time guarantee the ordinary man a reasonable security of livelihood and prevent the accumulation of wealth (and, what is still more important, the concentration of power over wealth) in the hands of a minority of the community? In the pamphlet under review, Professor Hayek hints at the possibility of such a programme.[104]

In due course Hayek responded to Dickinson's challenge, though the framework of *The Constitution of Liberty* would be quite different from the one hoped for by Dickinson. Though Hayek did not want it to be considered a blueprint, the book contained a fairly detailed account of the institutional settting that would permit a liberal democratic state to flourish.[105]

In "Freedom and the Economic System" Hayek signalled a second significant shift in his thinking. Up till then when he had argued against socialism, he had restricted himself to making economic arguments. By 1939 Hayek probably felt that he had successfully refuted socialism on economic grounds. But one can also see him coming to the realization that, having concentrated on winning the economic battle, he had placed himself in danger of losing the larger war.

> Many planners would be willing to put up with a considerable decrease of efficiency if at that price greater distributive justice could be achieved.

---

[103]Stuart Warner pointed out to the editor that "in the 1940s, Hayek's lists of phenomena which were the results of human action but not design include language, the market, money, and morals; law is not on the lists." Hayek's understanding of the law changed through time.

[104]H. D. Dickinson, "Review, *Freedom and the Economic System*", *Economica*, N. S., vol. 7, November 1940, pp. 435–437.

[105]F. A. Hayek, *The Constitution of Liberty*, op. cit.

And this, indeed, brings us to the crucial question. The ultimate decision for and against socialism cannot rest on purely economic grounds, and cannot be based merely on the determination of whether a greater or smaller output of society is likely to be obtained under the alternative systems in question. The aims of socialism as well as the costs of its achievement are mainly in the moral sphere.[106]

Henceforth, Hayek in his writings against socialism would add political, ethical, and historical arguments to the economic ones.

A third theme that Hayek mentions in passing in the essay concerns the origins of the belief that central planning is necessary for productive efficiency:

It would be interesting, but it is not possible within the space available, to show how this belief is largely due to the intrusion into the discussion of social problems of the preconceptions of the pure scientist and the engineer, which have dominated the outlook of the educated man during the past hundred years.[107]

Normally, of course, one thinks of Hayek as debating with other economists. But it is evident that what increasingly worried Hayek in the late 1930s was the enthusiasm for all sorts of planning among the non-economist intelligentsia of Britain, and especially among the natural scientists whose enthusiasm attracted much public attention and who, in this heyday of positivism, were accorded great respect. The group against which Hayek struggled has since come to be called the 'Social Relations of Science' movement.

Members of the movement generally adhered to three fundamental theses. First, science serves a social function, and it reflects the class interests of the society in which it is embedded. Second, though science in the past assisted the development of capitalism, its further advance has been hindered under monopoly capitalism. Finally, under socialism science would be planned and thereby could once again be made to serve the needs of society.

One of the leaders of the movement was the Cambridge-trained physicist J. D. Bernal. He had been introduced to socialist ideas during his student days by his friend H. D. Dickinson and was a Communist Party

---

[106]F. A. Hayek, this volume, p. 198.
[107]*Ibid.*, p. 197.

member in the 1920s and early 1930s. In his popular book *The Social Function of Science,* Bernal first offered a bleak description of the way that science was carried on, then provided a utopian vision of what a properly planned science could look like.[108] As one of his biographers put it, "The central purpose behind all of Bernal's writings is to show that only in socialist society can science take its rightful place as the chief servant of human liberation."[109] Bernal did not limit himself to writing. He was "a model Popular Front intellectual, involving himself at one count in more than sixty committees devoted to peace, anti-fascism, civil liberties, Spanish aid, friendship with the USSR, etc., ad infinitum."[110]

There were many others, and all were highly visible. J. B. S. Haldane was a biochemist and geneticist, for a time the Chairman of the Editorial Board of *The Daily Worker,* and one of the first to write popular science. His fluid style, frequent speaking engagements (by the mid–1930s he was averaging about 100 speeches a year), and willingness to break social conventions soon gained him a huge public; early in his career he was the model for characters in two different fictional works. The mathematician Hyman Levy was a great popularizer of science. The titles of his book series, the Library of Science and Culture, and of his BBC broadcasts ("Scientific Research and Social Needs", "Science in a Changing World", "The Web of Thought and Action") reveal his conviction that science is properly viewed as an agent of societal change. Lancelot Hogben held a chair in social biology at the London School of Economics from 1930 to 1936. In such books as *Mathematics for the Million* and *Science for the Citizen,*[111] Hogben made sure that his descriptions of the facts of science were accompanied by his own particular analyses of its social history. J. G. Crowther was the science correspondent for the *Manchester Guardian.* Though he hoped for a communistic scientific community, he also suspected that many scientists would not share his goals, writing in *The Social Relations of Science* that "the material conditions of scientists contain elements that dispose them to fascism. . . . The immediate economic and class interests of scientists tend to make them fall in with authority."[112] P. M. S. Blackett would win the Nobel Prize in physics in 1948. In 1935,

[108]J. D. Bernal, *The Social Function of Science* (New York: Macmillan, 1939; 2nd corrected edition, London: Routledge, 1940).

[109]Gary Werskey, *The Visible College: The Collective Biography of British Scientific Socialists of the 1930s* (New York: Holt, Rinehart and Winston, 1978), p. 185.

[110]*Ibid.,* p. 167.

[111]Lancelot Hogben, *Mathematics for the Million* (New York: Norton, 1938); *Science for the Citizen: A Self-Educator Based on the Social Background of Scientific Discovery* (London: Allen and Unwin, 1938).

[112]J. G. Crowther, *The Social Relations of Science* (London and New York: Macmillan, 1941; rev. ed., London: Cresset, 1967), p. 648.

he contributed the title essay to *The Frustration of Science,* a book whose main theme was that scientific advance would be frustrated so long as the capitalist system was maintained.[113] As a radical historian of the movement wrote:

> This theme—that it was the advancement of science, not the actions of the working class, which would bring about the downfall of capitalism (and vice versa)—became a significant one in any country where the Communist Party was allowed to operate in the 1930s. Nevertheless, no left-wing movement ever became quite so obsessional about the scientific road to socialism as the one in Britain.[114]

These were some of the people that Hayek had in mind when he wrote against the 'men of science'. One of his most explicit statements can be found in his 1941 piece, "Planning, Science, and Freedom".[115] The article appeared in the influential weekly *Nature,* which guaranteed that his challenge would reach the scientific elite of Britain. The war was under way, and Hayek was more explicit than he had been before about the similarities between the dark future he could foresee and conditions then evident in Germany. In the second sentence of the article he mentions France in conjunction with Germany as one of the places where the modern passion for planning originated. This theme was carefully developed in Hayek's just-published series of essays, "The Counter-Revolution of Science", where he traced the "source of the scientistic hubris" to the engineers of L'Ecole Polytechnique, Henri de Saint-Simon, Auguste Comte, and their apostles.[116]

Hayek notes in the *Nature* article:

> The attempts to advance the social sciences by a more or less close imitation of the methods of the natural sciences, far from being new, have been a constant feature for more than a century. The same objections

[113]Sir Daniel Hall and others, *The Frustration of Science* (London: Allen and Unwin, 1935; reprinted, New York: Arno Press, 1975).

[114]Gary Werskey, *The Visible College,* op. cit., p. 178.

[115]F. A. Hayek, "Planning, Science, and Freedom", *Nature,* vol. 143, November 15, 1941, pp. 580–584, reprinted as chapter 10, this volume.

[116]F. A. Hayek, "The Counter-Revolution of Science", *Economica, N. S.,* vol. 8, February 1941, pp. 9–36; May 1941, pp. 119–150; August 1941, pp. 281–320; reprinted in *The Counter-Revolution of Science: Studies on the Abuse of Reason* (Glencoe, Ill.: Free Press, 1952; second edition, Indianapolis, Ind.: Liberty*Press,* 1979), pp. 185–363.

against 'deductive' economics, the same proposals to make it at last 'scientific', and it must be added, the same characteristic errors and primitive mistakes to which the natural scientists approaching this field seem to be prone, have been repeated and discussed over and over again by successive generations of economists and sociologists and have led precisely nowhere. All the progress in the understanding of the phenomena which has been achieved has come from the economists patiently developing the technique which has grown out of their peculiar problems.[117]

Hayek's battle was a lonely one. As he put it, "for a hundred men of science who attack competition and 'capitalism' scarcely one can be found who criticizes the restrictionist and protectionist policies which masquerade as 'planning' and which are the true causes of the 'frustration of science'."[118] But he did have some companions besides Mises and Robbins, and he participated in a number of initiatives to stem the tide. One of his allies was the American journalist and critic Walter Lippmann. In *An Inquiry into the Principles of the Good Society*, Lippmann offered arguments similar to those of Hayek about planning, collectivism, and totalitarianism, and praised both Hayek and Mises in his book for their insights.[119] A French translation of *The Good Society* appeared the next year, and in August 1938 a five-day colloquium organized by Louis Rougier was held in Paris to honour Lippmann and to inquire into the prospects for democratic liberalism. Hayek, Mises, and Robbins were among those in attendance, as well as a number of Continental liberals, including Wilhelm Roepke, Raymond Aron, and Jacques Rueff. The meeting led to the creation of the short-lived Centre International des Etudes pour la Rénovation du Libéralisme, which lasted only until 1940, another victim of the war. Another compatriot was the physical chemist and philosopher Michael Polanyi, who attacked the science planning movement in his book *The Contempt of Freedom*, which Hayek reviewed.[120] In the early 1940s Hayek attempted to raise funds to finance the publication of an outlet for

[117]F. A. Hayek, "Planning, Science, and Freedom", pp. 216–217, this volume.

[118]*Ibid.*, p. 216. Hayek identifies some of his opponents in the chapter titled "The Totalitarians in Our Midst" in *The Road to Serfdom*, op. cit.

[119]Walter Lippmann, *An Inquiry into the Principles of the Good Society* (Boston: Little, Brown, 1937). I thank Julian Ellison for providing me with information concerning the existence and significance of the Lippmann colloquium.

[120]Michael Polanyi, *The Contempt of Freedom: The Russian Experiment and After* (London: Watts, 1940; reprinted, New York: Arno Press, 1975). Hayek's review appears in the Appendix of this volume. In a letter dated July 1, 1941, Hayek wrote Polanyi: "I attach very great importance to these pseudo-scientific arguments on social organization being effectively met and I am getting more and more alarmed by the effect of the propaganda of the Haldanes, Hogbens, Needhams, etc., etc." The Polanyi Archives, University of Chicago Library. The editor thanks Philip Mirowski for bringing the Polanyi-Hayek letters to his attention.

liberal thought, one that he thought should be named *Common Affairs*,[121] but the project was not realized. Hayek's organizational efforts did not bear fruit until April 1947, when the Mont Pèlerin Society was founded.

The final paper in this volume is "The Intellectuals and Socialism".[122] It was first published in 1949, five years after *The Road to Serfdom*. Hayek's initial attack was directed against a specifically British movement. By 1949 it was evident that socialist ideology was on the upswing among the intellectual elite worldwide, which may account for the resignation, and even self-pity, that one occasionally glimpses in the article. But at its conclusion one can also begin to see the outline of a program: "What we lack is a liberal Utopia, a program which seems neither a mere defense of things as they are nor a diluted kind of socialism, but truly liberal radicalism. . . ."[123] A decade later he provided his first comprehensive statement of the principles underlying a liberal Utopia in *The Constitution of Liberty*.[124]

The volume concludes with an Appendix in which are gathered a number of Hayek's book reviews from this period, wherein one may see some of the books that Hayek was reading at the time and how his reactions to them helped shape both his critical and positive writings.

6. Conclusion

This introduction is being written in 1995, only six years after the collapse of Communist regimes in the Soviet Union and Eastern Europe. As might be expected, most advocates of socialism, particularly those who had favoured extensive central planning, have been chastened by recent events. Such regimes continue, of course, to persist: Totalitarians rarely go gently into the night. But few intellectuals now seem prepared to defend anything resembling Soviet-style central planning.

Yet at the same time there has been a renewal of interest in market socialism. Ironically, the failures of the central-planning model have given advocates of market socialism the opportunity for a renewed claim on the

---

[121]On the choice of the title, Hayek remarked to Polanyi: "What appeals to me most in that title is that it would to some extent take the wind out of the sails of the socialists, who so far seem to have had all the advantage of the names which appeal to the man of goodwill." Hayek to Polanyi, letter of February 4, 1940, the Polanyi Archives, University of Chicago Library.

[122]F. A. Hayek, "The Intellectuals and Socialism", *University of Chicago Law Review*, volume 16, Spring 1949, pp. 417–433; reprinted in Hayek, *Studies in Philosophy, Politics and Economics* (Chicago: University of Chicago Press, 1967), pp. 178–194, which appears as chapter 11, this volume. Presumably Hayek would not share in the tiresome periodic outpouring of despair over 'the disappearance of the intellectual' from American public culture.

[123]*Ibid.*, p. 237, this volume.

[124]F. A. Hayek, *The Constitution of Liberty*, op. cit.

attention of the intelligentsia. As the socialist John Roemer succinctly states, "Clearly the Soviet model of socialist society is dead, but that does not mean that the other, untried forms of socialism should be buried along with it. This essay is a defense of an alternative socialism, market socialism."[125] Two recent collections of articles contain a variety of proposed market socialist alternatives.[126]

This development may seem incredible to those who know the history of the socialist calculation debates or, more fundamentally, to those who have followed the fortunes of various socialist 'experiments' in the twentieth century. It is essential for advocates of the market system to understand why socialist hopes for a New Jerusalem are so difficult to extinguish. There are three reasons for the persistence of such visions, and all of them were well understood by Hayek.

1) Dreams for a socialist utopia tap two deep and basic human impulses. The first is the quest for "social justice", for a society that is better, perhaps more egalitarian but certainly less unfair, than the one in which one lives. The second is the hope, and in more optimistic (or arrogant) times the expectation, that with reason, planning, and adequate forethought, such a society can actually be constructed. To possess these impulses, the desire for a better society and the willingness to try to construct one, is part of what it means to be human. Hayek knew this, which is why despite his strong disagreements with them, he never questioned the motivation of his socialist opponents.[127]

But Hayek also knew of the dangers of such hopes. He understood, in the first instance, that many human actions have beneficial though unintended consequences, and that through them a complex web of social institutions had emerged which served mankind remarkably well. He also understood that attempts to reconstruct society anew were virtually destined to fail. Since human comprehension of the functions of existing institutional structures is in the nature of things severely limited, changes in the structures could easily produce unintended adverse consequences. In particular, changes that failed to understand, as economists do, the functions performed by market institutions were bound to have disas-

---

[125]John Roemer, *A Future for Socialism* (Cambridge: Harvard University Press, 1994), p. 1.

[126]Pranab Bardhan and John Roemer, eds, *Market Socialism* (New York and Oxford: Oxford University Press, 1993), and Frank Roosevelt and David Belkin, eds, *Why Market Socialism? Voices from Dissent* (Armonk, N. Y., and London: M. E. Sharpe, 1994). Unfortunately there is not space here for a discussion of the new literature on market socialism and the economics of information, and their relationship to the earlier writings of Hayek and others.

[127]Hayek accordingly dismisses Schumpeter's cynical charge that it is 'politeness' that accounts for his failure to attack his opponents' motivations. See p. 227, this volume.

trous consequences, yet these were the very institutions that socialists seemed most intent on altering.

Because it drew on many disciplines, Hayek's message was not an easy one to grasp. And since it emphasized the limits of our capacity to change the world, neither was it an easy one for intellectuals or reformers to accept, particularly in the age in which he was writing, which was the heyday of positivism. We live today in a post-positivist world, one which has witnessed firsthand the unintended consequences of the engineering mentality, so perhaps there is reason to hope that Hayek's arguments may finally be allowed a fair hearing. In his last book, Hayek offered this final observation:

> It is a betrayal of concerns for others, then, to theorize about 'the just society' without carefully considering the economic consequences of implementing such views. Yet, after seventy years of experience with socialism, it is safe to say that most intellectuals outside the areas—Eastern Europe and the Third World—where socialism has been tried remain content to brush aside what lessons might lie in economics, unwilling to wonder whether there might not be a *reason* why socialism, as often as it is attempted, never seems to work out as its intellectual leaders *intended.*[128]

2) A second problem is that there are as many variants of socialism as there are blueprints for socialist utopias. This was a problem that both Mises and Hayek faced. Each time they attempted to show the flaws in one plan, another was proposed in its place. In the end the Austrians proposed general arguments against socialism, a strategy which under the circumstances made good sense, but which has its own shortcomings. Even general arguments may not apply to all conceivable socialist systems. But even more important, because general arguments do not address the specifics of particular plans, they can be ignored by socialist opponents who will insist that their own specific blueprints have not been adequately addressed.[129] The plethora of plans also explains how social-

[128]F. A. Hayek, *The Fatal Conceit: The Errors of Socialism,* ed. W. W. Bartley III, which is vol. 1 (1988) of *The Collected Works of F. A. Hayek,* op. cit., p. 85, emphasis in the original.

[129]Thus Evan Durbin, in his "Professor Hayek on Economic Planning and Political Liberty", *Economic Journal,* volume 55, December 1945, questioned Hayek's claim that socialism requires that planners impose a single set of values on the rest of society. Durbin argued that Hayek's criticism did not count as an argument against market socialism, under which production plans for private goods are supposed to reflect consumers' diverse preferences. In a footnote in *The Road to Serfdom,* op. cit., p. 40, Hayek had noted that his criticism of 'competitive socialism' could be found elsewhere, a point that Durbin conveniently ignored.

ists can continue to keep their hopes for a socialist utopia alive, even in the face of overwhelming countervailing evidence. Every failure convinces the committed socialist not of a flaw in socialism, but that the wrong blueprint has been used.

3) There is a final reason, a profound one, why dreams for a socialist utopia may never die. Hayek's case against socialism makes sense; it is reasonable, as is his case for viewing the market system as a mechanism for the discovery, creation, and coordination of knowledge. But these cases are not susceptible to any ultimate empirical test; there are no crucial experiments; ultimately his claims are not provable. Hayek recognizes this in his essay "Competition as a Discovery Procedure".

> The necessary consequence of the reason why we use competition is that, *in those cases in which it is interesting,* the validity of the theory can never be proved empirically. We can test it on conceptual models, and we might conceivably test it in artificially created real situations, where the facts which competition is intended to discover are already known to the observer. . . . If we do not know the facts we hope to discover by means of competition, we can never ascertain how effective it has been in discovering those facts that might be discovered. . . . The peculiarity of competition—which it has in common with the scientific method—is that its performance cannot be tested in particular instances where it is significant, but is shown only by the fact that the market will prevail in comparison with any alternative arrangements.[130]

Because of obstacles of this sort, Hayek's arguments presumably will make little headway with the committed socialist. But perhaps they can serve as a counterweight to the perennial socialist vision of a just society, a vision the implementation of which has been the source of much human suffering. Hayek's arguments should also help to convince those who have yet to make up their minds, and so may keep good-hearted people from repeating, always in the name of human decency, some of the twentieth century's most terrible mistakes.

Bruce Caldwell

This nicely illustrates the difficulty of formulating an effective critique of the many-headed Hydra.

[130]F. A. Hayek, "Competition as a Discovery Procedure", op. cit., p. 180, emphasis in the original.

PART I

MARKET SOCIALISM AND THE SOCIALIST CALCULATION DEBATE

ONE

THE NATURE AND HISTORY OF THE PROBLEM[1]

1. The Unseen Problem

There is reason to believe that we are at last entering an era of reasoned discussion of what has long uncritically been assumed to be a reconstruction of society on rational lines. For more than half a century, the belief that deliberate regulation of all social affairs must necessarily be more successful than the apparent haphazard interplay of independent individuals has continuously gained ground until today there is hardly a political group anywhere in the world which does not want central direction of most human activities in the service of one aim or another. It seemed so easy to improve upon the institutions of a free society which had come more and more to be considered as the result of mere accident, the product of a peculiar historical growth which might as well have taken a different direction. To bring order to such a chaos, to apply reason to the organization of society, and to shape it deliberately in every detail according to human wishes and the common ideas of justice seemed the only course of action worthy of a reasonable being.

But at the present day it is clear—it would probably be admitted by all sides—that during the greater part of the growth of this belief, some of the most serious problems of such a reconstruction have not even been recognized, much less successfully answered. For many years discussion of socialism—and for the greater part of the period it was only from socialism proper that the movement sprang—turned almost exclusively on ethical and psychological issues. On the one hand there was the general question whether justice required a reorganization of society on socialist lines and what principles of the distribution of income were to be regarded as just. On the other hand there was the question whether men in general could be trusted to have the moral and psychological qualities

---

[1][Published as "The Nature and History of the Problem", which constitutes the introduction to *Collectivist Economic Planning: Critical Studies on the Possibilities of Socialism*, ed. F. A. Hayek (London: George Routledge and Son, 1935; reprinted, Clifton, N. J.: Kelley, 1975), pp. 1–20. Reprinted in F. A. Hayek, ed., *Individualism and Economic Order*, op. cit.—Ed.]

which were dimly seen to be essential if a socialist system was to work. But although this latter question does raise some of the real difficulties, it does not really touch the heart of the problem. What was questioned was only whether the authorities in the new state would be in a position to make people carry out their plans properly. Only the practical possibility of the execution of the plans was called in question, not whether planning, even in the ideal case where these difficulties were absent, would achieve the desired end. The problem seemed therefore to be 'only' one of psychology or education, the 'only' meaning that after initial difficulties these obstacles would certainly be overcome.

If this were true, then the economist would have nothing to say on the feasibility of such proposals, and indeed it is improbable that any scientific discussion of their merits would be possible. It would be a problem of ethics, or rather of individual judgements of value, on which different people might agree or disagree, but on which no reasoned arguments would be possible. Some of the questions might be left to the psychologist to decide, if he has really any means of saying what men would be like under entirely different circumstances. Apart from this no scientist, and least of all the economist, would have anything to say about the problems of socialism. And many people believing that the knowledge of the economist is only applicable to the problems of a capitalist society (i.e., to problems arising out of peculiar human institutions which would be absent in a world organized on different lines) still think this to be the case.

2. Economic and Technological Problems

Whether this widespread belief is based on a clear conviction that there would be no economic problems in a socialist world, or whether it simply proves that the people who hold it do not know what economic problems are, is not always evident. Probably usually the latter. This is not at all surprising. The big economic problems which the economist sees and which he contends will also have to be solved in a collectivist society are not problems which at present are solved deliberately by anybody in the sense in which the economic problems of a household reach solution. In a purely competitive society nobody bothers about any but his own economic problems. There is therefore no reason why the existence of economic problems, in the sense in which the economist uses the term, should be known to others. But the distribution of available resources between different uses which is the economic problem is no less a problem for society than for the individual, and although the decision is not consciously made by anybody, the competitive mechanism does bring about some sort of solution.

No doubt if it were put in this general way everybody would be ready to admit that such a problem exists. But few realize that it is fundamentally different not only in difficulty but also in character from the problems of engineering. The increasing preoccupation of the modern world with problems of an engineering character tends to blind people to the totally different character of the economic problem, and is probably the main cause why the nature of the latter was less and less understood. At the same time, everyday terminology used in discussing either sort of problem has greatly enhanced the confusion. The familiar phrase of 'trying to get the greatest results from the given means' covers both problems. The metallurgist who seeks for a method which will enable him to extract a maximum amount of metal from a given quantity of ore, the military engineer who tries to build a bridge with a given number of men in the shortest possible time, or the optician who endeavours to construct a telescope which will enable the astronomer to penetrate to still more distant stars, all are concerned solely with technological problems. The common character of these problems is determined by the singleness of their purpose in every case, the absolutely determined nature of the ends to which the available means are to be devoted. Nor does it alter the fundamental character of the problem if the means available for a definite purpose is a fixed amount of money to be spent on factors of production with given prices. From this point of view the industrial engineer who decides on the best method of production of a given commodity on the basis of given prices is concerned only with technological problems although he may speak of his trying to find the most economical method. But the only element which makes his decision *in its effects* an economic one is not any part of his calculations but only the fact that he uses, as a basis for these calculations, prices as he finds them on the market.

The problems which the director of all economic activities of a community would have to face would only be similar to those solved by an engineer if the order of importance of the different needs of the community were fixed in such a definite and absolute way that provision for one could always be made irrespective of cost. If it were possible for him first to decide on the best way to produce the necessary supply of, say, food as the most important need, as if it were the only need, and would think about the supply, say, of clothing, only if and when some means were left over after the demand for food had been fully satisfied, then there would be no economic problem. For in such a case nothing would be left over except what could not possibly be used for the first purpose, either because it could not be turned into food or because there was no further demand for food. The criterion would simply be whether the possible maximum of foodstuffs had been produced or whether the application of different methods might not lead to a greater output. But the task would cease to be merely technological in character and would assume an entirely different nature if it were further postulated that as many resources as possible should be left over for other purposes. Then the question arises what *is* a greater quantity of resources. If one engineer proposed a method which would leave a great deal of land but only little labour for other purposes, while another would leave much labour and little land, how in the absence of any standard of value could it be decided which was the greater quantity? If there were only one factor of production this could be decided unequivocally on merely technical grounds, for then the main problem in every line of production would again be reduced to one of getting the maximum quantity of product out of any given amount of the same resources. The remaining economic problem of how much to produce in every line of production would in this case be of a very simple and almost negligible nature. As soon as there are two or more factors, however, this possibility is not present.

The economic problem arises therefore as soon as different purposes compete for the available resources. And the criterion of its presence is that costs have to be taken into account. Cost here, as anywhere, means nothing but the advantages to be derived from the use of given resources in other directions. Whether this is simply the use of part of the possible working day for recreation or the use of material resources in an alternative line of production makes little difference. It is clear that decisions of this sort will have to be made in any conceivable kind of economic system, wherever one has to choose between alternative employments of given resources. But the decisions between two possible alternative uses cannot be made in the absolute way which was possible in our earlier example. Even if the director of the economic system were quite clear in his mind that the food of one person is always more important than the clothing of another, that would by no means necessarily imply that it is also more important than the clothing of two or ten others. How critical the question is becomes clearer if we look at the less elementary wants. It may well be that although the need for one additional doctor is greater than the need for one additional schoolteacher, yet under conditions where it costs three times as much to train an additional doctor as it costs to train an additional schoolteacher, three additional schoolteachers may appear preferable to one doctor.

As has been said before, the fact that in the present order of things such economic problems are not solved by the conscious decision of anybody has the effect that most people are not conscious of their existence. Decisions whether and how much of a thing to produce are economic decisions in this sense. But the making of such a decision by a single

56

individual is only part of the solution of the economic problem involved. The person making such a decision makes it on the basis of given prices. The fact that by this decision he influences these prices to a certain, probably very small, extent will not influence his choice. The other part of the problem is solved by the functioning of the price system. But it is solved in a way which only a systematic study of the working of this system reveals. It has been already suggested that it is not necessary for the working of this sytem that anybody should understand it. But people are not likely to let it work if they do not understand it.

The real situation in this respect is very well reflected in the popular estimate of the relative merits of the economists and the engineer. It is probably no exaggeration to say that to most people the engineer is the person who actually does things and the economist the odious individual who sits back in his armchair and explains why the well-meaning efforts of the former are frustrated. In a sense this is not untrue. But the implication that the forces which the economist studies and the engineer is likely to disregard are unimportant and ought to be disregarded is absurd. It needs the special training of the economist to see that the spontaneous forces which limit the ambitions of the engineer themselves provide a way of solving a problem which otherwise would have to be solved deliberately.

3. The Decay of Economic Insight

There are, however, other reasons besides the increasing conspicuousness of the elaborate modern technique of production which are responsible for our contemporary failure to see the existence of economic problems. It was not always so. For a comparatively short period in the middle of the last century, the degree to which the economic problems were seen and understood by the general public was undoubtedly much higher than it is at present. But the classical system of political economy whose extraordinary influence facilitated this understanding had been based on insecure and in parts definitely faulty foundations, and its popularity had been achieved at the price of a degree of oversimplification which proved to be its undoing. It was only much later, after its teaching had lost influence, that the gradual reconstruction of economic theory showed that what defects there were in its basic concepts had invalidated its explanation of the working of the economic system to a much smaller degree than had at first seemed probable. But in the interval irreparable harm had been done. The downfall of the classical system tended to discredit the very idea of theoretical analysis, and it was attempted to substitute for an understanding of the why of economic phenomena a mere description of their occurrence. In consequence, the comprehension of the nature of the economic problem, the achievement of generations of teaching, was lost. The economists who were still interested in general analysis were far too much concerned with the reconstructing of the purely abstract foundations of economic science to exert a noticeable influence on opinion regarding policy.

It was largely owing to this temporary eclipse of analytical economics that the real problems connected with the suggestions of a planned economy have received so surprisingly little careful examination. But this eclipse itself was by no means only due to the inherent weaknesses and the consequent need for reconstruction of the old economics. Nor would it have had the same effect if it had not coincided with the rise of another movement definitely hostile to rational methods in economics. The common cause which at the same time undermined the position of economic theory and furthered the growth of a school of socialism, which positively discouraged any speculation of the actual working of the society of the future, was the rise of the so-called historical school in economics.[2] For it was the essence of the standpoint of this school that the laws of economics could only be established by the application to the material of history of the methods of the natural sciences. And the nature of this material is such that any such attempt is bound to degenerate into mere record and description and a total scepticism concerning the existence of any laws at all.

It is not difficult to see why this should happen. In all sciences except those which deal with social phenomena all that experience shows us is the result of processes which we cannot directly observe and which it is our task to reconstruct. All our conclusions concerning the nature of these processes are of necessity hypothetical, and the only test of the validity of these hypotheses is that they prove equally applicable to the explanation of other phenomena. And what enables us to arrive by this process of induction at the formulation of general laws or hypotheses regarding the process of causation is the fact that the possibility of experi-

---

[2]Some of the points on which I can only touch here I have developed at somewhat greater length in my inaugural address on "The Trend of Economic Thinking", *Economica*, vol. 13, May 1933, pp. 121–137. [Reprinted in *The Trend of Economic Thinking*, op. cit., chapter 1. The German Historical School was the chief rival of the Austrian School of Economics at the end of the nineteenth century. There were also historical movements in England and the United States; for more on this, see A. W. Coats, "The Historist Reaction in English Political Economy", *Economica, N. S.*, vol. 21, May 1954, pp. 143–153; Joseph Dorfman, "The Role of the German Historical School in American Economic Thought", *American Economic Review Papers and Proceedings*, vol. 45, May 1955, pp. 17–28; and Gerard Koot, *English Historical Economics 1870–1926: The Rise of Economic History and Neomercantilism* (Cambridge: Cambridge University Press, 1987).—Ed.]

menting, of observing the repetition of the same phenomena under identical conditions, shows the existence of definite regularities in the observed phenomena.

In the social sciences, however, the situation is the exact reverse. On the one hand, experiment is impossible, and we have therefore no knowledge of definite regularities in the complex phenomena in the same sense as we have in the natural sciences. But on the other hand the position of man, midway between natural and social phenomena—of the one of which he is an effect and of the other a cause—brings it about that the essential basic facts which we need for the explanation of social phenomena are part of common experience, part of the stuff of our thinking. In the social sciences it is the elements of the complex phenomena which are known beyond the possibility of dispute. In the natural sciences they can only be at best surmised. The existence of these elements is so much more certain than any regularities in the complex phenomena to which they give rise that it is they which constitute the truly empirical factor in the social sciences. There can be little doubt that it is this different position of the empirical factor in the process of reasoning in the two groups of disciplines which is at the root of much of the confusion with regard to their logical character. There can be no doubt, the social as well as natural sciences have to employ deductive reasoning. The essential difference is that in the natural sciences the process of deduction has to start from some hypothesis which is the result of inductive generalizations, while in the social sciences it starts directly from known empirical elements and uses them to find the regularities in the complex phenomena which direct observations cannot establish. They are, so to speak, empirically deductive sciences, proceeding from the known elements to the regularities in the complex phenomena which cannot be directly established. But this is not the place to discuss questions of methodology for their own sake. Our concern is only to show how it came that in the era of the great triumphs of empiricism in the natural sciences the attempt to force the same empirical methods on the social sciences was bound to lead to disaster. To start here at the wrong end, to seek for regularities of complex phenomena which could never be observed twice under identical conditions, could not but lead to the conclusion that there were no general laws, no inherent necessities determined by the permanent nature of the constituting elements, and that the only task of economic science in particular was a description of historical change. It was only with this abandonment of the appropriate methods of procedure, well established in the classical period, that it began to be thought that there were no other laws of social life than those made by men, that all observed phenomena were all only the product of social or legal institutions, merely 'historical categories' and not in any way arising out of the basic economic problems which humanity has to face.

4. The Attitude of Marxism

In many respects the most powerful school of socialism the world has so far seen is essentially a product of this kind of 'Historismus'. Although in some points Karl Marx adopted the tools of the classical economists, he made little use of their main permanent contribution, their analysis of competition. But he did wholeheartedly accept the central contention of the historical school that most of the phenomena of economic life were not the result of permanent causes but only the product of a special historical development. It is no accident that the country where the historical school had had the greatest vogue, Germany, was also the country where Marxism was most readily accepted.

The fact that this most influential school of socialism was so closely related to the general antitheoretical tendencies in the social sciences of the time had a most profound effect on all further discussion of the real problems of socialism. Not only did the whole outlook create a peculiar inability to see any of the permanent economic problems which are independent of the historical framework, but Marx and the Marxians also proceeded, quite consistently, positively to discourage any inquiry into the actual organization and working of the socialist society of the future. If the change was to be brought about by the inexorable logic of history, if it was the inevitable result of evolution, there was little need for knowing in detail what exactly the new society would be like. And if nearly all the factors which determined economic activity in the present society would be absent, if there would be no problems in the new society except those determined by the new institutions which the process of historical change would have created, then there was indeed little possibility of solving any of its problems beforehand. Marx himself had only scorn and ridicule for any such attempt deliberately to construct a working plan of such an 'utopia'. Only occasionally, and then in this negative form, do we find in his works statements about what the new society would *not* be like. One may search his writings in vain for any definite statement of the general principles on which the economic activity in the socialist community would be directed.[3]

[3]A useful collection of the different allusions to this problem in Marx's works, particularly in the *Randglossen zum Gothaer Programm* (1875), will be found in K. Tisch, *Wirtschaftsrechnung und Verteilung im zentralistisch organisierten sozialistischen Gemeinwesen* (doctoral thesis, University of Bonn, 1932), pp. 110–115. [Hayek refers to Marx's *Critique of the Gotha Programme* (English translation, New York: International Publishers, 1938). The critique was originally a letter in the form of marginal notes criticizing the proposed German Social Democratic Party platform, especially those statements which reflected the influence of Marx's rival,

Marx's attitude on this point had a lasting effect on the socialist of his school. To speculate about the actual organization of the socialist society immediately stigmatized the unfortunate writer as being 'unscientific', the most dreaded condemnation to which a member of the 'scientific' school of socialism could expose himself. But even outside the Marxian camp the common descent of all modern branches of socialism from some essentially historical or 'institutional' view of economic phenomena had the effect of successfully smothering all attempts to study the problems any constructive socialist policy would have to solve. As we shall see later, it was only in reply to criticism from the outside that this task was ultimately undertaken.

5. Socialism and Planning

We have now reached a point where it becomes necessary clearly to separate several different aspects of the programmes which we have so far lumped together as socialistic. For the earlier part of the period in which the belief in central planning grew it is historically justified to identify, without much qualification, the idea of socialism and that of planning. And in so far as the main economic problems are concerned, this is still the case today. Yet it must be admitted that in many other respects modern socialists and other modern planners are fully entitled to disclaim any responsibility for each other's programmes. What we must distinguish here are the ends aimed at and the means which have been proposed or are in fact necessary for the purpose. The ambiguities which exist in this connection arise out of the fact that the means necessary to achieve the ends of socialism in the narrower sense may be used for other ends, and that the problems with which we are concerned arise out of the means and not the ends.

The common end of all socialism in the narrower sense, of 'proletarian' socialism, is the improvement of the position of the propertyless classes of society by a redistribution of income derived from property. This implies collective ownership of the material means of production and collectivist direction and control of their use. The same collectivist methods may, however, be applied in the service of quite different ends. An aristocratic dictatorship, for example, may use the same methods to further the interest of some racial or other elite or in the service of some other decidedly anti-egalitarian purpose. The situation is further complicated by the fact that the method of collectivist ownership and control which is essential for any of these attempts to dissociate the distribution of income from the

---

Ferdinand Lassalle, whose followers were uniting with the Social Democrats. The Party Congress was held May 22–27, 1875, in the town of Gotha.—Ed.]

61

private ownership of the means of production admits of application in different degrees. For the present it will be convenient to use the term 'socialism' to describe the traditional socialist ends and to use the term 'planning' to describe the method, although later we shall use socialism in the wider sense. In the narrower sense of the term it can be said, then, that it is possible to have much planning with little socialism or little planning and much socialism. The method of planning in any case can certainly be used for purposes which have nothing to do with the ethical aims of socialism. Whether it is equally possible to dissociate socialism completely from planning—and the criticism directed against the method has led to attempts in this direction—is a question which we shall have to investigate later.

That it is possible, not only in theory but also in practice, to separate the problem of the method from that of the end is very fortunate for the purposes of scientific discussion. On the validity of the ultimate ends science has nothing to say. They may be accepted or rejected, but they cannot be proved or disproved. All that we can rationally argue about is whether and to what extent given measures will lead to the desired results. If, however, the method in question were only proposed as a means for one particular end it might prove difficult, in practice, to keep the argument about the technical question and the judgements of value quite apart. But since the same problem of means arises in connection with altogether different ethical ideals, one may hope that it will be possible to keep value judgements altogether out of the discussion.

The common condition necessary for the achievement of a distribution of income which is independent of individual ownership of resources—the common proximate end of socialism and other anti-capitalistic movements—is that the authority which decides on the principles of this distribution should also have control over the resources. Now whatever the substance of these principles of distribution, these ideas about the just or otherwise desirable division of income, they must be similar in one purely formal but highly important respect: They must be stated in the form of a scale of importance of a number of competing individual ends. It is this formal aspect, this fact that one central authority has to solve the economic problem of distributing a limited amount of resources between a practically infinite number of competing purposes, that constitutes the problem of socialism as a method. And the fundamental question is whether it is possible under the complex conditions of a large modern society for such a central authority to carry out the implications of any such scale of values with a reasonable degree of accuracy, with a degree of success equalling or approaching the results of competitive capitalism, not whether any particular set of values of this sort is in any way superior to another. It is the methods common to socialism in the narrower sense and all the other modern movements for a planned society, not the particular ends of socialism, with which we are here concerned.

6. The Types of Socialism

Since in all that follows we shall be concerned only with the methods to be employed and not with the ends aimed at, from now onwards it will be convenient to use the term socialism in this wider sense. In this sense it covers therefore any case of collectivist control of productive resources, no matter in whose interest this control is used. But while we need for our purpose no further definition of the concrete ends followed, there is still need for a further definition of the exact methods we want to consider. There are, of course, many kinds of socialism, but the traditional names of these different types, like communism, syndicalism, guild socialism, have never quite corresponded to the classification of methods which we want, and most of them have in recent times become so closely connected with political parties rather than with definite programmes that they are hardly useful for our purpose. What is relevant for us is essentially the degree to which the central control and direction of the resources is carried in each of the different types. To see to what extent variation on this point is possible it is perhaps best to begin with the most familiar type of socialism and then examine to what extent its arrangements can be altered in different directions.

The programme which is at once the most widely advocated and has the greatest prima facie plausibility provides not only for collective ownership but also for unified central direction of the use of all material resources of production. At the same time it envisages continued freedom of choice in consumption and continued freedom of the choice of occupation. At least it is essentially in this form that Marxism has been interpreted by the social-democratic parties on the Continent, and it is the form in which socialism is imagined by the greatest number of people. It is in this form too that socialism has been most widely discussed; most of the more recent criticism is focused on this variety. Indeed, so widely has it been treated as the only important socialist programme that in most discussions on the economic problems of socialism the authors concerned have neglected to specify which kind of socialism they had in mind. This has had somewhat unfortunate effects. For it never became quite clear whether particular objections or criticisms applied only to this particular form or to all the forms of socialism.

For this reason right from the outset it is necessary to keep the alternative possibilities in mind, and to consider at every stage of the discussion carefully whether any particular problem arises out of the assumptions which must underlie any socialist programme or whether they are only due to assumptions made in some particular case. Freedom of the choice of the consumer or freedom of occupation, for example, are by no means necessary attributes of any socialist programme, and although earlier socialists have generally repudiated the suggestion that socialism would abolish these freedoms, more recently criticisms of the socialist position have been met by the answer that the supposed difficulties would arise only if they were retained, and that it was by no means too high a price for the other advantages of socialism if their abolition should prove necessary. It is therefore necessary to consider this extreme form of socialism equally with the others. It corresponds in most respects to what in the past used to be called communism, i.e., a system where not only the means of production but all goods were collectively owned and where, in addition to this, the central authority would also be in a position to order any person to do any task.

This kind of society where everything is centrally directed may be regarded as the limiting case of a long series of other systems of a lesser degree of centralization. The more familiar type discussed already stands somewhat further in the direction of decentralization. But it still involves planning on a most extensive scale—minute direction of practically all productive activity by one central authority. The earlier systems of more decentralized socialism like guild-socialism or syndicalism need not concern us here since it seems now to be fairly generally admitted that they provide no mechanism whatever for a rational direction of economic activity. More recently, however, there has arisen, again mainly in response to criticism, a tendency among socialist thinkers to reintroduce a certain degree of competition into their schemes in order to overcome the difficulty which they admit would arise in the case of completely centralized planning. There is no need at this stage to consider in detail the forms in which competition between individual producers may be combined with socialism. This will be done later on. But it is necessary from the outset to be aware of them. This for two reasons: In the first place, in order to remain conscious throughout the further discussion that the completely centralized direction of all economic activity which is generally regarded as typical of all socialism may conceivably be varied to some extent; secondly—and even more important—in order that we may see clearly what degree of central control must be retained in order that we may reasonably speak of socialism, or what are the minimum assumptions which will still entitle us to regard a system as coming within our field. Even if collective ownership of productive resources should be found to be compatible with competitive determination of the purposes for which individual units of resources are to be used and the method of their employment, we must still assume that the question, who is to exercise command over a given quantity of resources for the community, or with what amount of resources the different 'entrepreneurs' are to be entrusted, will have to be decided by one central authority. This seems to be the minimum assumption consistent with the idea of collective ownership, the smallest degree of central control which would still enable the community to retain command over the income derived from the material means of production.

7. Planning and Capitalism

Without some such central control of the means of production, planning in the sense in which we have used the term ceases to be a problem. It becomes unthinkable. This would probably be agreed by the majority of economists of all camps, although most other people who believe in planning still think of it as something which could be rationally attempted inside the framework of a society based on private property. In fact, however, if by planning is meant the actual direction of productive activity by authoritative prescription, either of the quantities to be produced, the methods of production to be used, or the prices to be fixed, it can be easily shown, not that such a thing is impossible, but that any isolated measure of this sort will cause reactions which will defeat its own end, and that any attempt to act consistently will necessitate further and further measures of control until all economic activity is brought under one central authority.

It is impossible within the scope of this discussion of socialism to enter further into this separate problem of state intervention in a capitalistic society. It is mentioned here only to say explicitly that it is excluded from our considerations. In our opinion, well-accepted analysis shows that it does not provide an alternative which can be rationally chosen or which can be expected to provide a stable or satisfactory solution of any of the problems to which it is applied.[4]

But here again it is necessary to guard against misunderstanding. To say that partial planning of the kind we are alluding to is irrational is, however, not equivalent to saying that the only form of capitalism which can be rationally advocated is that of complete laissez faire in the old sense. There is no reason to assume that the historically given legal insti-

---

[4]Cf. Ludwig von Mises, *Kritik des Interventionismus* (Jena: Gustav Fischer, 1929). [This was later published as *A Critique of Interventionism*, trans. Hans Sennholz (New Rochelle, N.Y.: Arlington House, 1977). Mises (1881–1973) was Hayek's mentor; for more on their relationship, see F. A. Hayek, *Hayek on Hayek*, op. cit., pp. 67–73.—Ed.]

tutions are necessarily the most 'natural' in any sense. The recognition of the principle of private property does not by any means necessarily imply that the particular delimitation of the contents of this right as determined by the existing laws are the most appropriate. The question as to which is the most appropriate permanent framework which will secure the smoothest and most efficient working of competition is of the greatest importance and one which it must be admitted has been sadly neglected by economists.

But on the other hand, to admit the possibility of changes in the legal framework is not to admit the possibility of a further type of planning in the sense in which we have used the word so far. There is an essential distinction here which must not be overlooked; the distinction between a permanent legal framework so devised as to provide all the necessary incentives to private initiative to bring about the adaptations required by any change, and a system where such adaptations are brought about by central direction. And it is this, and not the question of the maintenance of the existing order versus the introduction of new institutions, which is the real issue. In a sense both systems can be described as being the product of rational planning. But in the one case this planning is concerned only with the permanent framework of institutions and may be dispensed with if one is willing to accept the institutions which have grown in a slow historical process, while in the other it has to deal with day-to-day changes of every sort.

There can be no doubt that planning of this sort involves changes of a type and magnitude hitherto unknown in human history. It is sometimes urged that the changes now in progress are merely a return to the social forms of the pre-industrial era. But this is a misapprehension. Even when the medieval guild system was at its height, and when restrictions to commerce were most extensive, they were not used as a means to actually direct individual activity. They were probably not the most rational permanent framework for individual activity which could have been devised, but they were essentially only a permanent framework inside which current activity by individual initiative had free play. With our attempts to use the old apparatus of restrictionism as an instrument of almost day-to-day adjustment to change we have probably already gone much further in the direction of central planning of current activity than has ever been attempted before. And if we follow the path on which we have started, if we try to act consistently and to combat the self-frustrating tendencies of any isolated act of planning, we shall certainly embark upon an experiment which has no parallel in history. But even at this stage we have gone very far. If we are to judge the potentialities aright it is necessary to realize that the system under which we live choked up with attempts at partial planning and restrictionism is almost as far from any system of capitalism which could be rationally advocated as it is different from any consistent system of planning. It is important to realize in any investigation of the possibilities of planning that it is a fallacy to suppose capitalism as it exists today is the alternative. We are certainly as far from capitalism in its pure form as we are from any system of central planning. The world of today is just interventionist chaos.

8. The Basis of Modern Criticism

Classical political economy broke down mainly because it failed to base its explanation of the fundamental phenomenon of value on the same analysis of the springs of economic activity which it had so successfully applied to the analysis of the more complex phenomena of competition. The labour theory of value was the product of a search after some illusory substance of value rather than an analysis of the behaviour of the economic subject. The decisive step in the progress of economics was taken when economists began to ask what exactly were the circumstances which made individuals behave towards goods in a particular way. And to ask the question in this form led immediately to the recognition that to attach a definite significance or value to the units of different goods was a necessary step in the solution of the general problem which arises everywhere when a multiplicity of ends compete for a limited quantity of means.

The omnipresence of this problem of value wherever there is rational action was the basic fact from which a systematic exploration of the forms under which it would make its appearance under different organizations of economic life could proceed. And up to a certain point from the very beginning the problems of a centrally directed economy found a prominent place in the expositions of modern economics. It was obviously so much simpler to discuss the fundamental problems on the assumption of the existence of a *single* scale of values consistently followed than on the assumption of a multiplicity of individuals following their personal scales that in the early chapters of the new systems the assumption of a communist state was frequently used—and used with considerable advantage—as an expository device.[5] But it was used only to demonstrate that any solution would necessarily give rise to essentially the same value phenomena—rent, wages, and interest, etc.—which we actually observe in a competitive society, and the authors then generally proceeded to show how the interaction of independent activities of the individuals produced these phenomena spontaneously without inquiring further whether they

---

[5]Cf. particularly Friedrich von Wieser, *Natural Value*, ed. William Smart, trans. Christian Malloch (London and New York: Macmillan, 1893), passim. [Wieser (1851–1926) taught Hayek at the University of Vienna; see the translation of Hayek's obituary notice in *The Fortunes of Liberalism*, op. cit., chapter 3.—Ed.]

could be produced in a complex modern society by any other means. The mere absence of an agreed common scale of values seemed to deprive that problem of any practical importance. It is true that some of the earlier writers of the new school not only thought that they had actually solved the problem of socialism but also believed that their utility calculus provided a means which made it possible to combine individual utility scales into a scale of ends objectively valid for society as a whole. But it is now generally recognized that this latter belief was just an illusion and that there is no scientific criterion which would enable us to compare or assess the relative importance of needs of different persons, although conclusions implying such illegitimate interpersonal comparisons of utilities can probably still be found in discussions of special problems.

But it is evident that as the progress of the analysis of the competitive system revealed the complexity of the problems which it solved spontaneously, economists became more and more sceptical about the possibility of solving the same problems by deliberate decision. It is perhaps worth noting that as early as 1854 the most famous among the predecessors of the modern 'marginal utility' school, the German H. H. Gossen, had come to the conclusion that the central economic authority projected by the communists would soon find that it had set itself a task which far exceeded the powers of individual men.[6] Among the later economists of

---

[6]H. H. Gossen, *Entwicklung der Gesetze des menschlichen Verkehrs und der daraus fließenden Regeln für menschliches Handeln* (Braunschweig: Vieweg, 1854), p. 231: "Dazu folgt aber außerdem aus den im vorstehenden gefundenen Sätzen über das Genießen, und infolgedessen über das Steigen und Sinken des Werthes jeder Sache mit Verminderung und Vermehrung der Maße und der Art, *daß nur durch Feststellung des Privateigenthums der Maßstab gefunden wird zur Bestimmung der Quantität, welche den Verhältnissen angemessen am Zweckmäßigsten von jedem Gegenstand zu produzieren ist.* Darum würde denn die von Communisten projectierte Zentralbehörde zur Verteilung der verschiedenen Arbeiten sehr bald die Erfahrung machen, daß sie sich eine Aufgabe gestellt habe, deren Lösung die Kräfte einzelner Menschen weit übersteigt" (italics in the original). ["Moreover, *only with the establishment of private property can the yardstick be found for the determination of the optimal quantity of each commodity to be produced under given circumstances.* This follows from the previously found laws of pleasure and the related rise and fall in the value of any commodity (with the decrease or increase of its quantity) and the manner by which prices are determined. Consequently, the central authority—projected by the communist—for the purpose of allocating the different types of labour and their rewards would soon find that it has set itself a task that far exceeds the powers of any individual." *The Laws of Human Relations and the Rules of Human Action Derived Therefrom*, trans. R. C. Blitz (Cambridge, Mass.: MIT Press, 1983), pp. 254–255. Hermann Heinrich Gossen (1810–1858) anticipated the 'Marginal Revolution' of the 1870s with his two 'Laws', the first postulating diminishing marginal utility, the second the equimarginal principle that total utility is maximized when the marginal utility of all activities is equalized. Hayek provided an introductory essay to the third German edition of the book; a translation of his essay may be found in *The Trend of Economic Thinking*, op. cit., pp. 352–371.—Ed.]

the modern school the point in which already Gossen based his objection, the difficulty of rational calculation when there is no private property, was frequently hinted at. It was particularly clearly put by Edwin Cannan, who stressed the fact that the aims of socialists and communists could only be achieved by "abolishing both the institution of private property and the practice of exchange, without which value, in any reasonable sense of the word, cannot exist."[7] But beyond general statements of this sort, critical examination of the possibilities of a socialist economic policy made little headway, for the simple reason that no concrete socialist proposal of how these problems would be overcome existed to be examined.[8]

It was only early in the present century that at last a general statement of the kind we have just examined concerning the impracticability of socialism by the eminent Dutch economist, N. G. Pierson,[9] provoked K. Kautsky, then the leading theoretician of Marxian socialism, to break the traditional silence about the actual working of the future socialist state, and to give in a lecture, still somewhat hesitantly and with many apologies, a description of what would happen on the Morrow of the Revolution.[10] But Kautsky only showed that he was not even really aware of the problem which the economists had seen. He thus gave Pierson the opportunity to demonstrate in detail, in an article which first appeared in the Dutch *Economist*, that a socialist state would have its problems of value just as any other economic system and that the task socialists had to solve

[7]Edwin Cannan, *A History of the Theories of Production and Distribution* [1893], 3rd edition (London: P. S. King, 1917; reprinted, New York: Kelley, 1967), p. 395. Professor Cannan has later also made an important contribution to the problem of international relations between socialist states. Cf. his essay on "The Incompatibility of Socialism and Nationalism" in *The Economic Outlook* (London: T. Fisher Unwin, 1912). [Edwin Cannan (1861–1935) taught at the London School of Economics from 1895 to 1926. For more on Cannan, see Hayek's obituary notice in F. A. Hayek, *Contra Keynes and Cambridge: Essays and Correspondence*, op. cit., Addendum to chapter 1.—Ed.]

[8]A completely neglected attempt to solve the problem from the socialist side, which shows at least some realization of the real difficulty, was made by Georg Sulzer, *Die Zukunft des Sozialismus* (Dresden: O. V. Bohmert, 1899).

[9][The Dutch economist Nikolaas G. Pierson (1839–1909) popularized the Austrian approach in Holland. His article, "Het waardeproblem in een socialistische Maatschappij", *De Economiste*, vol. 41, 1902, pp. 423–456, was translated by Hayek into German in 1925. The English version, translated by G. Gardiner, bore the title "The Problem of Value in the Socialist Society" and appeared as chapter 2 of *Collectivist Economic Planning*, op. cit.—Ed.]

[10]An English translation of this lecture, originally given in Delft on April 24, 1902, and soon afterwards published in German, together with that of another lecture given two days earlier at the same place, was published under the title, *The Social Revolution and On the Morrow of the Social Revolution* (London: Twentieth Century Press, 1903). [The Marxist Karl Kautsky (1854–1938) was the leading theoretician of the German Social Democratic Party. He was the architect of the Erfurt Program, passed by the Party Congress in 1891, which in supplanting the Gotha Program returned the Social Democrats to the Marxian fold.—Ed.]

was to show how in the absence of a pricing system the value of different goods was to be determined. This article is the first important contribution to the modern discussion of the economic aspects of socialism, and although it remained practically unknown outside of Holland and was only made accessible in a German version after the discussion had been started independently by others, it remains of special interest as the only important discussion of these problems published before the [First World] War. It is particularly valuable for its discussion of the problems arising out of the international trade between several socialist communities.[11]

All the further discussions of the economic problems of socialism which appeared before the war confined themselves more or less to the demonstration that the main categories of prices, as wages, rent and interest, would have to figure at least in the calculations of the planning authority in the same way in which they appear today and would be determined by essentially the same factors. The modern development of the theory of interest played a particularly important role in this connection, and after Böhm-Bawerk[12] it was particularly Gustav Cassel[13] who showed convincingly that interest would have to form an important element in the rational calculation of economic activity. But none of these authors even attempted to show how these essential magnitudes could be arrived at in practice. The one author who at least approached the problem was the Italian economist Enrico Barone who in 1908 in an article on the Ministry of Production in the Collectivist State developed certain suggestions of

[11][Hayek noted in the original publication of this article that an English translation is now reproduced in *Collectivist Economic Planning*, op. cit., as chapter 2.—Ed.]

[12]In addition to his general work on interest, his essay on "Macht oder ökonomisches Gesetz?", *Zeitschrift für Volkswirtschaft, Sozialpolitik und Verwaltung*, vol. 23, 1914, pp. 205–271, reprinted in Böhm-Bawerk's *Gesammelte Schriften*, vol. 1 (Vienna: Hölder-Pichler-Tempsky, 1924) should be specially mentioned, which in many ways must be regarded as a direct predecessor of the later critical work. [Eugen von Böhm-Bawerk (1851–1914) was, with Friedrich von Wieser, a prominent member of the 'second generation' of Austrian economists. Among those who attended his famous seminar at the University of Vienna prior to the First World War were Ludwig von Mises and Joseph Schumpeter. Böhm-Bawerk's most important work was *Kapital und Kapitalzins* [1884–1912], 3 vols, 4th edition (Jena: Gustav Fischer, 1921), published in English as *Capital and Interest*, trans. George Huncke and Hans Sennholz, 3 vols (South Holland, Ill.: Libertarian Press, 1959). A translation by John Richard Mez of the article cited above appears as "Control or Economic Law?" in *Shorter Classics of Böhm-Bawerk* (South Holland, Ill.: Libertarian Press, 1962), pp. 139–199.—Ed.]

[13][The Swedish economist Gustav Cassel (1866–1944) taught at the University of Stockholm. His students included future Nobel laureates in economics Bertil Ohlin and Gunnar Myrdal. Cassel's work on interest is contained in *The Nature and Necessity of Interest* (London and New York: Macmillan, 1903; reprinted, New York: Kelley and Millman, 1957).—Ed.]

Pareto's.[14] This article is of considerable interest as an example of how it was thought that the tools of mathematical analysis of economic problems might be utilized to solve the tasks of the central planning authority.[15]

9. The War and Its Effects on Continental Socialism

When, with the end of the [First World] War, socialist parties came into power in most of the states of central and Eastern Europe, the discussion on all these problems necessarily entered a new and decisive phase. The victorious socialist parties had now to think of a definite programme of action and the socialist literature of the years immediately following the war was for the first time largely concerned with the practical question how to organize production on socialist lines. These discussions were very much under the influence of the experience of the war years, when the states had set up food and raw material administrations to deal with the serious shortage of the most essential commodities. It was generally assumed that this had shown that not only was central direction of economic activity practicable and even superior to a system of competition, but also that the special technique of planning developed to cope with the problems of war economics might be equally applied to the permanent administration of a socialist economy.

Apart from Russia, where the rapidity of change in the years immediately following the revolution left little time for quiet reflection, it was mainly in Germany and even more so in Austria that these questions were most seriously debated. Particularly in the latter country, whose socialists had always played a leading role in the intellectual development of socialism, and where a strong and undivided socialist party had probably exercised a greater influence on its economic policy than in any other country outside of Russia, the problems of socialism had assumed enormous practical importance. It may perhaps be mentioned in passing that it is rather curious how little serious study has been devoted to the economic experiences of this country in the decade after the war, although they are prob-

---

[14]Vilfredo Pareto, *Cours d'Economie Politique*, vol. 2 (Lausanne: Librarie de l'Université, 1897), pp. 364 et seq. [The Italian economist Vilfredo Pareto (1848–1923), successor to the chair of Léon Walras at the University of Lausanne, expanded upon Walras's general equilibrium approach in his *Cours*. Enrico Barone (1859–1924) taught economics in Rome and also contributed to the development of general equilibrium theory. "The Ministry of Production in the Collectivist State" originally appeared as "Il Ministro della Produzione nello Stato Collettivista", *Giornale degli Economisti*, vol. 37, September/October 1908, pp. 267–293, 391–414.—Ed.]

[15][In the original publication of this article, Hayek noted that an English translation of the Barone article was published as an appendix to *Collectivist Economic Planning*, op. cit.—Ed.]

ably more relevant to the problems of a socialist policy in the Western world than anything that has happened in Russia. But whatever one may think about the importance of the actual experiments made in Austria, there can be little doubt that the theoretical contributions made there to the understanding of the problems will prove to be a considerable force in the intellectual history of our time.

Among these early socialist contributions to the discussions, in many ways the most interesting and in any case the most representative for the still very limited recognition of the nature of the economic problems involved, is a book by Otto Neurath which appeared in 1919,[16] in which the author tried to show that war experiences had shown that it was possible to dispense with any considerations of value in the administration of the supply of commodities and that all the calculations of the central planning authorities should and could be carried out *in natura*, i.e., that the calculations need not be carried through in terms of some common unit of value but that they could be made in kind. Neurath was quite oblivious of the insuperable difficulties which the absence of value calculations would put in the way of any rational economic use of the resources and even seemed to consider it as an advantage. Similar strictures apply to the works published about the same time by one of the leading spirits of the Austrian Social Democratic Party, Otto Bauer.[17] It is impossible here to give any detailed account of the argument of these and a number of other related publications of that time.[18] They have to be mentioned, however, because they are important as representative expressions of socialist thought just before the impact of the new criticism and because much of this criticism is naturally directly or implicitly concerned with these works.

In Germany discussion centred round the proposals of the 'socialization commission' set up to discuss the possibilities of the transfer of individual industries to the ownership and control of the state. It was this

---

[16]Otto Neurath, *Durch die Kriegswirtschaft zur Naturalwirtschaft,* op. cit. [The philosopher and sociologist Otto Neurath (1882–1945) attended, along with von Mises, Böhm-Bawerk's economics seminar and was later a member of the 'Vienna Circle' of logical positivists. According to Hayek, Neurath's book helped to "provoke" von Mises's work on socialist calculation; see F. A. Hayek, Foreword to Ludwig von Mises, *Socialism: An Economic and Sociological Analysis,* in *The Fortunes of Liberalism,* op. cit., p. 136.—Ed.]

[17]Otto Bauer, *Der Weg zum Sozialismus* (Vienna: Ignaz Brand, 1919). [Otto Bauer (1881–1938) was a leader of the Austrian Socialist Party following the First World War and a theoretician of Austro-Marxism. He, too, participated in Böhm-Bawerk's seminar; for more on Bauer, see Ludwig von Mises, *Notes and Recollections,* op. cit., pp. 16–19, 39–40, passim. —Ed.]

[18][For more on the Austrian contribution, see Günther Chaloupek, "The Austrian Debate on Economic Calculation in a Socialist Society", op. cit.—Ed.]

commission or in connection with its deliberations that economists like Professor Emil Lederer and Professor Eduard Heimann and the ill-fated Walther Rathenau developed plans for socialization which became the main topic of discussion among economists.[19] For our purpose, however, these proposals are less interesting than their Austrian counterparts because they did not contemplate a completely socialized system but were mainly concerned with the problem of the organization of individual socialized industries in an otherwise competitive system. For this reason their authors did not have to confront the main problems of a really socialist system. They are important, nevertheless, as symptoms of the state of public opinion at the time and in the nation where the more scientific examination of these problems began. One of the projects of this period deserves perhaps special mention not only because its authors are the inventors of the now-fashionable term 'planned economy', but also because it so closely resembles the proposals for planning now so prevalent in this country. This is the plan developed in 1919 by the Reichswirtschaftsminister Rudolf Wissell and his undersecretary of state Wichard von Möllendorff.[20] But interesting as their proposals of organization of individual industries are and relevant, as is the discussion to which they gave rise, to many of the problems discussed in England at the present moment, they cannot be regarded as socialist proposals of the kind discussed here, but belong to the halfway house between capitalism and socialism, discussion of which for reasons mentioned above has been deliberately excluded from the present work.

10. Mises, Max Weber, and Brutzkus

The distinction of having first formulated the central problem of socialist economics in such a form as to make it impossible that it should ever

---

[19][The German economist and sociologist Emil Lederer (1882–1939), another member of the Böhm-Bawerk seminar, taught at Heidelberg from 1918 to 1931 and at Berlin as the successor to Sombart from 1931 to 1933. He then emigrated to the United States and became the first Dean of the Faculty of Political and Social Sciences at the New School for Social Research in New York. Eduard Heimann (1889–1967) taught at the University of Hamburg from 1925 to 1933, when he also left Germany for a post at the New School. The German industrialist Walther Rathenau (1867–1922) was head of the electrical cartel and helped to organize the procurement of raw materials for the German war effort during the First World War. Rathenau was assassinated by right-wing fanatics soon after becoming Foreign Minister of the Weimar Republic.—Ed.]

[20]This plan was originally developed in a memorandum submitted to the Cabinet of the Reich on May 7, 1919, and later developed by R. Wissell in two pamphlets, *Die Planwirtschaft* (Hamburg: Hamburger Buchdruckerei, 1920) and *Praktische Wirtschaftspolitik* (Berlin: Gesellschaft und Erziehung, 1919). [Rudolf Wissell (1869–1962) and Wichard G. O. von Möllendorff (1881–1937) were leaders of the German Social Democrats.—Ed.]

again disappear from the discussion belongs to the Austrian economist Ludwig von Mises. In an article on "Economic Calculation in a Socialist Community" which appeared in the spring of 1920,[21] he demonstrated that the possibility of rational calculation in our present economic system was based on the fact that prices expressed in money provided the essential condition which made such reckoning possible. The essential point where Mises went far beyond anything done by his predecessors was the detailed demonstration that an economic use of the available resources was only possible if this pricing was applied not only to the final product but also to all the intermediate products and factors of production, and that no other process was conceivable which would take in the same way account of all the relevant facts as did the pricing process of the competitive market.[22] Together the two works represent the starting point from which all the discussions of the economic problems of socialism, whether constructive or critical, which aspire to be taken seriously must necessarily proceed.

While Mises's writings contain beyond doubt the most complete and successful exposition of what from then onwards became the central problem, and while they had by far the greatest influence on all further discussions, it is an interesting coincidence that about the same time two other distinguished authors arrived independently at very similar conclusions. The first was the great German sociologist Max Weber,[23] who in his posthumous magnum opus, *Wirtschaft und Gesellschaft*, which appeared in 1921, dealt expressly with the conditions which in a complex economic system made rational decisions possible. Like Professor Mises (whose article he quotes as having come to his notice only when his own discussion was already set up in print), he insisted that the *in natura* calculations proposed by the leading advocates of a planned economy could not pro-

[21]"Die Wirtschaftsrechnung im sozialistischen Gemeinwesen", *Archiv für Sozialwissenschaften und Sozialpolitik*, op. cit., pp. 86–121. Most of this article has been embodied in the more elaborate discussion of the economic problems of a socialist community in Part 2 of Professor Mises's *Die Gemeinwirtschaft: Untersuchungen über den Sozialismus*.

[22][In the original publication of this article, Hayek noted that the translation was contained in *Collectivist Economic Planning* and that he hoped that the larger work in which it was later incorporated would soon be available in an English edition. The translation of the second edition appeared in 1936; see *Socialism: An Economic and Sociological Analysis*, op. cit.—Ed.]

[23][The German sociologist Max Weber (1864–1920) wrote extensively on the nature of capitalism, the methodology of the social sciences, and the sociology of religion. He was also the original editor of the *Grundriss der Sozialökonomik*, op. cit., a multi-volume reference work in the social sciences to which Hayek was to contribute a volume on money and monetary theory. For more on this, see F. A. Hayek, *The Trend of Economic Thinking*, op. cit., p. 127.—Ed.]

74

vide a rational solution of the problems which the authorities in such a system would have to solve. He emphasized in particular that the rational use and the preservation of capital could be secured only in a system based on exchange and the use of money, and that the wastes due to the impossibility of rational calculation in a completely socialized system might be serious enough to make it impossible to maintain alive the present populations of the more densely inhabited countries.

> The assumption that some system of accounting would in time be found or invented if one only tried seriously to tackle the problem of a moneyless economy does not help here: The problem is the fundamental problem of any complete socialization and it is certainly impossible to talk of a *rationally* 'planned economy' while in so far as the all-decisive point is concerned no means for the construction of a 'plan' is known.[24]

A practically simultaneous development of the same ideas is to be found in Russia. Here in the summer of 1920 in the short interval after the first military successes of the new system, when it had for once become possible to utter criticisms in public, Professor Boris Brutzkus, a distinguished economist mainly known for his studies in the agricultural problems of Russia, subjected to a searching criticism in a series of lectures the doctrines governing the action of the communist rulers. These lectures, which appeared under the title "The Problems of Social Economy under Socialism" in a Russian journal and were only many years later made accessible to a wider public in a German translation,[25] show in their main conclusion a remarkable resemblance to the doctrines of Professor Mises and Max Weber, although they arose out of the study of the concrete problems which Russia had to face at that time, and although they were written at a time when their author, cut off from all

[24]Max Weber, *Wirtschaft und Gesellschaft*, vol. 3 of *Grundriss der Sozialökonomik* (Tübingen: J. C. B. Mohr (P. Siebeck)), pp. 55–56. [Weber's great posthumous work appears in English as *Economy and Society*, Claus Wittich and Guenther Roth, eds, 2 vols (Berkeley: University of California Press, 1978). The first English translation of *Wirtschaft und Gesellschaft* was published in three volumes in New York: Bedminster Press, in 1968.—Ed.]

[25]The original title under which these lectures appeared in the winter 1921–22 in the Russian journal *Ekonomist* was "The Problems of Social Economy under Socialism". They were later reprinted in Russian as a pamphlet which appeared in Berlin, 1923, and a German translation under the title "Die Lehren des Marxismus im Lichte der russischen Revolution" was published in Berlin, 1928. [Further publication of the *Ekonomist* was forbidden by the Soviet authorities in the summer of 1922. Many members of the editorial staff of the journal, including Boris Davidovich Brutzkus (1874–1938), were briefly imprisoned before being forced to leave the country. The German government granted them visas.—Ed.]

communication with the outside world, could not have known of the similar efforts of the Austrian and German scholars. Like Professor Mises and Max Weber, his criticism centres round the impossibility of a rational calculation in a centrally directed economy from which prices are necessarily absent. An English translation of this essay, together with discussion of the development of economic planning in Russia which conforms in a remarkable way to the expectations which could be based on such theories, will appear simultaneously with the present book as a companion volume to it.[26]

11. More Recent Continental Discussion

Although to some extent Max Weber and Professor Brutzkus share the credit of having pointed out independently the central problem of the economics of socialism, it was the more complete and systematic exposition of Professor Mises, particularly in his larger work on *Die Gemeinwirtschaft*, which has mainly influenced the trend of further discussion on the Continent. In the years immediately succeeding its publication, a number of attempts were made to meet his challenge directly and to show that he was wrong in his main thesis, and that even in a strictly centrally directed economic system values could be exactly determined without any serious difficulties. But although the discussion on this point dragged on for several years, in the course of which Mises twice replied to his critics,[27] it became more and more clear that in so far as a strictly centrally directed planned system of the type originally proposed by most socialists was concerned, his central thesis could not be refuted. Much of the objections made at first were really more a quibbling about words caused by the fact that Mises had occasionally used the somewhat loose statement that socialism was impossible, while what he meant was that socialism made rational calculation impossible. Of course any proposed course of action, if the proposal has any meaning at all, is possible in the strict sense of the word, i.e., it may be tried. The question can only be whether it will lead to the expected results, that is, whether the proposed course of action is consistent with the aims which it is intended to serve. And in so far as it had been hoped to achieve by means of central direction of all economic activity *at one and the same time* a distribution of income indepen-

[26][The book to which Hayek refers is Boris Brutzkus, *Economic Planning in Soviet Russia*, op. cit. Hayek's Foreword to the book appears as an appendix to the present chapter.—Ed.]

[27][Hayek refers to two articles by von Mises, "Neue Beiträge zum Problem der sozialistischen Wirtschaftsrechnung", *Archiv für Sozialwissenschaft und Sozialpolitik*, vol. 51, 1923–24, pp. 488–500, and "Neue Schriften zum Problem der sozialistischen Wirtschaftsrechnung", *ibid.*, vol. 60, 1928, pp. 187–190. Part of the first essay has been translated into English and appears as the appendix to Mises's *Socialism*, op. cit., pp. 473–478.—Ed.]

dent of private property in the means of production and a volume of output which was at least approximately the same or even greater than that procured under free competition, it was more and more generally admitted that this was not a practicable way to achieve these ends.

But it was only natural that even where Professor Mises's main thesis was conceded this did not mean an abandonment of the search for a way to realize the socialist ideals. Its main effect was to divert attention from what had so far been universally considered as the most practicable forms of socialist organization to the exploration of alternative schemes. It is possible to distinguish two main types of reaction among those who conceded his central argument. In the first place there were those who thought that the loss of efficiency, the decline in general wealth which will be the effect of the absence of a means of rational calculation, would not be too high a price for the realization of a more just distribution of this wealth. Of course if this attitude is based on a clear realization of what this choice implies there is no more to be said about it, except that it seems doubtful whether those who maintain it would find many who will agree with their idea. The real difficulty here is, of course, that for most people the decision on this point will depend on the extent to which the impossibility of rational calculation would lead to a reduction of output in a centrally directed economy compared with that of a competitive system. And although in the opinion of the present writer it seems that careful study can leave no doubt about the enormous magnitude of that difference, it must be admitted that there is no simple way to prove how great that difference would be. The answer here cannot be derived from general considerations but will have to be based on a careful comparative study of the working of the two alternative systems, and presupposes a much greater knowledge of the problems involved than can possibly be acquired in any other way but by a systematic study of economics.[28]

The second type of reaction to Professor Mises's criticism was to regard it as valid only as regards the particular form of socialism against which it was mainly directed, and to try to construct other schemes that would be immune against that criticism. A very considerable and probably the more interesting part of the later discussions on the Continent tended to move in that direction. There are two main tendencies of speculation. On

---

[28]It is perhaps necessary in this connection to state explicitly that it would be wholly inconclusive if such a comparison were made between capitalism as it exists (or is supposed still to exist) and socialism as it might work under ideal assumptions—or between capitalism as it might be in its ideal form and socialism in some imperfect form. If the comparison is to be of any value for the question of principle, it has to be made on the assumption that either system is realized in the form which is most rational under the given condition of human nature and external circumstances which must of course be accepted.

the one hand, it was attempted to overcome the difficulties in question by extending the element of planning even further than had been contemplated before, so as to abolish completely the free choice of the consumer and the free choice of occupation. Or on the other hand it was attempted to introduce various elements of competition. To what extent these proposals really overcome any of the difficulties and to what extent they are practical will be considered in later sections of this volume. In so far as the result of the German discussions are concerned, Professor Georg Halm, who has taken a very active part in these debates, summarizes in his contribution to the present volume [*Collectivist Economic Planning*] the present state of opinion among those who take a critical attitude to the present.[29]

12. The Purpose of the Present Volume [Collectivist Economic Planning]

In the English-speaking world the discussion of these problems began at a considerably later date than on the Continent, and, although it probably began on a somewhat higher level, thus avoiding many of the more elementary mistakes, and has in the last few years produced a number of important studies, it has made little use of the results of the discussions on the Continent.[30] Yet clearly it is wasted effort to disregard these precedents. It is the purpose of this volume therefore to present within two covers the main results of the critical analysis of socialist planning attempted by Continental scholars. Together with the translation of Professor Mises's major work and the companion volume containing Professor Brutzkus's studies on Russia it should give a fairly comprehensive survey of the problems raised by any kind of planning.

The present volume, accordingly, is a collection of material which may serve as a basis for further discussion, rather than a systematic or connected exposition of a single point of view. The individual essays here collected were not intended for publication in a single volume, but were written at different times and for different purposes. In nearly all cases the later articles were written in ignorance of the earlier ones. The inevi-

[29][Hayek noted that a list of all the more important contributions made in this debate from both sides can be found in an appendix to *Collectivist Economic Planning*, op. cit. H. E. Batson's translation of Georg Halm's article appears as chapter 4 of that volume under the title "Further Considerations on the Possibility of Adequate Calculation in a Socialist Community".—Ed.]

[30]A noteworthy early and independent exposition of the way in which the problem of value will make itself felt in a socialist society and of the difficulties which would impede the rational distribution of resources in such a society occurs in a little-known small book by John Bowen, *Conditions of Social Welfare* (London: C. W. Daniel, 1926), particularly pp. 23 et seq.

table effect of this is some degree of repetition and occasional differences of opinion between the authors represented. The arrangement follows the chronological order of appearance of the original essays, excepting that of Barone, which is relegated to an appendix only because it is decidedly more technical than the rest of the book. The second appendix contains a bibliography of the more important works on the same subject which have been published since 1920.

In a concluding essay the editor has attempted to follow up some of these lines of thought and to examine in their light some of the more recent developments of English speculation.[31] It is in this connection also that an attempt is made to assess the importance of the conclusions so far arrived at and to judge their relevance to the practical problems of our day.

Addendum: Review of Planwirtschaft und Verkehrswirtschaft[32]

Landauer describes his book, which in his concluding remarks he defines as an "attempt to bring socialist aspirations—which are a political and intellectual reality, even though Marxism's failure to come to terms with modern problems has deprived them of their theoretical underpinnings—face to face with the findings of modern economic theory".[33] It is a stimulating and interesting work which is written clearly and fluently, and in undoctrinaire fashion Landauer frequently demonstrates real courage in not flinching before uncomfortable findings of modern economic theory, a courage seldom found among socialist writers. By its tone and approach, this is one of those rare works with which one is eager to come to grips. Yet the book is disappointing particularly where one would least expect it in light of the author's earlier theoretical writings as well as its purported aim, as stated in the above quotation. It slights the critical theoretical questions concerning the possibility of an economic calculus in a socialist commonwealth, and its theoretical arguments, moreover, seem to be open to many objections. The main source of these deficiencies probably lies in Landauer's odd views about value theory (which in fact already manifested themselves in his previous work on "Grundprobleme der funktionellen Verteilung des wirtschaftlichen Werts" (fun-

---

[31][Hayek's concluding essay, "The Present State of the Debate", appears as chapter 2 of the present volume.—Ed.]

[32][F. A. Hayek, "Review of Carl Landauer, *Planwirtschaft und Verkehrswirtschaft*", op. cit. Hayek's review originally appeared in German in *Zeitschrift für Nationalökonomie*, vol. 4 (1933), pp. 294–298. The translation is provided by Dr. Grete Heinz. The German academician and editor Carl Landauer (1891–1983) fled Berlin in 1933. He taught economics at the University of California, Berkeley, from 1934 to 1959.—Ed.]

[33][Landauer, *Planwirtschaft und Verkehrswirtschaft*, op. cit., p. 223.—Ed.]

damental problems with respect to the functional distribution of economics value) in 1923).[34] We refer to his attempt to explain price phenomena directly in terms of the laws on subjective value formation rather than by a two-step method, the approach rightly favoured by most authors, who explain prices not only by subjective value but by the differences in purchasing power between the various persons involved. This leads Landauer to the clearly erroneous assertions that *"in both a planned economy and a market economy, given the same consumer needs and the same supply of goods, labour resources, and technical knowledge, the same processes will be appropriate"*[35] and "goods will have the same value in both a competitive economy and a planned economy given the same consumer needs and production facilities".[36] In reality a planned economy necessitates state control over the larger portion of productive facilities, and this precludes an unchanged distribution of incomes and hence an unaltered demand. Landauer admittedly states further on that "actually" comparison between a market economy and a planned economy requires the additional assumption that "the social qualification of the individual consumer, insofar as it determines the satisfaction of consumption needs, remains unchanged".[37] However, this reference to the relatively small "differences in income in the two types of economy operating with the same production facilities and especially with the same technology and the same population size" is no adquate proof that, as Landauer believes, "production overall would remain the same in its basic features if complete equality of income were attained, despite striking differences in specific aspects"[38] and that "the comparison of a market economy and a planned economy in terms of productivity is not invalidated by leaving standards of social qualification out of account".[39]

It is difficult to accept Landauer's assumption that the goal to "satisfy needs as amply as possible" by itself determines unambiguously the direc-

[34][Carl Landauer, *Grundprobleme der funktionellen Verteilung des wirtschaftlichen Werts* (Jena: G. Fischer, 1923).—Ed.]

[35]Landauer, *Planwirtschaft und Verkehrswirtschaft*, op. cit., p. 9, italics in the original.

[36]*Ibid.*, p. 10. Landauer follows the comment cited above with a short attack on the opponents of value theory, culminating in the assertion that the concept of value satisfied the terminological need for a higher-order concept which encompasses market prices for goods in a market economy and scientific value judgements about goods in a planned economy. This analysis is valid only if one identified the concept of objective value or exchange value as it exists in a market economy with the 'subjective' value of all individuals, on the basis of a uniform ranking of these needs (which "scientific evaluation in a planned economy" presupposes). This can actually occur in its pure form either in an individualist economy or in a strictly communist economy. I feel that Landauer uses the concept of value in a misleading way and thus supplies the opponents of value theory with pertinent arguments.

[37]*Ibid.*, p. 11.

[38]*Ibid.*, p. 13.

[39]*Ibid.*, p. 14.

tion taken by production, since he fails to take into account the relative importance attached to the needs of particular individuals. This neglect also casts doubt on his assumption that "the very same processes unfold in a completely rational planned economy based on this goal as they do in an ideal market economy".[40] Landauer continues as follows: "An ideal market economy is just as much an optimal economy as a completely rational planned economy. Both are equally impossible to implement in practice. Does a real market economy more closely approximate the ideal version than a planned economy, or can a planned economy offering better guarantees for optimal economic processes be more easily realized? Therein lies the controversy to be settled between liberals and socialists".[41] All this assumes an unambiguous yardstick for global social satisfaction, which does not in fact yet exist. Landauer must know perfectly well at heart that this is so, but he is tempted to disregard this fact because of his peculiar notions on the theory of value mentioned above.[42]

It goes without saying that, given this basic point of departure, Landauer focuses on the argument that a planned economy would attain a higher "productivity" than a market economy. He therefore looks somewhat askance at pure "distributive socialists"[43] who set their sights on merely changing the distribution of the social product that has already been attained. His arguments are weakened by the absence of a yardstick, which precludes such a comparison in principle, unless one is willing to assume that some dictatorial power would rank-order individual needs in a uniform fashion that corresponds to the prevailing opinion about the importance of these individual needs. But even if one were to assume, for the sake of argument, that there existed in principle a possible way to make such a comparison, the result remains unconvincing, since we are comparing the actual market economy as it exists today which, as Landauer himself concedes, is "more of a market economy than a planned economy",[44] with a planned economy that is purely a mental construct. Landauer attempts to justify this approach by attributing all the "antiproductive manifestations in the market economy", especially its monopolistic tendencies, as inevitable developments[45] without taking into account how significantly the tendencies in question have in fact been fostered by interventionist measures. Specifically, Landauer completely disregards

---

[40]*Ibid.*, p. 15.

[41]*Ibid.*, p. 15f.

[42]See on this point the particularly glaring remark on p. 33, "One might just as well refer to buyers with more purchasing power as to buyers with more pressing needs for a particular commodity than other individuals."

[43]Landauer, *Planwirtschaft und Verkehrswirtschaft,* op. cit., p. 113.

[44]*Ibid.*, p. 16.

[45]*Ibid.*, p. 21.

the importance of tariff protection with respect to the formation of cartels and pays little attention to government measures that encourage cartellization. Thus he fails to demonstrate that tendencies he derives from his observation of today's market economy are equally applicable to any conceivable market economy, and it is this conceivable market economy, which would be free of any socialist influences, to which his potential planned economy should be compared. The section entitled "Do declining costs interfere with monopolization?"[46] would deserve a special discussion if there were space for it in this review. We will mention here only its peculiar conclusion that "the law of declining costs . . ." may well prevent trusts from exploiting their monopoly position in a certain phase of development".[47]

One of the topics discussed under "antiproductive phenomena in market economies" is cyclical unemployment. Here Landauer displays unusually profound insight into business cycle theory, which stands in heartening contrast to the usual socialist literature in which underconsumption theories are almost always singled out. In view of his knowledgeable treatment of the subject, it is all the more incomprehensible that he feels no qualms about possible misinvestments in a planned economy. Along these lines it is worth mentioning that Landauer in various places[48] very aptly criticizes "purchasing power theories" and shows a highly commendable grasp of the importance of capital maintenance and formation in his book. Among the "additional flaws in the functioning of market economies" Landauer discusses here, we would like to quote one passage that shows clearly how differently the same objective content can be evaluated in the light of different world views. Landauer writes, "A state which constitutes a cost factor within the private economy can never take over more than a very limited fraction of the social product, a fraction that can easily fall below the level at which all communal needs are fully met. We have every reason to assume that notwithstanding the gigantic budgets of our public bodies, even today certain specific communal needs are underfinanced. Perhaps resources for them could be raised if waste were reduced in the public budget. But even if the resources saved in this manner could suffice at present, they would surely be insufficient in the future."[49]

We would like to single out here the excellent discussion concerning the problems of state control over monopolies, which appears in the short second section of the book under the heading of "economic planning

[46]*Ibid.*, pp. 26–34.
[47]*Ibid.*, p. 29.
[48]*Ibid.*, p. 50 and especially pp. 86ff.
[49]*Ibid.*, p. 65.

organs of market societies". This section is remarkable for a similar reason as the discussion on business cycle theories to which we alluded earlier. Here Landauer has a clear view of all the difficulties, which he is then far too inclined to overlook when he describes the socialist economic order. But it is at the very least striking to read the following sentence in the work of a socialist writer: "If officials in charge of controlling [monopoly prices] could really form an objectively valid judgement about such matters, the best would be to let them act as entrepreneurs themselves."[50]

In the last three sections of the book, which delineate the "basic features of a socialist economic order" and the "road to socialism", Landauer displays much "confidence in utopia" (his own heading for the first subsection of this part of the book). In this respect he consciously adopts the opposite stance to Marxist socialism, which chose to take the easy way out by refusing, on principle, to envisage the problems of a socialist economic order. Here we find at last the chapter on a "socialist calculus", which he unfortunately confines to a very brief, seven-page chapter. All it states about the socialist economy, as Landauer really conceives it, is that "not only the consumption goods market, but also the production goods market, should generally be maintained" and individual enterprises should be able to buy from each other just as capitalist entrepreneurs do".[51]

He then deals exclusively with the possibility of carrying out an economic calculus without price formation for the means of production. He answers this question in the affirmative on the basis of value attribution. But we fail to be informed about his views on the really interesting question how price formation could serve as a regulator for the utilization of the means of production when these means of production are without exception state-owned. Landauer's optimistic presentation of the ways in which the state could regulate capital formation and capital utilization is also less than convincing. His assertion that "the state can thus draw up an investment program for the economy as a whole and harmonize investments with the resources available in the economy"[52] is not backed up by any evidence. How can this conceivably be done in the absence of a free capital market in which an interest rate is formed and which serves to ascertain which investments are appropriate and which are not? The problem is certainly not solved by Landauer's proposal that the socialist state develop a scientific calculus as a control mechanism for the monetary calculus.[53] According to Landauer's odd notion, this control mechanism should reveal whether "these are burdens that can be imposed on

[50]*Ibid.*, p. 99.
[51]*Ibid.*, p. 114.
[52]*Ibid.*, p. 122.
[53]*Ibid.*, see also p. 128.

the economy".[54] There is no space here to analyze the deficiencies of this entire construct, as it would mean repeating all the arguments raised by Pierson, Mises,[55] and their followers against the possibility of running an economy in this manner. Landauer unfortunately does not come to grips with these arguments, as mentioned earlier.

We cannot take up here the final sections of the book consisting of the subsection "on the sociology of socialism", two major sections on "the road to socialism" and "the goal of the socialist labour movement and present-day socialist possibilities", since this review is already overly long and these sections are of relatively less interest to economists. We would like to point out, however, that here too, in addition to a number of remarks that can make sense only in the light of "socialist aspirations", there are many perceptive and accurate insights to be found of a kind that is rare in socialist writings. It should be emphasized once more, in conclusion, that the book as a whole reflects a spirit that makes it seem a far from hopeless undertaking to reach common grounds about most of the major problems.

Addendum: Foreword to Brutzkus, Economic Planning in Soviet Russia [1935][56]

It can hardly be said that the intense interest with which, for more than fifteen years, all the world has been watching the developments in Russia has been rewarded with an amount of instruction at all commensurate with the space it has occupied among the topics of general discussion. Few of those who have been following the ever-increasing stream of litera-ture on the subject can have felt satisfied that they ever really knew what was happening in that country, and a great many have by now practically abandoned the attempt to form a clear opinion of the results so far achieved. It is fashionable to speak of it as the great experiment and to emphasize its importance for the future of the human race, but how many who use these phrases really know what the whole thing actually means.

To some degree this unsatisfactory state of affairs is due to the political passions involved which inevitably deprive much of the available informa-tion of reliability. But this cannot fully account for the existing situation. During the last few years there has certainly been no lack of dispassionate

---

[54]*Ibid.,* p. 123.

[55][Translations of the articles by Pierson and Mises appeared in F. A. Hayek, *Collectivist Economic Planning,* op. cit.—Ed.]

[56][Foreword by F. A. Hayek to Boris Brutzkus, *Economic Planning in Soviet Russia,* op. cit.—Ed.]

attempts at a serious examination of the problem, and yet in most cases the outcome has been singularly inconclusive. About the central problem, the advantages or disadvantages of centralized economic planning, the difficulties which the Soviet government has met and the degree to which it has solved them, our knowledge has not much increased. The reason for this is the extraordinary scarcity of information on which conclusions of this sort could be based. The difficulties which have to be overcome in this respect are so immense that only an investigator of quite exceptional qualifications could hope to overcome them.

But among those who have been attracted to such investigations, the majority have lacked even the first requisite for really successful researches—mastery of the Russian language. Where most of the really relevant information has to be laboriously collected from occasional statements in internal Russian discussions, and where all information made available in foreign language is notoriously misleading, it is impossible for anyone who does not possess a full command of the language to hope to get very far. But a qualification no less important but much more rare is such an intimate knowledge of the country, its history and institutions, and of the psychology of its people, as will enable the observer to separate what is specifically Russian and independent of the system by which that country is at present governed from the consequences which can be said properly to derive from the existing system. It is not really surprising that most of the accounts of modern Russia hardly penetrate at all below the surface. No doubt as the impressions of intelligent men they have a certain interest. But they certainly contain little answer to the main question.

But beyond this there is a further qualification necessary. Even the most careful study of the Russian facts cannot lead very far if it is not guided by a clear conception of what the problem is; i.e., if it is not undertaken by a person who, before he embarks on the investigations of the special problems of Russia, has arrived at a clear idea of the fundamental task that economic planning involves.

It is improbable that anyone but a Russian economist will ever combine the qualifications required for the successful conduct of such a study. But the number of Russian economists who still really know their country and who at the same time are in the position to speak freely about the present events has become very limited. Among those who remain, the author of the present volume may claim to speak with special authority. Professor of agricultural economics at Petersburg from 1907 to 1922 and long recognized as one of the first authorities on Russian agriculture, Professor Brutzkus has followed the developments with an active interest at close quarters. In his book on the *Agricultural Development and Agricultural Revo-*

lution in Russia[57] he has given us a most illuminating and certainly not unsympathetic account of the trends that led to the Revolution. From the very beginning of the new regime he devoted himself to an intense study of the tasks it had set itself, and as early as 1920 he produced, under circumstances which he describes in his preface, the remarkable survey of the economic problems raised by socialism, which in a slightly abridged English translation forms now the first part of the present volume. If one reads it today, in the light of the developments that have since taken place in Russia and of the extensive discussions which have been devoted to the problem of collectivist planning, one is still struck by the extraordinary clarity with which at that early date its author had grasped the really central problems. Together with the works of Professor Mises and Max Weber,[58] which appeared in Germany only a few months earlier, this book must indeed be regarded as one of the chief of those studies which initiated the modern discussion of the economic problems of socialism.

This critical analysis of the problems of socialism assumes special significance from the fact that it deals not only with socialism in general, but also with the concrete problems of a country which for more than a dozen years has actually had to try to solve the problems. The attentive reader who keeps in mind the date when it was written will again and again be struck by the extraordinary foresight shown by the author and the degree to which his predictions have been verified by actual events. Not only the more spectacular changes of economic policy which have occurred during the period but also many of the minor events in the history of the Russian experiment are clearly foreshadowed in his discussion. This is clearly demonstrated in the second part of the volume where the developments of the past fifteen years are analyzed.

For some time after the publication of this criticism, Professor Brutzkus was still allowed to remain in the country, and for a time in 1922 he even acted as chairman of the agricultural planning commission for the Petrograd district in the people's commissariat for agriculture. But at the end of that year he was compelled to leave the country and settled in Germany where, for a period of ten years, he was Professor at the Russian Scientific Institute at Berlin, a position which he lost after the National Socialist Revolution. This position enabled him, however, to follow events in Russia closely and to study all aspects of the further economic developments of that country in great detail. Numerous publications (mostly in Ger-

---

[57]This work was published in German. Its original title is *Agrarentwicklung und Agrarrevolution in Russland.* Mit einem Vorwort von Max Sering (Berlin: "Quellen und Studien" herausagegeben vom Osteuropa-Institut in Breslau, Abt. Wirtschaft, 1926).

[58][Hayek refers to Mises's *Die Gemeinwirtschaft: Untersuchungen über den Sozialismus,* op. cit., and to Weber's *Wirtschaft und Gesellschaft,* op. cit.—Ed.]

man) which appeared during the course of this period bear witness to the uninterrupted attention which he devoted to every phase of that phenomenon. A short study reviewing the results of the First Five Year Plan, which appeared in 1932, has attracted particularly wide attention.[59] In the second part of the present volume he has now elaborated this into a more comprehensive survey of economic planning in Russia from the revolution to the present time. It seems to me that in it he has succeeded in throwing more light on the history of this experiment than any other work known to me. His familiarity with the Russian scene has enabled him to draw on relatively inaccessible sources which, just because they were not prepared for foreign consumption, tell more about the actual situation than volumes of official statistics. Yet, as the reader will notice, the fragments of information from which he pieces together his surprisingly complete and illuminating picture are all gathered from statements from the most authoritative sources. I do not hesitate to place his work as it is now collected in the present volume in the very first rank of the really scientific literature on present-day Russia. It is to be hoped that in its English form it will have the same success as its German predecessors.

[59]Boris Brutzkus, *Der Fünfjahresplan und seine Erfüllung* (Leipzig: Verlag Deutsche Wissenschaftliche Buchhandlung, 1932).

TWO

THE PRESENT STATE OF THE DEBATE[1]

1. The Effects of Criticism

In spite of a natural tendency on the part of socialists to belittle its importance, it is clear that the criticism of socialism epitomized in the foregoing
chapters has already had a very profound effect on the direction of socialist thought. The great majority of 'planners' are, of course, still unaf-
fected by it: The great mass of the hangers-on of any popular movement
are always unconscious of the intellectual currents which produce a
change of direction.[2] Moreover, the actual existence in Russia of a system,
which professes to be planned, has led many of those who know nothing
of its development to suppose that the main problems are solved; in fact,
as we shall see, Russian experience provides abundant confirmation of
the doubts already stated. But among the leaders of socialist thought not
only is the nature of the central problem more and more recognized, but
the force of the objections raised against the types of socialism which in
the past used to be considered as most practicable is also increasingly
admitted. It is now rarely denied that, in a society which is to preserve
freedom of choice of the consumer and free choice of occupation, central
direction of all economic activity presents a task which cannot be ratio-

---

[1][Published as "The Present State of the Debate", which constitutes chapter 5 of *Collectivist
Economic Planning: Critical Studies on the Possibilities of Socialism*, op. cit. (see chapter 1, note 1,
above), pp. 210–243. Reprinted in F. A. Hayek, ed., *Individualism and Economic Order*, op.
cit.—Ed.]

[2]This applies, unfortunately, also to most of the organized collective efforts which profess
to be devoted to the scientific study of the problem of planning. Anyone who studies such
publications as the *Annales de l'economie collective*, or the material contributed to the "World
Social Economic Congress, Amsterdam, 1931", and published by the "International Relations Institute" under the title *World Social Economic Planning*, 2 vols (The Hague: International Industrial Relations Institute, 1931–32), will search in vain for any sign that the problems are even recognized. [Hayek refers to two international organizations which published
studies advocating extensive economic planning. The *Annales de l'economie collective* was is-
sued in French, German, and English, and began publication in Geneva in 1925. The World
Social Economic Congress was held in Amsterdam in 1931. The two-volume work Hayek
cites was an addendum to the material contributed to the conference.—Ed.]

nally solved under the complex conditions of modern life. It is true, as we shall see, that even among those who see the problem, this position is not yet completely abandoned; but its defence is more or less of the nature of a rearguard action where all that is attempted is to prove that 'in principle' a solution is conceivable. Little or no claim is made that such a solution is practicable. We shall later have occasion to discuss some of these attempts. But the great majority of the more recent schemes try to get around the difficulties by the construction of alternative socialist systems which differ more or less fundamentally from the traditional types against which the criticism was directed in the first instance and which are supposed to be immune against the objections to which the latter are subject.

In the preceding section, Professor Halm has examined some of the solutions proposed by Continental writers.[3] In this concluding essay, the recent English literature of the subject will be considered and an attempt will be made to evaluate the recent proposals which have been devised to overcome the difficulties which have now been recognized. Before we enter into this discussion, however, a few words on the relevance of the Russian experiment to the problems under discussion may be useful.

2. The Lessons of the Russian Experiment

It is of course neither possible nor desirable to enter at this point into an examination of the concrete results of this experiment. In this respect it is necessary to refer to detailed special investigations, particularly to that of Professor Brutzkus, which will appear simultaneously with the present volume and which forms an essential complement to the more abstract considerations presented here.[4] At this moment we are only concerned with the more general question of how the established results of such an examination of the concrete experiences fit in with the more theoretical argument, and how far the conclusions reached by a priori reasoning are confirmed or contradicted by empirical evidence.

It is perhaps not unnecessary to remind the reader at this point that it was not the possibility of planning as such which has been questioned on the grounds of general considerations, but the possibility of successful planning, of achieving the ends for which planning was undertaken. Therefore we must first be clear as to the tests by which we are to judge

[3][Georg Halm surveyed the recent continental literature on socialism in his contribution to *Collectivist Economic Planning*, op. cit., pp. 131–200, entitled "Further Considerations on the Possibility of Adequate Calculation in a Socialist Community".—Ed.]

[4]Boris Brutzkus, *Economic Planning in Russia*, op. cit. [See chapter 1, note 25, for more on Brutzkus, and the addendum to chapter 1 for Hayek's Foreword to Brutzkus's book.—Ed.]

success, or the forms in which we should expect failure to manifest itself. There is no reason to expect that production would stop, or that the authorities would find difficulty in using all the available resources somehow, or even that output would be permanently lower than it had been before planning started. What we should anticipate is that output, where the use of the available resources was determined by some central authority, would be lower than if the price mechanism of a market operated freely under otherwise similar circumstances. This would be due to the excessive development of some lines of production at the expense of others, and the use of methods which are inappropriate under the circumstances. We should expect to find overdevelopment of some industries at a cost which was not justified by the importance of their increased output, and to see unchecked the ambition of the engineer to apply the latest developments made elsewhere, without considering whether they were economically suited in the situation. In many cases the use of the latest methods of production, which could not have been applied without central planning, would then be a symptom of a misuse of resources rather than a proof of success.

It follows therefore that the excellence, from a technological point of view, of some parts of the Russian industrial equipment, which most strikes the casual observer and which is commonly regarded as evidence of success, has little significance in so far as the answer to the central question is concerned. Whether the new plant will prove to be a useful link in the industrial structure for increasing output depends not only on technological considerations, but even more on the general economic situation. The best tractor factory may not be an asset, and the capital invested in it is a sheer loss, if the labour which the tractor replaces is cheaper than the cost of the material and labour which goes to make a tractor, *plus* interest.

But once we have freed ourselves from the misleading fascination of the existence of colossal instruments of production, which is likely to captivate the uncritical observer, only two legitimate tests of success remain: the goods which the system actually delivers to the consumer, and the rationality or irrationality of the decisions of the central authority. There can be no doubt that the first test would lead to a negative result, for the present at any rate, or if applied to the whole population and not to a small privileged group. Practically all observers seem to agree that even compared with prewar Russia the position of the great masses has deteriorated. Yet such a comparison still makes the results appear too favourable. It is admitted that Tsarist Russia did not offer conditions very favourable to capitalist industry, and that under a more modern regime capitalism would have brought about rapid progress. It must also be taken into account that the suffering in the past fifteen years, that 'starving to greatness' which was supposed to be in the interest of later progress, should by now have borne some fruits. It would provide a more appropriate basis of comparison if we assumed that the same restriction of consumption, which has actually taken place, had been caused by taxation, the proceeds of which had been lent to competitive industry for investment purposes. It can hardly be denied that this would have brought about a rapid and enormous increase of the general standard of life beyond anything which is at present even remotely possible.

There only remains, then, the task of actually examining the principles on which the planning authority has acted. And although it is impossible to trace here, even shortly, the varied course of that experiment, all we know about it, particularly from Professor Brutzkus's study referred to above, fully entitles us to say that the anticipations based on general reasoning have been thoroughly confirmed. The breakdown of 'war-communism' occurred for exactly the same reasons, the impossibility of rational calculation in a moneyless economy, which Professor Mises and Professor Brutzkus had foreseen.[5] The development since, with its repeated reversals of policy, has only shown that the rulers of Russia had to learn by experience all the obstacles which a systematic analysis of the problem reveals. But it has raised no important new problems, still less has it suggested any solutions. Officially the blame for nearly all the difficulties is still put on the unfortunate individuals who are persecuted for obstructing the plan by not obeying the orders of the central authority or by carrying them too literally. But although this means that the authorities only admit the obvious difficulty of making people follow out the plan loyally, there can be no doubt that the more serious disappointments are really due to the inherent difficulties of any central planning. In fact, from accounts such as that of Professor Brutzkus, we gather that, far from advancing towards more rational methods of planning, the present tendency is to cut the knot by abandoning the comparatively scientific methods employed in the past. Instead are substituted more and more arbitrary and uncorrelated decisions of particular problems as they are suggested by the contingencies of the day. In so far as political or psychological problems are concerned, Russian experience may be very instructive. But to the student of economic problems of socialism it does little more than furnish illustrations of well-established conclusions. It gives us no help towards an answer to the intellectual problem which the desire for a rational reconstruction of society raises. To this end we shall have to proceed with our systematic survey of the different conceivable systems

[5][*Ibid.*, and Mises, *Socialism*, op. cit.—Ed.]

92

which are no less important for only existing so far as theoretical suggestions.

3. The Mathematical Solution

As has been pointed out in the Introduction, discussion of these questions in the English literature began relatively late and at a comparatively high level. Yet it can hardly be said that the first attempts really met any of the main points. Two Americans, Professor F. M. Taylor and W. C. Roper, were first in their field. Their analyses, and to some extent also that of H. D. Dickinson in this country,[6] were directed to show that on the assumption of a complete knowledge of all relevant data, the values and quantities of the different commodities to be produced might be determined by the application of the apparatus by which theoretical economics explains the formation of prices and the direction of production in a competitive system. Now it must be admitted that this is not an impossibility in the sense that it is logically contradictory. But to argue that a determination of prices by such a procedure being logically conceivable in any way invalidates the contention that it is not a possible solution only proves that the real nature of the problem has not been perceived. It is only necessary to attempt to visualize what the application of this method would imply in practice in order to rule it out as humanly impracticable and impossible. It is clear that any such solution would have to be based on the solution of some such system of equations as that developed in Barone's article in the Appendix.[7] But what is practically relevant here is not the formal structure of this system, but the nature and amount of concrete information required if a numerical solution is to be attempted and the magnitude of the task which this numerical solution must involve in any mod-

---

[6][The works that Hayek refers to include Fred M. Taylor, "The Guidance of Production in a Socialist State", *American Economic Review,* volume 19, March 1929, pp. 1–8, reprinted in *On the Economic Theory of Socialism*, ed., with an introduction, by Benjamin E. Lippincott, op. cit., pp. 41–54; W. Crosby Roper, *The Problem of Pricing in a Socialist State* (Cambridge: Harvard University Press, 1931); and H. D. Dickinson, "Price Formation in a Socialist Community", *Economic Journal,* op. cit., pp. 237–250. Fred M. Taylor (1855–1932) taught economics at the University of Michigan from 1904 until his death. The article cited here by Taylor, the author of a popular textbook, was his presidential address read before the American Economics Association on December 27, 1928. Willet Crosby Roper (1910–) saw the book begun as his honours thesis at Harvard published as part of a series of Harvard Undergraduate Essays. Henry Douglas Dickinson (1899–1969) was educated at Cambridge and the LSE and taught economics at Leeds and Bristol. Hayek discusses his *Economics of Socialism*, op. cit., at length in chapter 3 of the present volume.—Ed.]

[7][Enrico Barone's paper, "The Ministry of Production in the Collectivist State", appeared as Appendix A to *Collectivist Economic Planning*, op. cit. See chapter 1, note 14, for more on Barone.—Ed.]

ern community. The problem here is, of course, not how detailed this information and how exact the calculation would have to be in order to make the solution perfectly exact, but only how far one would have to go to make the result at least comparable with that which the competitive system provides. Let us look into this a little further.

In the first place it is clear that if central direction is really to take the place of the initiative of the manager of the individual enterprise and is not simply to be a most irrational limitation of his discretion in some particular respect, it will not be sufficient that it takes the form of mere general direction, but it will have to include and be intimately responsible for details of the most minute description. It is impossible to decide rationally how much material or new machinery should be assigned to any one enterprise and at what price (in an accounting sense) it will be rational to do so, without also deciding at the same time whether and in which way the machinery and tools already in use should continue to be used or be disposed of. It is matters of this sort, details of technique, the saving of one material rather than the other or any other of the small economies which cumulatively decide the success or failure of a firm, and in any central plan which is not to be hopelessly wasteful, they must be taken account of. In order to be able to do so it will be necessary to treat every machine, tool, or building not just as one of a class of physically similar objects, but as an individual whose usefulness is determined by its particular state of wear and tear, its location, and so on. The same applies to every batch of commodities which is situated at a different spot or which differs in any other respect from other batches. This means that in order to achieve that degree of economy in this respect which is secured by the competitive system, the calculations of the central planning authority would have to treat the existing body of instrumental goods as being constituted of almost as many different types of goods as there are individual units. And so far as ordinary commodities, i.e., non-durable semi-finished or finished goods, are concerned, it is clear that there would be many times more different types of such commodities to consider than we should imagine if they were classified only by their technical characteristics. Two technically similar goods in different places or in different packings or of a different age cannot possibly be treated as equal in usefulness for most purposes if even a minimum of efficient use is to be secured.

Now since in a centrally directed economy the manager of the individual plant would be deprived of the discretion of substituting at will one kind of commodity for another, all this immense mass of different units would necessarily have to enter *separately* into the calculations of the planning authority. It is obvious that the mere statistical task of enumeration exceeds anything of this sort hitherto undertaken. But that is not all. The information which the central planning authority would need would also include a complete description of all the relevant technical properties of every one of these goods, including costs of movement to any other place where it might possibly be used with greater advantage, cost of eventual repair or changes, etc., etc.

But this leads to another problem of even greater importance. The usual theoretical abstractions used in the explanation of equilibrium in a competitive system include the assumption that a certain range of technical knowledge is 'given'. This, of course, does not mean that all the best technical knowledge is concentrated anywhere in a single head, but that people with all kinds of knowledge will be available and that among those competing in a particular job, speaking broadly, those that make the most appropriate use of the technical knowledge will succeed. In a centrally planned society this selection of the most appropriate among the known technical methods will only be possible if all this knowledge can be used in the calculations of the central authority. This means in practice that this knowledge will have to be concentrated in the heads of one or at best a very few people who actually formulate the equations to be worked out. It is hardly necessary to emphasize that this is an absurd idea even in so far as that knowledge is concerned which can properly be said to 'exist' at any moment of time. But much of the knowledge that is actually utilized is by no means 'in existence' in this readymade form. Most of it consists in a technique of thought which enables the individual engineer to find new solutions rapidly as he is confronted with new constellations of circumstances. To assume the practicability of these mathematical solutions, we should have to assume that the concentration of knowledge at the central authority would also include a capacity to discover any improvement of detail of this sort.[8]

There is a third set of data which would have to be available before the actual operation of working out the appropriate method of production and quantities to be produced could be undertaken, data relative to importance of the different kinds and quantities of consumers' goods. In a society where the consumer was free to spend his income as he liked, these data would have to take the form of complete lists of the different quantities of all commodities which would be bought at any possible combination of prices of the different commodities which might be available. These figures would inevitably be of the nature of estimates for a future

---

[8]On the more general problem of experimentation and the utilization of really new inventions, etc., see this chapter, section 7.

period based upon past experience. But past experience cannot provide the range of knowledge necessary. And as tastes change from moment to moment, the lists would have to be in process of continuous revision.

It is probably evident that the mere assembly of these data is a task beyond human capacity. Yet if the centrally run society were to work as efficiently as the competitive society, which as it were decentralizes the task of collecting them, they would have to be present. But let us assume for the moment that this difficulty, the 'mere difficulty of statistical technique', as it is contemptuously referred to by most planners, is actually overcome. This would be only the first step in the solution of the main task. Once the material is collected it would still be necessary to work out the concrete decisions which it implies. Now the magnitude of this essential mathematical operation will depend on the number of unknowns to be determined. The number of these unknowns will be equal to the number of commodities which are to be produced. As we have seen already, we have to take as different commodities all the final products to be completed at different moments, whose production has to be started or to be continued at present. At present we can hardly say what their number is, but it is hardly an exaggeration to assume that in a fairly advanced society, the order of magnitude would be at least in the hundreds of thousands. This means that, at each successive moment, every one of the decisions would have to be based on the solution of an equal number of simultaneous differential equations, a task which, with any of the means known at present, could not be carried out in a lifetime. And yet these decisions would not only have to be made continuously, but they would also have to be conveyed continuously to those who had to execute them.

It will probably be said that such a degree of exactitude would not be necessary, since the working of the present economic system itself does not come anywhere near it. But this is not quite true. It is clear that we never come near the state of equilibrium described by the solution of such a system of equations. But that is not the point. We should not expect equilibrium to exist unless all external change had ceased. The essential thing about the present economic system is that it does react to some extent to all those small changes and differences which would have to be deliberately disregarded under the system we are discussing if the calculations were to be manageable. In this way rational decision would be impossible in all these questions of detail, which in the aggregate decide the success of productive effort.

It is improbable that any one who has realized the magnitude of the task involved has seriously proposed a system of planning based on comprehensive systems of equations. What has actually been in the minds of those who have mooted this kind of analysis has been the belief that, starting from a given situation, which was presumably to be that of the pre-existing capitalistic society, the adaptation to the minor changes which occur from day to day could be gradually brought about by a method of trial and error. This suggestion suffers, however, from two fundamental mistakes. In the first instance, as has been pointed out many times, it is inadmissible to assume that the changes in relative values brought about by the transition from capitalism to socialism would be of a minor order, so permitting the prices of the pre-existing capitalistic system to be used as a starting point, and making it possible to avoid a complete rearrangement of the price system. But even if we neglect this very serious objection, there is not the slightest reason to assume that the task could be solved in this way. We need only to remember the difficulties experienced with the fixing of prices, even when applied to a few commodities only, and to contemplate further that, in such a system, price-fixing would have to be applied not to a few but to all commodities, finished or unfinished, and that it would have to bring about as frequent and as varied price changes as those which occur in a capitalistic society every day and every hour, in order to see that this is not a way in which the solution provided by competition can even be approximately achieved. Almost every change of any single price would make changes of hundreds of other prices necessary and most of these other changes would by no means be proportional but would be affected by the different degrees of elasticity of demand, by the possibilities of substitution and other changes in the method of production. To imagine that all this adjustment could be brought about by successive orders by the central authority when the necessity is noticed, and that then every price is fixed and changed until some degree of equilibrium is obtained, is certainly an absurd idea. That prices may be fixed on the basis of a total view of the situation is at least conceivable, although utterly impracticable; but to base authoritative price-fixing on the observation of a small section of the economic system is a task which cannot be rationally executed under any circumstances. An attempt in this direction will either have to be made on the lines of the mathematical solution discussed before, or else entirely abandoned.

4. Abrogation of the Sovereignty of the Consumer

In view of these difficulties, it is not surprising that practically all who have really tried to think through the problem of central planning have despaired of the possibility of solving it in a world in which every passing whim of the consumer is likely to upset completely the carefully worked out plans. It is more or less agreed now that free choice of the consumer (and presumably also free choice of occupation) and planning from the centre are incompatible aims. But this has given the impression that the unpredictable nature of the tastes of the consumers is the only or the main obstacle to successful planning. Dr. Maurice Dobb[9] has recently followed this to its logical conclusion by asserting that it would be worth the price of abandoning the freedom of the consumer if by the sacrifice socialism could be made possible. This is undoubtedly a very courageous step. In the past, socialists have consistently protested against any suggestion that life under socialism would be like life in a barracks, subject to regimentation of every detail. Dr. Dobb considers these views as obsolete. Whether he would find many followers if he professed these views to the socialist masses is not a question which need concern us here. The question is, would it provide a solution to our problem?

Dr. Dobb openly admits that he has abandoned the view, now held by H. D. Dickinson and others, that the problem could or should be solved by a kind of pricing system under which the prices of the final products and the prices of the original agents would be determined in some kind of a market while the prices of all other products would be derived from these by some system of calculation. But he seems to suffer from the curious delusion that the necessity of any pricing is only due to the prejudice that consumers' preferences should be respected, and that in consequence the categories of economic theory and apparently all problems of value would cease to have significance in a socialist society. "If equality of reward prevailed, market valuations would ipso facto lose their alleged significance, since money cost would have no meaning."[10]

Now it is not to be denied that the abolition of free consumers' choice would simplify the problem in some respects. One of the unpredictable variables would be eliminated and in this way the frequency of the necessary readjustments would be somewhat reduced. But to believe, as Dr. Dobb does, that in this way the necessity of some form of pricing, of an exact comparison between costs and results, would be eliminated, surely indicates a complete unawareness of the real problem. Prices would only cease to be necessary if one could assume that in the socialist state production would have no definite aim whatever—that it would not be directed according to some well-defined order of preferences, however

---

[9]See the article in *Economic Journal* quoted in Appendix B. [The article to which Hayek refers is Maurice Dobb, "Economic Theory and the Problem of a Socialist Economy", *Economic Journal*, op. cit. The British Marxist Maurice Dobb (1900–1976) taught at Cambridge from 1924 to 1965. In the article Hayek cites, Dobb is critical of market socialism and argues against the proposition that "the categories of economic theory are equally valid in a socialist as in an individualist order" (p. 589).—Ed.]

[10][Dobb, *ibid.*, p. 592.—Ed.]

arbitrarily fixed, but that the state would simply proceed to produce something and consumers would then have to take what had been produced. Dr. Dobb asks what would be the loss. The answer is: almost everything. His attitude would only be tenable if costs determined value, so that so long as the available resources were used somehow, the way in which they were used would not affect our well-being, since the very fact that they had been used would confer value on the product. But the question whether we have more or less to consume, whether we are to maintain or to raise our standard of life, or whether we are to sink back to the state of savages always on the edge of starvation, depends mainly on how we use our resources. The difference between an economic and an uneconomic distribution and combination of resources among the different industries is the difference between scarcity and plenty. The dictator, who himself ranges in order the different needs of the members of the society according to his views about their merits, has saved himself the trouble of finding out what people really prefer and avoided the impossible task of combining the individual scales into an agreed common scale which expresses the general ideas of justice. But if he wants to follow this norm with any degree of rationality or consistency, if he wants to realize what he considers to be the ends of the community, he will have to solve all the problems which we have discussed already. He will not even find that his plans are not upset by unforeseen changes, since the changes in tastes are by no means the only, and perhaps not even the most important, changes that cannot be foreseen. Changes in the weather, changes in the numbers or the state of health of the population, a breakdown of machinery, the discovery or the sudden exhaustion of a mineral deposit, and hundreds of other constant changes will make it no less necessary for him to reconstruct his plans from moment to moment. The distance to the really practicable and the obstacles to rational action will have been only slightly reduced at the sacrifice of an ideal which few who realized what it meant would readily abandon.

5. Pseudo-Competition

In these circumstances it is easy to understand that Dr. Dobb's radical solution has not had many followers and that many of the younger socialists seek for a solution in quite the opposite direction. While Dr. Dobb wants to suppress the remnants of freedom or competition which are still assumed in the traditional socialist schemes, much of the more recent discussion aims at a complete reintroduction of competition. In Germany such proposals have actually been published and discussed. But in this country thought on these lines is still in a very embryonic stage. Dickinson's suggestions are a slight step in this direction. But it is known that some of the younger economists who have given thought to these problems have gone much farther and are prepared to go the whole hog and to restore competition completely, as least so far as in their view this is compatible with the state retaining the ownership of all the material means of production. Although it is not yet possible to refer to published work on these lines, what one has learnt about them in conversations and discussions is probably sufficient to make worthwhile some examination of their content.

In many respects these plans are very interesting. The common fundamental idea is that there should be markets and competition between independent entrepreneurs or managers of individual firms, and that in consequence there should be money prices, as in the present society, for all goods, intermediate or finished, but that these entrepreneurs should not be owners of the means of production used by them but salaried officials of the state, acting under state instructions and producing, not for profit, but so as to be able to sell at prices which will just cover costs.

It is idle to ask whether such a scheme still falls under what is usually considered as socialism. On the whole, it seems it should be included under that heading. More serious is the question whether it still deserves the designation of planning. It certainly does not involve much more planning than the construction of a rational legal framework for capitalism. If it could be realized in a pure form in which the direction of economic activity would be wholly left to competition, the planning would also be confined to the provision of a permanent framework within which concrete action would be left to individual initiative. And the kind of planning or central organization of production which is supposed to lead to organization of human activity more rational than 'chaotic' competition would be completely absent. But how far this would be really true would depend of course on the extent to which competition was reintroduced—that is to say, on the crucial question which is here crucial in every respect, namely of what is to be the independent unit, the element which buys and sells on the markets. At first sight there seem to be two main types of such systems. We may assume either that there will be competition between industries only, and that each industry is represented as it were by one enterprise, or that within each industry there are many independent firms which compete with each other. It is only in this latter form that this proposal really evades most of the objections to central planning as such and raises problems of its own. These problems are of an extremely interesting nature. In their pure form they raise the question of the rationale of private property in its most general and fundamental aspect. The question, then, is not whether all problems of production and distribution can be rationally decided by one central authority but whether decisions and responsibility can be successfully left to competing individuals who are not owners or are otherwise directly interested in the means of production under their charge. Is there any decisive reason why the responsibility for the use made of any part of the existing productive equipment should always be coupled with a personal interest in the profits or losses realized on them, or would it really be only a question whether the individual managers, who deputize for the community in the exercise of its property rights under the scheme in question, served the common ends loyally and to the best of their capacity?

6. A World of Competing Monopolies

We may best discuss this question when we come to deal with the schemes in detail. Before we can do that, however, it is necessary to show why, if competition is to function satisfactorily, it will be necessary to go all the way and not to stop at a partial reintroduction of competition. The case which we have therefore to consider next is that of completely integrated industries standing under a central direction but competing with other industries for the custom of the consumer and for the factors of production. This case is of some importance beyond the problems of socialism which we are here chiefly concerned with, since it is by means of creating such monopolies for particular products that those who advocate planning within the framework of capitalism hope to 'rationalize' the so-called chaos of free competition. This raises the general problem, whether it is ever in the general interest to plan or rationalize individual industries where this is only possible through the creation of a monopoly, or whether, on the contrary, we must not assume that this will lead to an uneconomic use of resources and that the supposed economies are really diseconomies from the point of view of society.

   The theoretical argument which shows that under conditions of widespread monopoly there is no determinate equilibrium position and that in consequence under such conditions there is no reason to assume that resources would be used to best advantage is now fairly well accepted. It is perhaps not inappropriate to open the discussion of what this would mean in practice by a quotation from the work of the great scholar who has been mainly responsible for establishing it.

   It has been proposed as an economic ideal [wrote the late F. Y. Edgeworth[11]] that every branch of trade and industry should be formed into

[11]Cf. F. Y. Edgeworth, *Papers Relating to Political Economy*, vol. 1 (London: Macmillan, 1925; reprinted, New York: Franklin, 1970), pp. 138–139. [Francis Ysidro Edgeworth (1845–

a separate union. The picture has some attractions. Nor is it at first sight morally repulsive: since, where all are monopolists, no one will be the victim of monopoly. But an attentive consideration will disclose an incident very prejudicial to industry—instability in the value of all those articles the demand for which is influenced by the prices of other articles, a class which is probably very extensive.

Among those who would suffer by the new regime there would be one class which particularly interests readers of this Journal,[12] namely abstract economists, who would be deprived of their occupation, the investigation of the conditions which determine value. There would survive only the empirical school, flourishing in the chaos congenial to their mentality.

Now the mere fact that the abstract economists would be deprived of their occupation would probably be only a matter of gratification to most advocates of planning if it were not that at the same time the order which they study would also cease to exist. The instability of values, of which Edgeworth speaks, or the indeterminateness of equilibrium, as the same fact can be described in more general terms, is by no means a possibility only to disturb theoretical economists. It means in effect that in such a system there will be no tendency to use the available factors to the greatest advantage, to combine them in every industry in such a way that the contribution which every factor makes is not appreciably smaller than that which it might have made if used elsewhere. The actual tendency prevailing would be to adjust output in such a way, not that the greatest return is obtained from every kind of available resources, but so that the difference between the value of factors which can be used elsewhere and the value of the product is maximized. This concentration on maximum monopoly profits rather than on making the best use of the available factors is the necessary consequence of making the right to produce a good itself a 'scarce factor of production'. In a world of such monopolies this may not have the effect of reducing production all around in the sense that some of the factors of production will remain unemployed, but it will certainly have the effect of reducing output by bringing about an

---

1926), Drummond Professor of Political Economy at Oxford from 1891 to 1922, was editor of the *Economic Journal* from 1890 to 1911 and co-editor with J. M. Keynes from 1919 until his death. Author of *Mathematical Psychics* (London: Kegan Paul, 1881; reprinted, New York: Kelley, 1967), he pioneered the use of mathematics and statistical inference in economics.—Ed.]

[12][The paper from which Hayek's quote is drawn, "The Pure Theory of Monopoly", is a translation of an article that was first published in 1897 in the Italian journal *Giornale degli Economisti.*—Ed.]

uneconomic distribution of factors between industries. This will remain true even if the instability feared by Edgeworth should prove to be of a minor order. The equilibrium that would be reached would be one in which the best use would have been made only of one scarce factor: the possibility of exploiting consumers.

7. The 'Economies' of Rationalization

This is not the only disadvantage of a general reorganization of industry on monopolistic lines. The so-called economies which it is claimed would be made possible if industry were 'reorganized' on monopolistic lines prove on closer examination to be sheer waste. In practically all the cases where the planning of individual industries is advocated at present, the object is to deal with the effects of technical progress.[13] Sometimes it is claimed that the desirable introduction of a technical innovation is made impossible by competition. On other occasions it is objected against competition that it causes waste by forcing the adoption of new machines, etc., when producers would prefer to continue using the old ones. But in both cases, as can be easily shown, planning which aims to prevent what would happen under competition would lead to social waste.

Once productive equipment of any kind is already in existence it is desirable that it should be used so long as the costs of using it (the 'prime costs')[14] are lower than the total cost of providing the same service in an alternative way. If its existence prevents the introduction of more modern equipment this means that the resources which are necessary to produce the same product with more modern methods can be used with greater advantage in some other connection. If older and more modern plants exist side by side and the more modern firms are threatened by the 'cut-throat competition' of the more obsolete works, this may mean either of two things. Either the newer method is not really better, i.e., its introduction has been based on a miscalculation and should never have taken place. In such a case, where operating costs under the new method are actually higher than under the old, the remedy is, of course, to shut down the new plant, even if it is in some sense 'technically' superior. Or—and this is the more probable case—the situation will be that while operating costs under the new method are lower than under the old, they are not

[13]On these problems see A. C. Pigou, *The Economics of Welfare*, 4th edition (London: Macmillan, 1932), p. 188, and F. A. Hayek, "The Trend of Economic Thinking", op. cit., p. 132. [A. C. Pigou (1877–1959) was the successor to Alfred Marshall's chair at Cambridge, which he held from 1908 to 1943. In his book he articulated the English variant of welfare economics, sometimes dubbed the 'Old Welfare Economics'.—Ed.]

[14]["Prime costs" was the term that the British economist Alfred Marshall used to refer to "variable costs".—Ed.]

sufficiently lower to leave at a price which covers the operating costs of the old plant a margin sufficient to pay interest and amortization on the new plant. In this case, too, miscalculation has taken place. The new plant should never have been built. But once it exists the only way in which the public can derive at least some benefit from the capital which has been misdirected is for prices to be allowed to fall to the competitive level and part of the capital value of the new firms to be written off. Artificially to maintain capital values of the new plant by compulsory shutting down the old would simply mean to tax the consumer in the interest of the owner of the new plants without any compensating benefit in the form of increased or improved production.

All this is even clearer in the not infrequent case where the new plant is really superior in the sense that if it had not already been built it would be advantageous to build it now, but where the firms using it are in financial difficulties because it has been erected at a time of inflated values they are in consequence loaded with an excessive debt. Instances like this, where the technically really most efficient firms are at the same time the financially most unsound, are said to be not infrequent in some English industries. But here again any attempt to preserve capital values by suppressing competition from the less modern firms can only have the effect of enabling producers to keep prices higher than they otherwise would be, solely in the interests of the bondholders. The right course from the social point of view is to write down the inflated capital to a more appropriate level, and potential competition from the less modern concerns has therefore the beneficial effect of bringing prices down to a level appropriate to present costs of production. The capitalists who have invested at an unfortunate moment may not like this, but it is clearly in the social interest.

The effects of planning in order to preserve capital values are perhaps even more harmful when it takes the form of retarding the introduction of new inventions. If we abstract, as we are probably entitled to do, from the case where there is reason to assume that the planning authority possesses greater foresight and is better qualified to judge the probability of further technical progress than the individual entrepreneur, it should be clear that any attempt in this direction must have the effect that that which is supposed to eliminate waste is in fact the cause of waste. Given reasonable foresight on the part of the entrepreneur, a new invention will only be introduced if it makes it either possible to provide the same services as were available before at a smaller expenditure of current resources (i.e., at a smaller sacrifice of other possible uses of these resources) or to provide better services at an expenditure which is not proportionately greater. The fall in the capital values of existing instruments which will undoubtedly follow is in no way a social loss. If they can be used for other purposes, a fall of their value in their present use below that which they would attain elsewhere is a distinct indication that they should be transferred. And if they have no other use but their present one, their former value is of interest only as an indication how much cost of production must be lowered by the new invention before it becomes rational to abandon them entirely. The only persons who are interested in the maintenance of the value of already-invested capital are its owners. But the only way this can be done in these circumstances is by withholding from the other members of society the advantages of the new invention.

8. The Criterion of Marginal Costs

It will probably be objected that these strictures may be true of capitalist monopolies aiming at maximum profits, but that they would certainly not be true of the integrated industries in a socialist state whose managers would have instructions to charge prices which just covered costs. And it is true that the last section has been essentially a digression into the problem of planning under capitalism. But it has enabled us not only to examine some of the supposed advantages which are commonly associated with any form of planning but also to indicate certain problems which will necessarily accompany planning under socialism. We shall meet some of these problems again at a later stage. For the moment, however, we must once more concentrate upon the case where the monopolized industries are conducted not so as to make the greatest profit but where it is attempted to make them act as if competition existed. Does the instruction that they should aim at prices which will just cover their (marginal) cost really provide a clear criterion of action?

It is in this connection that it almost seems as if perhaps excessive preoccupation with the conditions of a hypothetical state of stationary equilibrium has led modern economists in general, and especially those who propose this particular solution, to attribute to the notion of costs in general a much greater precision and definiteness than can be attached to any cost phenomenon in real life. Under conditions of widespread competition the term 'cost of production' has indeed a very precise meaning. But as soon as we leave the realm of extensive competition and a stationary state and consider a world where most of the existing means of production are the product of particular processes that will probably never be repeated; where, in consequence of incessant change, the value of most of the more durable instruments of production has little or no connection with the costs which have been incurred in their production but depends only on the services which they are expected to render in the future, the question of what exactly are the costs of production of a given product is a question of extreme difficulty which cannot be answered definitely on the basis of any processes which take place inside the individual firm or industry. It is a question which cannot be answered without first making some assumption as regards the prices of the products in the manufacture of which the same instruments will be used. Much of what is usually termed cost of production is not really a cost element that is given independently of the price of the product but a quasi-rent, or a depreciation quota which has to be allowed on the capitalized value of expected quasi-rents, and is therefore dependent on the prices which are expected to prevail.

For every single firm in a competitive industry these quasi-rents, although dependent on price, are not a less reliable and indispensable guide for the determination of the appropriate volume of production than true cost. On the contrary, it is only in this way that some of the alternative ends which are affected by the decision can be taken into account. Take the case of some unique instrument of production which will never be replaced and which cannot be used outside the monopolized industry and which therefore has no market price. Its use does not involve any costs which can be determined independent from the price of its product. Yet if it is at all durable and may be used up either more or less rapidly, its wear and tear must be counted as true cost if the appropriate volume of production at any one moment is to be rationally determined. And this is not only true because its possible services in the future have to be compared with the results of a more intensive use at present, but also because while it exists it saves the services of some other factor which would be needed to replace it and which can meanwhile be used for other purposes. The value of the services of this instrument is here determined by the sacrifices involved in the next best way of producing the same product; and these services have therefore to be economized because some alternative satisfactions depend on them in an indirect way. But their value can only be determined if the real or potential competition of the other possible methods of producing the same product is allowed to influence its price.

The problem which arises here is well known from the field of public utility regulation. The problem how, in the absence of real competition, the effects of competition could be simulated and the monopolistic bodies be made to charge prices equivalent to competitive prices, has been widely discussed in this connection. But all attempts at a solution have failed, and, as has recently been demonstrated by R. F. Fowler,[15] they were bound to fail because fixed plant is extensively used and one of the most important cost elements, interest and depreciation on such plant, can only be determined after the price which will be obtained for the product is known.

Again it may be objected that this is a consideration which may be relevant in a capitalistic society, but that since even in a capitalistic society fixed costs are disregarded in determining the short run volume of production, they might also with much more reason be disregarded in a socialist society. But this is not so. If rational disposition of resources is to be attempted, and particularly if decisions of this sort are to be left to the managers of the individual industry, it is certainly necessary to provide for the replacement of the capital out of the gross proceeds of the industry, and it will also be necessary that the returns from this reinvested capital should be at least as high as they would be elsewhere. And it would be as misleading under socialism as it is in a capitalistic society to determine the value of the capital which has thus to be recouped on some historic basis such as the past cost of production of the instruments concerned. The value of any particular instrument and therefore the value of its services which have to be counted as cost must be determined from a consideration of the returns expected, having regard to all the alternative ways in which the same result may be obtained and to all the alternative uses to which it may be put. All those questions of obsolescence due to technical progress or change of needs, which were discussed in the last section, enter here into the problem. To make a monopolist charge the price that would rule under competition, or a price that is equal to the necessary cost, is impossible, because the competitive or necessary cost cannot be known unless there is competition. This does not mean that the manager of the monopolized industry under socialism will go on, against his instructions, to make monopoly profits. But it does mean that since there is no way of testing the economic advantages of one method of production as compared with another, the place of monopoly profits will be taken by uneconomic waste.

There is also the further question whether under dynamic conditions profits do not serve a necessary function, whether they are not the main equilibrating force which brings about the adaptation to any change. Cer-

---

[15]R. F. Fowler, *The Depreciation of Capital, Analytically Considered* (London: P. S. King, 1934; reprinted, Nendeln, Liechtenstein: Kraus, 1970), pp. 74 et seq. [The British academic and civil servant Ronald Frederick Fowler (1910–) was a Lecturer in Commerce at the LSE from 1932 to 1940, and the Director of Statistics at the Ministry of Labour from 1950 to 1968.—Ed.]

tainly when there is competition within the industry the question whether it is advisable to start a new firm or not can only be decided on the basis of the profits made by the already existing industries. At least in the case of the more complete competition which we have yet to discuss, profits as an inducement to change cannot be dispensed with. But one might conceive that where any one product is manufactured only by one single concern it will adapt the volume of its output to the demand without varying the price of the product except in so far as cost changes. But how is it then to be decided who is to get the products before supply has caught up with an increased demand? And even more important, how is the concern to decide whether it is justified in incurring the initial cost of bringing additional factors to the place of production? Much of the cost of movement, of transfer of labour and of other factors is of the nature of a non-recurrent investment of capital which is only justified if interest at the market rate can permanently be earned on the sums involved. The interest on such non-tangible investments connected with the establishment or expansion of a plant (the 'goodwill', which is not only a question of popularity with the buyers but equally one of having all the required factors assembled in the proper place) is certainly a very essential factor in such calculations. But once these investments have been made it cannot in any sense be regarded as cost but will appear as profit which shows that the original investment was justified.

And these are by no means all the difficulties which arise in connection with the idea of an organization of production on state monopolistic lines. We have said nothing about the problem of the delimitation of the individual industries, the problem of the status of a firm providing equipment needed in many different lines of production, nor of the criteria on which the success or failure of any of the managers would be judged. Is an 'industry' to include all processes that lead up to any single final product or is it to comprise all plants which turn out the same immediate product, in whatever further process it is used? In either case the decision will involve also a decision on the methods of production to be adopted. Whether every industry is to produce its own tools or whether it has to buy them from another industry which produces them at large scale will essentially affect the question whether it will be advantageous to use a particular instrument at all. But these or very similar problems will have to be discussed in some detail in connection with proposals for readmitting competition in a much more complete form. What has been said here seems however sufficient to show that if one wants to preserve competition in the socialist state in order to solve the economic problem, it would not really help to get a satisfactory solution to go only halfway. Only if competition exists not only *between* but also *within* the different industries can we expect it to serve its purpose. It is to the examination of such a more completely competitive system that we have now to turn.

9. The Possibility of Real Competition under Socialism

At first sight it is not evident why such a socialist system with competition within industries as well as between them should not work as well or as badly as competitive capitalism. All the difficulties one might expect to arise seem likely to be only of that psychological or moral character about which so little definite can be said. And it is true that the problems which arise in connection with such a system are of a somewhat different nature from those arising in a 'planned' system, although on examination they prove not to be so different as may appear at first.

The crucial questions in this case are, What is to be the independent business unit? Who is to be the manager? What resources are to be entrusted to him and how his success or failure is to be tested? As we shall see, these are by no means only minor adminstrative problems, questions of personnel such as those which have to be solved in any large organization today, but major problems whose solution will affect the structure of industry almost as much as the decisions of a real planning authority.

To begin with, it must be clear that the need for some central economic authority will not greatly diminish. It is clear, too, that this authority will have to be almost as powerful as in a planned system. If the community is the owner of all material resources of production, somebody will have to exercise this right for it, at least in so far as the distribution and the control of the use of these resources is concerned. It is not possible to conceive of this central authority simply as a kind of super-bank which lends the available funds to the highest bidder. It would lend to persons who have no property of their own. It would therefore bear all the risk and would have no claim for a definite amount of money as a bank has. It would simply have rights of ownership of all real resources. Nor can its decisions be confined to the redistribution of free capital in the form of money, and perhaps of land. It would also have to decide whether a particular plant or piece of machinery should be left further to the entrepreneur who has used it in the past, at his valuation, or whether it should be transferred to another who promises a higher return from it.

In imagining a system of this sort it is most charitable to assume that the initial distribution of resources between individual firms will be made on the basis of the historically given structure of industry and that the selection of the managers is made on the basis of some efficiency test and of previous experience. If the existing organization of industry were not accepted it could be improved or rationally changed only on the basis of very extensive central planning, and this would land us back with the systems which the competitive system is an attempt to replace. But acceptance of the existing organization would solve the difficulties only for the moment. Every change in circumstance will necessitate changes in this organization and in the course of a comparatively short space of time the central authority will have to effect a complete reorganization.

On what principles will it act?

It is clear that in such a society change will be quite as frequent as under capitalism. It will also be quite as unpredictable. All action will have to be based on anticipation of future events and the expectations on the part of different entrepreneurs will naturally differ. The decision to whom to entrust a given amount of resources will have to be made on the basis of individual promises of future return. Or, rather, it will have to be made on the statement that a certain return is to be expected with a certain degree of probability. There will, of course, be no objective test of the magnitude of the risk. But who is then to decide whether the risk is worth taking? The central authority will have no other grounds on which to decide but the past performance of the entrepreneur. But how are they to decide whether the risks he has run in the past were justified? And will its attitude towards risky undertakings be the same as if he risked his own property?

Consider first the question how his success or failure will be tested. The first question will be whether he has succeeded in preserving the value of the resources entrusted to him. But even the best entrepreneur will occasionally make losses and sometimes even very heavy losses. Is he to be blamed if his capital has become obsolete because of an invention or a change in demand? How is it to be decided whether he was entitled to take a certain risk? Is the man who never makes losses because he never takes a risk necessarily the man who acts most in the interest of the community? There will certainly be a tendency to prefer the safe to the risky enterprise.

But risky and even the purely speculative undertakings will be no less important here as under capitalism. Specialization in the function of risk-bearing by professional speculators in commodities will be as desirable a form of division of labour as it is today. But how is the magnitude of the capital of the speculator to be determined and how is his remuneration to be fixed? How long is a formerly successful entrepreneur to be suffered to go on making losses? If the penalty for loss is the surrender of the position of 'entrepreneur' will it not be almost inevitable that the possible chance of making a loss will operate as so strong a deterrent that it will outbalance the chance of the greatest profit? Under capitalism, too, loss of capital may mean loss of status as capitalist. But against this deterrent is always the attraction of the possible gain. Under socialism this cannot exist. It is even conceivable that general reluctance to undertake any risky business might drive the rate of interest down to nearly zero. But would this be an advantage to society? If it were only due to the satiation of all the absolutely safe channels of investment it would be bought at a sacrifice of all experimentation with new and untried methods. Even if progress is inevitably connected with what is commonly called waste, is it not worth having if on the whole gains exceed losses?

But, to turn back to the problem of the distribution and control of resources: There remains the very serious question of how to decide in the short run whether a going concern is making the best use of its resources. Even whether it is making profit or losses is a matter which will depend on one's estimate of the future returns to be expected from its equipment. Its results can only be determined if a definite value is to be given to its existing plant. What is to be the decision if another entrepreneur promises to get a higher return out of the plant (or even an individual machine) than that on which the present user bases his valuation? Is the plant or machine to be taken from him and to be given to the other man in his mere promise? This may be an extreme case, yet it illustrates only the constant shift of resources between firms which goes on under capitalism and which would be equally advantageous in a socialist society. In a capitalist society the transfers of capital from the less to the more efficient entrepreneur is brought about by the former making losses and the latter making profits. The question of who is to be entitled to risk resources and with how much he is to be trusted is here decided by the man who has succeeded in acquiring and maintaining them. Will the question in the socialist state be decided on the same principles? Will the manager of a firm be free to reinvest profits wherever and whenever he thinks it is worth while? At present he will compare the risk involved in further expansion of this present undertaking with the income which he will obtain if he invests elsewhere or if he consumes his capital. Will consideration of the alternative advantages which society might derive from that capital have the same weight in this computation of risk and gain as would have his own alternative gain or sacrifice?

The decision about the amount of capital to be given to an individual entrepreneur and the decision thereby involved concerning the size of the individual firm under a single control are in effect decisions about the most appropriate combination of resources.[16] It will rest with the central

[16]For a more detailed discussion of how the size of the individual firm is determined under competition and of the way in which this affects the appropriateness of different methods of production and the costs of the product, cf. E. A. G. Robinson, *The Structure of Competitive Industry*, Cambridge Economic Handbooks, vol. 7 (London: Nisbet, 1931; re-

authority to decide whether one plant located at one place should expand rather than another plant situated elsewhere. All this involves planning on the part of the central authority on much the same scale as if it were actually running the enterprise. And while the individual entrepreneur would in all probability be given some definite contractual tenure for managing the plant entrusted to him, all new investment will necessarily be centrally directed. This division in the disposition over the resources would then simply have the effect that neither the entrepreneur nor the central authority would be really in a position to plan, and that it would be impossible to assess responsibility for mistakes. To assume that it is possible to create conditions of full competition without making those who are responsible for the decisions pay for their mistakes seems to be pure illusion. It will at best be a system of quasi-competition where the person really responsible will not be the entrepreneur but the official who approves his decisions and where in consequence all the difficulties will arise in connection with freedom of initiative and the assessment of responsibility which are usually associated with bureaucracy.[17]

10. The General Significance for Socialist Theory of the Recourse to the 'Competitive Solution'

Without pretending any finality for this discussion of pseudo-competition, it may at least be claimed that it has been shown that its successful administration presents considerable obstacles and that it raises numerous difficulties which must be surmounted before we can believe that its results will even approach those of competition which is based on private property of the means of production. It must be said that in their present state, even considering their very provisional and tentative character, these proposals seem rather more than less impracticable than the older socialist proposals of a centrally planned economic

---

vised ed., Cambridge: Cambridge University Press, 1968). [Cambridge economist Austin Robinson (1879–1993) served as co-editor of the *Economic Journal* from 1944 to 1970 and as Managing Editor of *The Collected Writings of John Maynard Keynes*, op. cit.—Ed.]

[17]For further very illuminating discussion of these problems, see the works of R. G. Hawtrey and J. Gerhardt quoted in Appendix B. [The works to which Hayek refers are the chapter entitled "Collectivism" in Ralph George Hawtrey, *The Economic Problem* (New York and London: Longmans, 1925), pp. 336–352; and Johannes Gerhardt, *Unternehmertum und Wirtschaftsführung* (Tübingen: J. C. B. Mohr, 1930). Hawtrey (1879–1975) wrote popular books and made a number of contributions to monetary economics during the interwar years. His article "Public Expenditure and the Demand for Labour", *Economica*, March 1925, pp. 38–48, provided the theoretical underpinning for the 'Treasury View'. Gerhardt (1895–1942?) taught economics at the University of Munich.—Ed.]

system. It is true, even more true than in the case of planning proper, that all the difficulties which have been raised are 'only' due to the imperfections of the human mind. But while this makes it illegitimate to say that these proposals are impossible in any absolute sense, it remains not the less true that these very serious obstacles to the achievement of the desired end exist and that there seems to be no way in which they can be overcome.

Instead of discussing any further the detailed difficulties which these proposals raise, it is perhaps more interesting to consider what it really implies that so many of those of the younger socialists who have seriously studied the economic problems involved in socialisms have abandoned the belief in a centrally planned economic system and pinned their faith on the hope that competition may be maintained even if private property is abolished. Let us assume for the moment that it is possible in this way to come very near the results which a competitive system based on private property achieves. Is it fully realized how much of the hopes commonly associated with a socialist system are already abandoned when it is proposed to substitute for the centrally planned system, which was regarded as highly superior to any competitive system, a more or less successful imitation of competition? And what are the advantages which will remain to compensate for the loss of efficiency which, if we take account of our earlier objections, it seems will be the inevitable effects of the fact that without private property competition will necessarily be somewhat restricted and that therefore some of the decisions will have to be left to the arbitrary decision of a central authority?

The illusions which have to be abandoned with the idea of a centrally planned system are indeed very considerable. The hope of a vastly superior productivity of a planned system over that of chaotic competition has had to give place to the hope that the socialist system may nearly equal the capitalist system in productivity. The hope that the distribution of income may be made entirely independent of the price of the services rendered and based exclusively on considerations of justice, preferably in the sense of an egalitarian distribution, has to be replaced by the hope that it will be possible to use part of the income from the material factors of production to supplement income from labour. The expectation that the 'wage system' would be abolished; that the managers of a socialized industry or firm would act on entirely different principles from the profit-seeking capitalist has proved to be equally wrong. And although there has been no occasion to discuss this point in detail, the same must be said of the hope that such a socialist system would avoid crises and unemployment. A centrally planned system, although it could not avoid making

113

even more serious mistakes of the sort which lead to crises under capitalism, would at least have the advantage that it would be possible to share the loss equally between all its members. It would be superior in this respect in that it would be possible to reduce wages by decree when it was found that this was necessary in order to correct the mistakes. But there is no reason why a competitive socialist system should be in a better position to avoid crises and unemployment than competitive capitalism. Perhaps an intelligent monetary policy may reduce their severity for both, but there are no possibilities in this respect under competitive socialism which would not equally exist under capitalism.

Against all this there is of course the advantage that it would be possible to improve the relative position of the working class by giving them a share in the returns from land and capital. And this is, after all, the main aim of socialism. But that it will be possible to improve their position relative to that of those who were capitalists does not mean that their absolute incomes will be increased or that they will even remain as high as before. What will happen in this respect depends entirely on the extent to which general productivity is reduced. It must again be pointed out here that general considerations of the kind which can be advanced in a short essay can lead to no decisive conclusions. Only by intensive application of analysis on these lines to the phenomena of the real world is it possible to arrive at approximate estimates of the quantitive importance of the phenomena which have been discussed here. On this point opinions will naturally differ. But even if it could be agreed that what exactly the effects of any of the proposed systems on the national income would be, there would still be the further question of whether any given reduction, either of its present absolute magnitude or its future rate of progress, is not too high a price for the achievement of the ethical ideal of greater equality of incomes. On this question, of course, scientific argument must give way to individual conviction.

But at least the decision cannot be made before the alternatives are known, before it is at least approximately realized what the price is that has to be paid. That there is still so little clarity on this point, that it is still possible to deny that it is impossible to have the best of both worlds, is mainly due to the fact that most socialists have little idea of what the system they advocate is really to be like, whether it is to be a planned or a competitive system. It is at present one of the strongest tactics of contemporary socialists to leave this point in the dark, and, while claiming all the benefits which used to be associated with central planning, refer to competition when they are asked how they are going to solve a particular difficulty. But nobody has yet demonstrated how planning and competition can be rationally combined; and so long as this is not done

one is certainly entitled to insist that these two alternatives are kept clearly separate, and that anybody who advocates socialism must decide for one or the other and then demonstrate how he proposes to overcome the difficulties inherent in the system he has chosen.

11. Conclusion

No pretence is made that the conclusions reached here in the examination of the alternative socialist constructions must necessarily be final. One thing, however, seems to emerge from the discussions of the last years with incontrovertible force: that today we are not intellectually equipped to improve the working of our economic system by 'planning' or to solve the problem of socialist production in any other way without very considerably impairing productivity. What is lacking is not 'experience' but intellectual mastery of a problem which so far we have only learnt to formulate but not to answer. No one would want to exclude every possibility that a solution may yet be found. But in our present state of knowledge serious doubt must remain whether such a solution can be found. We must at least face the possibility that for the past fifty years thought has been on the wrong lines, attracted by a notion which on examination at close range proved not to be realizable. If this were so, it would be no proof that it would have been desirable to stay where we were before this tendency set in, but only that a development in another direction would have been more advantageous. And there is indeed some reason to suppose that it might, for instance, have been more rational to seek for a smoother working of competition than to obstruct it so long with all kinds of attempts of planning that almost any alternative came to seem preferable to existing conditions.

But if our conclusions on the merits of the beliefs which are undoubtedly one of the main driving forces of our time are essentially negative, this is certainly no cause for satisfaction. In a world bent on planning, nothing could be more tragic than that the conclusion should prove inevitable that persistence on this course must lead to economic decay. Even if there is already some intellectual reaction under way, there can be little doubt that for many years the movement will continue in the direction of planning. Nothing, therefore, could do more to relieve the unmitigated gloom with which the economist today must look at the future of the world than if it could be shown that there is a possible and practicable way to overcome its difficulties. Even for those who are not in sympathy with all the ultimate aims of socialism there is strong reason to wish that now the world is moving in that direction it should prove practicable and a catastrophe be averted. But it must be admitted that today it seems, to say the least, highly unlikely that such a solution can be found. It is of some significance that so far the smallest contributions to such a solution have come from those who have advocated planning. If a solution should ever be reached this would be due more to the critics, who have at least shown what the problem is, even if they have despaired of finding a solution.

THREE

SOCIALIST CALCULATION:
THE COMPETITIVE 'SOLUTION'[1]

I

Two chapters in the discussion of the economics of socialism may now be regarded as closed. The first deals with the belief that socialism will dispense entirely with calculation in terms of value and will replace it with some sort of calculation *in natura* based on units of energy or of some other physical magnitude. Although this view is not yet extinct and is still held by some scientists and engineers, it has been definitely abandoned by economists. The second closed chapter deals with the proposal that values, instead of being left to be determined by competition, should be found by a process of calculations carried out by the planning authority which would use the technique of mathematical economics. With regard to this suggestion, V. Pareto (who, curiously enough, is sometimes quoted as holding this view) has already said what probably will remain the final word. After showing how a system of simultaneous equations can be used to explain what determines prices on a market he adds:

> It may be mentioned here that this determination has by no means the purpose to arrive at a numerical calculation of prices. Let us make the most favourable assumption for such a calculation, let us assume that we have triumphed over all the difficulties of finding the data of the problem and that we know the *ophélimités* of all the different commodities for each individual, and all the conditions of production of all the commodi-

---

[1][Published as "Socialist Calculation: The Competitive 'Solution'", *Economica*, N.S., vol. 7, May 1940, pp. 125–149; reprinted in Hayek, ed., *Individualism and Economic Order*, op. cit. —Ed.] The two recent books with which this article is mainly concerned are Oskar Lange and Fred M. Taylor, *On the Economic Theory of Socialism*, ed., with an introduction, by Benjamin E. Lippincott, op. cit., and H. D. Dickinson, *Economics of Socialism*, op. cit. [The Polish economist Oskar Lange (1904–1965) lectured on economics and statistics at the Universities of Cracow, California, Chicago, and Warsaw. His article "On the Economic Theory of Socialism", originally published in two parts in the *Review of Economic Studies*, op. cit., is regarded as one of the founding documents of market socialism. Benjamin E. Lippincott (1902–1988) was a professor of political science at the University of Minnesota. For more on Taylor and Dickinson, see chapter 2, note 6.—Ed.]

ties, etc. This is already an absurd hypothesis to make. Yet it is not sufficient to make the solution of the problem possible. We have seen that in the case of 100 persons and 700 commodities there will be 70,699 conditions (actually a great number of circumstances which we have so far neglected will still increase that number); we shall therefore have to solve a system of 70,699 equations. This exceeds practically the power of algebraic analysis, and this is even more true if one contemplates the fabulous number of equations which one obtains for a population of forty millions and several thousand commodities. In this case the roles would be changed: It would not be mathematics which would assist political economy, but political economy would assist mathematics. In other words, if one really could know all these equations, the only means to solve them which is available to human powers is to observe the practical solution given by the market.[2]

In the present article we shall be mainly concerned with a third stage in this discussion, for which the issue has now been clearly defined by the elaboration of proposals for a competitive socialism by Professor Lange and Dr. Dickinson. Since, however, the significance of the result of the past discussions is not infrequently represented in a way which comes very near to an inversion of the truth, and as at least one of the two books to be discussed is not quite free from this tendency, a few further remarks on the real significance of the past development seem not unnecessary.

The first point is connected with the nature of the original criticism directed against the more primitive conceptions of the working of a socialist economy which were current up to about 1920. The idea then current (and still advocated, e.g., by Dr. O. Neurath[3]) is well expressed by F. Engels in his *Anti-Dühring*, when he says that the social plan of production "will be settled very simply, without the intervention of the famous 'value'".[4] It was against this generally held belief that N. G. Pierson,

[2]Vilfredo Pareto, *Manuel d'économie politique*, 2nd edition (Paris: M. Giard, 1927), pp. 233–234. [Hayek refers to the French edition of Pareto's work, which was originally published in Italian. The English edition, translated from the French (hence twice removed from the original), is *Manual of Political Economy*, trans. Ann Schwier (New York: Kelley, 1971). For more on Pareto, see chapter 1, note 14.—Ed.]

[3][See chapter 1, note 16, for more on Neurath.—Ed.]

[4][Friedrich Engels, *Herrn Eugen Dühring's Umwälzung der Wissenschaft* (Leipzig: Genossenschafts-Buchdruckerei, 1877–78); translated as *Herr Eugen Dühring's Revolution in Science (Anti-Dühring)*, op. cit., p. 338. Engels (1820–1895) was Karl Marx's collaborator; *Anti-Dühring* was his polemic against the ideas of the blind German academic and rival socialist Eugen Karl Dühring (1833–1921). Three chapters from the book formed the basis for his *Socialism: Utopian and Scientific*, trans. Edward Aveling (New York: International Publishers, 1935), the most influential socialist pamphlet of the late nineteenth century.—Ed.]

L. von Mises, and others pointed out that if the socialist community wanted to act rationally its calculation would have to be guided by the same *formal* laws which applied to a capitalist society. It seems necessary especially to underline the fact that this was a point made by the critics of the socialist plans, since Professor Lange and particularly his editor[5] now seem inclined to suggest that the demonstration that the formal principles of economic theory apply to a socialist economy provides an answer to these critics. The fact is that it has never been denied by anybody, except socialists, that these formal principles *ought* to apply to a socialist society, and the question raised by Professor Mises and others was not whether they ought to apply but whether they could in practice be applied in the absence of a market. It is therefore entirely beside the point when Professor Lange and others quote Pareto and Barone as having shown that values in a socialist society would depend on essentially the same factors as in a competitive society. This of course had been shown long before, particularly by Wieser.[6] But none of these authors has made an attempt to show how these values, which a socialist society ought to use if it wanted to act rationally, could be found, and Pareto, as we have seen, expressly denied that they could be determined by calculation.

It seems then that, on this point, the criticisms of the earlier socialist schemes have been so successful that the defenders, with few exceptions,[7] have felt compelled to appropriate the argument of their critics, and have been forced to construct entirely new schemes of which nobody thought before. While against the older ideas that it was possible to plan rationally without calculation in terms of value it could be justly argued that they were logically impossible, the newer proposals designed to determine values by some process other than competition based on private property raise a problem of a different sort. But it is surely unfair to say, as Professor Lange does, that the critics, because they deal in a new way with the new schemes evolved to meet the original criticism, "have given up the essential point" and "retreated to a second line of defence".[8] Is this not rather a case of covering up their own retreat by creating confusion about the issue?

---

[5]See B. E. Lippincott in Lange and Taylor, op. cit., p. 7.

[6][Friedrich Wieser made this point in *Natural Value,* op. cit., pp. 60ff. For more on Wieser, see chapter 1, note 5.—Ed.]

[7]The most notable exception is Dr. M. Dobb. See his *Political Economy and Capitalism* (London: Routledge and Kegan Paul, 1937; revised edition, London: Routledge and Kegan Paul, 1940), chapter 8, and his review of Professor Lange's book, titled "Economists and the Economics of Socialism", in *The Modern Quarterly,* vol. 2, 1939, pp. 173–179. [For more on Maurice Dobb, see chapter 2, note 9.—Ed.]

[8]Lange and Taylor, op. cit., p. 63.

There is a second point on which Professor Lange's presentation of the present state of the debate is seriously misleading. The reader of his study can hardly avoid the impression that the idea that values should and could be determined by using the technique of mathematical economics, i.e., by solving millions of equations, is a malicious invention of the critics, intended to throw ridicule on the efforts of modern socialist writers. The fact, which cannot be unknown to Professor Lange, is of course that this procedure has more than once been seriously suggested by socialist writers as a solution of the difficulty—among others by Dr. Dickinson, who now, however, expressly withdraws this earlier suggestion.[9]

II

A third stage in the debate has now been reached with the proposal to solve the problems of determining values by the re-introduction of competition. When five years ago the present author tried to appraise the significance of these attempts[10] it was necessary to rely on what could be gathered from oral discussion among socialist economists, since no systematic exposition of the theoretical bases of competitive socialism was then available. This gap has now been filled by the two books here to be discussed. The first contains a reprint of an essay by Professor Lange, originally published in 1936 and 1937, together with an older article by the late Professor Taylor (dating from 1928) and an introduction by the editor, Professor B. E. Lippincott, which in addition to a quite unnecessary restatement of Professor Lange's argument in cruder terms does much by the unmeasured praise he bestows on this argument and the extravagant claims he advances for it[11] to prejudice the reader against the essentially scholarly piece of work that follows. Although written in a lively style and confining itself to the outlines of the subject, it does seriously grapple with some of the main difficulties in the field.

   H. D. Dickinson's more recent book is a far more comprehensive survey of the field, proposing essentially the same solution.[12] It is unquestionably a book of great distinction, well organized, lucid and concise, and should rapidly establish itself as the standard work on its subject. To the econo-

---

[9]Dickinson, op. cit., p. 104, and K. Tisch, *Wirtschaftsrechnung und Verteilung im zentralistisch organisierten sozialistischen Gemeinwesen*, op. cit.

[10]In *Collectivist Economic Planning*, op. cit., "The Present State of the Debate". [Reprinted as chapter 2 of the present volume.—Ed.]

[11]Dr. Lange's essay is described as the "first writing to make an advance on Barone's contribution" and to show by "irrefutable" argument the "evident feasibility and superiority" of a socialist system. (Lange and Taylor, op. cit., pp. 13, 24, 37).

[12]It is a curious fact that Dickinson nowhere in his book (except in the bibliography) refers to Lange's work.

mist, the reading of the book provides indeed the rare pleasure of feeling that recent advances of economic theory have not been in vain and have even helped to reduce political differences to points which can be rationally discussed. Dickinson himself would probably agree that he shares all his economics with—and indeed has learnt most of it from—non-socialist economists, and that in his essential conclusions on the desirable economic policy of a socialist community he differs much more from most of his socialist colleagues than from 'orthodox' economists. This, together with the open-mindedness with which the author takes up and considers the arguments advanced by his opponents, makes discussion of his views a real pleasure. If the socialists, like the economists, are ready to accept his book as the most up-to-date general treatment of the economics of socialism from the socialist point of view, it should provide the basis for much fruitful further discussion.

As has already been mentioned, the main outlines of the solution offered by the two authors are essentially the same. They both rely to some extent on the competitive mechanism for the determination of relative prices. But they both refuse to let prices be determined directly in the market and propose instead a system of price-fixing by a central authority, where the state of the market of a particular commodity, i.e., the relation of demand to supply, merely serves as an indication to the authority whether the prescribed prices ought to be raised or lowered. Neither of the two authors explains why he refuses to go the whole hog and to restore the price mechanism in full. But as I happen to agree (although probably for different reasons) that this would be impracticable in a socialist community, we can leave this question aside for the moment and shall take it for granted that in such a society competition cannot play quite the same role as it does in a society based on private property, and that, in particular, the rates at which commodities will be exchanged by the parties in the market will have to be decreed by the authority.

We shall leave the details of the proposed organization for later consideration and first consider the general significance of this solution under three aspects. We shall ask firstly how far this kind of socialist system still conforms to the hopes that were placed on the substitution of a planned socialist system for the chaos of competition; secondly, how far the proposed procedure is an answer to the main difficulty, and, finally, how far it is applicable.

The first and most general point can be dealt with fairly briefly, although it is not unimportant if one wants to see these new proposals in their proper light. It is merely a reminder of how much of the original claim for the superiority of planning over competition is abandoned if the planned society is now to rely for the direction of its industries to a large extent on competition. Until quite recently, at least, planning and competition used to be regarded as opposites, and this is unquestionably still true of nearly all planners except a few economists among them. I fear that the schemes of Lange and Dickinson will bitterly disappoint all those scientific planners who, in the recent words of B. M. S. Blackett, believe that "the object of planning is largely to overcome the results of competition".[13] This would be even more true if it were really possible to reduce the arbitrary elements in a competitive socialist system as much as is believed by Dickinson, who hopes that his "libertarian socialism" "may establish, for the first time in human history, an effective individualism".[14] Unfortunately, as we shall see, this is not likely to be the case.

III

The second general question we must consider is how far the proposed method of centralized price fixing, while leaving it to individual firms and consumers to adjust demand and supply to the given prices, is likely to solve the problem which admittedly cannot be solved by mathematical calculation. Here, I am afraid, I find it exceedingly difficult to understand the grounds on which such a claim is made. Lange as well as Dickinson assert that even if the initial system of prices were chosen entirely at random, it would be possible by such a process of trial and error gradually to approach to the appropriate system.[15] This seems to be much the same thing as if it were suggested that a system of equations which was too complex to be solved by calculation within reasonable time and whose values were constantly changing could be effectively tackled by arbitrarily inserting tentative values and then trying about till the proper solution was found. Or, to change the metaphor, the difference between such a system of regimented prices and a system of prices determined by the market seems to be about the same as that between an attacking army where every unit and every man could only move by special command and by the exact distance ordered by headquarters and an army where every unit and every man can take advantage of every opportunity offered to them. There is of course no *logical impossibility* of conceiving a directing organ of the collective economy which is not only "omnipresent and omniscient" as Dickinson conceives it,[16] but also omnipotent and

[13]See Sir Daniel Hall and others, *The Frustration of Science*, op. cit., p. 142. [The English physicist Patrick Maynard Stuart, Baron Blackett (1897–1974) received the Nobel prize in 1948; he contributed the article "The Frustration of Science" to the volume Hayek cites. —Ed.]

[14]Dickinson, op. cit., p. 26.

[15]Lange and Taylor, op. cit., pp. 70, 86, and Dickinson, op. cit., pp. 103 and 113.

[16]Dickinson, op. cit., p. 191.

which therefore would be in a position to change without delay every price by just the amount that is required. When, however, one proceeds to consider the actual apparatus by which this sort of adjustment is to be brought about, one begins to wonder whether anyone should really be prepared to suggest that, within the domain of practical possibility, such a system will ever even distantly approach the efficiency of a system where the required changes are brought about by the spontaneous action of the persons immediately concerned.

We shall later, when we consider the proposed institutional setting, come back to the question how this sort of mechanism is likely to function in practice. In so far as the general question is concerned, however, it is difficult to suppress the suspicion that this particular proposal has been born out of an excessive preoccupation with problems of the pure theory of stationary equilibrium. If in the real world we had to deal with approximately constant data, that is, if the problem were, to find a price system which then could be left more or less unchanged for long periods, then the proposal under consideration would not be so entirely unreasonable. With given and constant data such a state of equilibrium could indeed be approached by the method of trial and error. But this is far from being the situation in the real world, where constant change is the rule. Whether and how far anything approaching the desirable equilibrium is ever reached depends entirely on the speed with which the adjustments can be made. The practical problem is not whether a particular method would eventually lead to a hypothetical equilibrium, but which method will secure the more rapid and complete adjustment to the daily changing conditions in different places and different industries. How great the difference in this respect would be between a method where prices are currently agreed upon by the parties of the market and a method where these prices are decreed from above is of course a matter of practical judgement. But I find it difficult to believe that anybody should doubt that in this respect the inferiority of the second method would be very great indeed.

The third general point is also one where I believe that preoccupation with concepts of pure economic theory has seriously misled both our authors. In this case it is the concept of perfect competition which apparently has made them overlook a very important field to which their method appears to be simply inapplicable. Wherever we have a market for a fairly standardized commodity it is at least conceivable that all prices should be decreed in advance from above for a certain period. The situation is however very different with respect to commodities which cannot be standardized, and particularly for those which today are produced on individual orders, perhaps after invitation for tenders. A large part of the product of the 'heavy industries', which of course would be the first to be socialized, belongs to this category. Much machinery, most buildings and ships, and many parts of other products are hardly ever produced for a market, but only on special contract. This does not mean that there may not be intense competition in the market for the products of these industries, although it may not be 'perfect competition' in the sense of pure theory; the fact is simply that identical products are rarely produced twice in short intervals; and the circle of producers who will compete as alternative suppliers in each instance will be different in almost every individual case, just as the circle of potential customers who will compete for the services of a particular plant will differ from week to week. What basis is there in all these cases for fixing prices of the product so as 'to equalize demand and supply'? If prices are here to be fixed by the central authority, they will have to be fixed in every individual case and on the basis of an examination by that authority of the calculations of all potential suppliers and all potential purchasers. It is hardly necessary to point out the various complications that will arise according as the prices are fixed before or after the prospective buyer has decided on the particular piece of machinery or building which he wants. Presumably it will be the estimates of the producer which, before they are submitted to the prospective customer, will have to be approved by the authority. Is it not clear that in all these cases, unless the authority in effect takes all the functions of the entrepreneur on itself (i.e., unless the proposed system is abandoned and one of complete central direction substituted), the process of price fixing would either become exceedingly cumbersome and the cause of infinite delay, or a pure formality?

IV

All these considerations appear to be relevant whatever particular form of organization is chosen. Before we go further, however, it becomes necessary to consider somewhat more in detail the concrete apparatus of industrial control which the two authors propose. The sketches they provide of the organization are fairly similar, although in this respect Lange gives us somwhat more information than Dickinson, who, for most of the problems of economic organization, refers us to the works of the Webbs and G. D. H. Cole.[17]

----

[17]Dickinson, op. cit., p. 30. [The works to which Dickinson referred in his book are Sidney and Beatrice Webb, *Constitution for a Socialist Commonwealth of Great Britain* (London: Longmans, 1920; reprinted, Cambridge: Cambridge University Press, 1975); and G. D. H. Cole, *Principles of Economic Planning* (London: Macmillan, 1935; reprinted, Ann Arbor: University of Michigan Press, 1970), and *Britain without Capitalists: A Study of What Industry in a Soviet Britain Could Achieve* (London: Lawrence and Wishart, 1936). Sidney (1859–1947) and Be-

Both authors contemplate a socialist system in which the choice of occupation would be free and regulated mainly by the price mechanism (i.e., by the wage system) and in which the consumers also would be free to spend their incomes as they chose. Apparently both authors also want prices of consumers' goods to be fixed by the ordinary market processes (although Dickinson does not seem to be quite decided on this point),[18] and also to leave the determination of wages to the bargaining between the parties concerned.[19] Both also agree that for various reasons not the whole of industry should be socialized, but that besides the socialized there should also remain a private sector, consisting of small enterprises run on essentially capitalistic lines. I find it difficult to agree with their belief that the existence of such a private sector parallel with the socialized sector creates no special difficulties. But as it would be difficult within the space of this article to deal adequately with this problem, we shall, for the purposes of this discussion, disregard the existence of the private sector and assume that the whole of industry is socialized.

The determination of all prices, other than those of consumers' goods and of wages, is the main task of the central economic authority, Lange's Central Planning Board or Dickinson's Supreme Economic Council. (We shall, following Dickinson, henceforth refer to this body as the SEC.) As regards the technique of how particular prices are announced and changed we get more information, although by no means enough, from Lange, while Dickinson goes more fully into the question by what considerations the SEC should be guided in the fixing of prices. Both questions have a special importance and they must be considered separately.

According to Lange, the SEC would from time to time issue what, following Taylor, he calls 'factor valuation tables', that is, comprehensive lists of prices of all means of production (except labour).[20] These prices would have to serve as the sole basis for all transactions between different enterprises and the whole calculation of all the industries and plants during the period of their validity and the managers must treat these prices as constant.[21] What we are not told, however, either by Lange or by Dickinson, is for what period these prices are to be fixed. This is one of the more serious obscurities in the exposition of both authors, a gap in their exposition which makes one almost doubt whether they have made a real

atrice (1858–1943) Webb helped found both the Fabian Society and the London School of Economics; Hayek's review of their book on the Soviet Union is reprinted in the Appendix of the present volume. The British academic G. D. H. Cole (1889–1959), an architect of guild socialism, wrote numerous popular tracts on socialism.—Ed.]

[18]Lange and Taylor, op. cit., p. 78; Dickinson, op. cit., p. 60.

[19]Lange and Taylor, op. cit., p. 78; Dickinson, op. cit., p. 126.

[20]Lange and Taylor, op. cit., pp. 46, 52.

[21]Lange and Taylor, *ibid.*, p. 81.

effort to visualize their system at work. Are prices to be fixed for a definite period in advance, or are they to be changed whenever it seems desirable? F. M. Taylor seemed to suggest the former alternative when he wrote that the appropriateness of particular prices would show itself at the end of the "productive period";[22] and Lange, on at least one occasion, gives the same impression when he says that "any price different from the equilibrium price would show at the end of the accounting period a surplus or shortage of the commodity in question".[23] But on another occasion he says that "adjustments of those prices would be constantly made",[24] while Dickinson confines himself to stating that after, "by a process of successive approximation", "a set of prices can ultimately be established in consonance with the principles of scarcity and substitution", "small adjustments will be sufficient to keep the system in equilibrium except in the case of major technical innovations or of big changes in consumers' tastes".[25] Could the failure to understand the true function of the price mechanism, caused by the modern preoccupation with stationary equilibrium, be better illustrated?

While Dickinson is very uninformative on the mechanism of bringing price changes into effect, he goes much more fully than Lange into the considerations on which the SEC would have to base their decisions. Unlike Lange, Dickinson is not satisfied with the SEC merely watching the market and adjusting prices when an excess of demand or supply appears, and then trying to find by experimentation a new equilibrium level. He rather wants the SEC to use statistically established demand and supply schedules as a guide to determine the equilibrium prices. This is evidently a residue of his earlier belief in the possibility of solving the whole problem by the method of simultaneous equations. But although he has now abandoned this idea (not because he regards it as impossible, since he still believes it could be done by solving merely "two or three thousand simultaneous equations",[26] but because he realizes that "the data themselves, which would have to be fed into the equation-machine, are continually changing"), he still believes that the statistical determination of demand schedules would be useful as an aid to, if not as a substitute for, the method of trial and error, and that it would be well worth while to try and establish the numerical values of the constants (*sic*) in the Walrasian system of equilibrium.

[22]Lange and Taylor, *ibid.*, p. 53.
[23]Lange and Taylor, *ibid.*, p. 82.
[24]Lange and Taylor, *ibid.*, p. 86.
[25]Dickinson, op. cit., pp. 100, 102, 103.
[26]Dickinson, *ibid.*, p. 104.

V

Whatever the method by which the SEC fixes prices, and particularly whatever the periods at which and for which prices are announced, there are two points about which there can be little question: The changes will occur later than they would if prices were determined by the market parties, and there will be less differentiation between prices of commodities according to differences of quality and the circumstances of time and place. While with real competition price changes occur when the parties immediately concerned know that conditions have changed, the SEC will be able to act only after the parties have reported, the reports have been verified, contradictions cleared up, etc.; and the new prices will become effective only after all the parties concerned have been notified, that is, either a date will have to be fixed in advance at which the new prices will become effective, or the accounting will have to include an elaborate system by which every manager of production is constantly notified of the new prices upon which he has to base his calculations. Since in fact every manager would have to be informed constantly on many more prices than those of the commodities which he is actually using (at least of those of all possible substitutes), some sort of periodic publication of complete lists of all prices would be necessary. It is clear that while economic efficiency demands that prices should be changed as promptly as possible, practicability would confine actual changes to intervals of fair length.

That the price fixing process will be confined to establishing uniform prices for classes of goods and that therefore distinctions based on the special circumstances of time, place, and quality will find no expression in prices is probably obvious. Without some such simplification the number of different commodities for which separate prices would have to be fixed would be practically infinite. This means, however, that the managers of production will have no inducement and even no real possibility to make use of special opportunities, special bargains, and all the little advantages offered by their special local conditions, since all these things could not enter into their calculations. It would also mean, to give only one other instance of the consequences, that it would never be practicable to incur extra costs to remedy a sudden scarcity quickly, since a local or temporary scarcity could not affect prices until the official machinery had acted.

For both these reasons, because prices would have to be fixed for periods and because they would have to be fixed generically for categories of goods, a great many prices would be at most times in such a system substantially different from what they would be in a free system. This is very important for the functioning of the system. Lange makes great play with the fact that prices act merely as "indices of terms on which alterna-tives are offered"[27] and that this "parametric function of prices"[28] by which prices are guiding the action of individual managers without being directly determined by them, will be fully preserved under such a system where prices are fixed. As he himself points out, "the determinateness of the accounting prices holds, however, only if all discrepancies between demand and supply of a commodity are met by an appropriate change of price", and for this reason "rationing has to be excluded" and "the rule to produce at the minimum average cost has no significance unless prices represent the relative scarcity of the factors of production".[29] In other words, prices will provide a basis for rational accounting only if they are such that at the ruling prices anyone can always sell as much or buy as much as he wishes, or that anyone should be free to buy as cheaply or to sell as dearly as is made possible by the existence of a willing partner. If I cannot buy more of a factor so long as it is worth more to me than the price, and if I cannot sell a thing as soon as it is worth less to me than the price which somebody else would be willing to pay for it, prices are no longer indices of alternative opportunities.

We shall see the significance of this more clearly when we consider the action of the managers of the socialist industries. But before we can con-sider their action we must see who these people are and with what func-tions they are invested.

VI

The nature of the industrial unit under separate management and the factors which determine its size and the selection of its management is another point on which both our authors are deplorably vague. Lange seems to contemplate the organization of the different industries in the form of national trusts, although this important point is only just touched upon once when the National Coal Trust is mentioned as an example.[30] The very important and relevant question of what is *one* industry is nowhere discussed, but he apparently assumes that the various "man-agers of production" will have monopolistic control of the particular com-modities with which they are concerned. In general, Lange uses the term "managers of production" exceedingly vaguely,[31] leaving it obscure whether the directors of a whole "industry" or of a single unit are meant;

---

[27]Lange and Taylor, op. cit., p. 78.
[28]Lange and Taylor, *ibid.*, pp. 70, 86.
[29]Lange and Taylor, *ibid.*, pp. 93–94.
[30]Lange and Taylor, *ibid.*, p. 78.
[31]Lange and Taylor, *ibid.*, pp. 75, 79, 86.

but at critical points[32] a distinction between the managers of plant and the managers of a whole industry appears without any clear limitation of their function. Dickinson is even more vague when he speaks of economic activities being "decentralized and carried on by a large number of separate organs of collective economy" which will have "their own nominal capital and their own profit and loss account and will be managed very much as separate enterprises under capitalism".[33]

Whoever these managers of production are, their main function would appear to be to decide how much and how to produce on the basis of the prices fixed by the SEC (and the prices of consumers' goods and the wages determined by the market). They would be instructed by the SEC to produce at the lowest possible average costs[34] and to expand production of the individual plants till marginal costs are equal to price.[35] According to Lange, the directors of the industries (as distinguished from the managers of individual plants) would have also the further task of seeing that the amount of equipment in the industry as a whole is so adjusted that "the marginal cost incurred by the industry" in producing an output which "can be sold or 'accounted for' at a price which equals marginal cost" is the lowest possible.[36]

In this connection a special problem arises which unfortunately cannot be discussed here as it raises questions of such difficulty and complexity that a separate article would be required. It concerns the case of decreasing marginal costs where, according to both our authors, the socialist industries would act differently from capitalist industry by expanding production till prices are equal, not to average, but to marginal costs. Although the argument employed possesses a certain specious plausibility it can hardly be said even that the problem is adequately stated in either of the two books, still less that the conclusions drawn are convincing. Within the space available on this occasion, however, we can do no more than seriously question Dickinson's assertion that "under modern technical conditions, diminishing costs are far commoner than increasing costs"—a statement which in the context in which it occurs clearly refers to marginal costs.[37]

Here we shall confine ourselves to considering one question arising out of this part of the proposal, the question how the SEC will ensure that the principle that prices are equalized to the lowest marginal cost at which

[32]Lange and Taylor, *ibid.*, p. 76, 82n.
[33]Dickinson, op. cit., p. 213.
[34]Lange and Taylor, op. cit., p. 75.
[35]Lange and Taylor, *ibid.*, p. 76; Dickinson, op. cit., p. 107.
[36]Lange and Taylor, op. cit., p. 77.
[37]Dickinson, op. cit., p. 108.

the quantity concerned can be produced is actually put into force. The question which arises here is not 'merely' one of the loyalty or capacity of the socialist managers. For the purpose of this argument it may be granted that they will be as capable and as anxious to produce as cheaply as the average capitalist entrepreneur. The problem arises because one of the most important forces which in a truly competitive economy brings about the reduction of costs to the minimum discoverable will be absent, namely, price competition. In the discussion of this sort of problem, as in the discussion of so much of economic theory at the present time, the question is frequently treated as if the cost curves were objectively given facts. What is forgotten here is that the method which under given condi- tion is the cheapest is a thing which has to be discovered, and to be dis- covered anew sometimes almost from day to day, by the entrepreneur, and that, in spite of the strong inducement, it is by no means regularly the established entrepreneur, the man in charge of the existing plant, who will discover what is the best method. The force which in a competi- tive society brings about the reduction of price to the lowest cost at which the quantity saleable at that cost can be produced is the opportunity for anybody who knows a cheaper method to come in at his own risk and to attract customers by underbidding the other producers. But if prices are fixed by the authority this method is excluded. Any improvement, any adjustment of the technique of production to changed conditions will be dependent on convincing the SEC that the commodity in question can be produced cheaper and that therefore the price ought to be lowered. Since the man with the new idea will have no possibility of establishing himself by undercutting, the new idea cannot be proved by experiment till he has convinced the SEC that his way of producing the thing is cheaper. Or, in other words, every calculation by an outsider who believes that he can do better will have to be examined and approved by the authority, which in this connection will have to take over all the functions of the entre- preneur.

VII

Let us briefly consider a few of the problems arising out of the relations between the 'socialist managers of production' (whether of a plant or an industry) and the SEC. The manager's task is, as we have seen, to order production in such a way that his marginal costs are as low as possible and equal to price. How is he to do this and how is the fact of his success to be verified? He has to take prices as given. This turns him into what has recently been called a pure 'quantity adjuster', i.e., his decision is confined to the quantities of factors of production and the combination in which he uses them. But as he has no means of inducing his suppliers to offer more, or to induce his purchasers to buy more, than they want to at the prescribed price, he will frequently be simply unable to carry out his instructions; or at least, if he cannot get more of a material required at the prescribed price, the only way for him, e.g., to expand production so as to make his cost equal to price, would be to use inferior substitutes or to employ other uneconomic methods; and when he cannot sell at the prescribed price and until the price is lowered by decree, he will have to stop production where under true competition he would have lowered his prices.

Another great difficulty arising out of the periodic price changes by decree is the problem of anticipations of future price movements. Lange, somewhat too bravely, cuts this Gordian knot by prescribing that "for purposes of accounting, prices must be treated as constant, as they are treated by entrepreneurs on a competitive market"(!)[38] Does that mean that the managers, although they know for certain that a particular price will have to be raised or lowered, must act as if they did not know? Clearly this won't do. But if they are free to meet expected price movements by anticipatory action, are they to be allowed to take advantage of the administrative delays in making price changes effective? And who is to be responsible for losses caused by wrongly timed or wrongly directed price changes?

Closely connected with this problem is another one, to which we also get no answer. Both our authors speak about 'marginal costs' as if they were independent of the period for which the manager can plan. Clearly actual costs depend in many instances as much as anything on buying at the right time. And in no sense can costs during any period be said to depend solely on prices during that period. They depend as much on whether these prices have been correctly foreseen as on the views that are held about future prices. Even in the very short run, costs will depend on the effects which current decisions will have on future productivity. Whether it is economical to run a machine hard or to economize in lubricants, whether to make major adjustments to a given change in demand or to carry on as well as possible with the existing organization, in fact almost every decision on how to produce now depends at least in part on the views held about the future. But while the manager clearly must hold some views on these questions, he can hardly be held responsible for anticipating future changes correctly if these changes depend entirely on the decision of the authority.

Not only, however, will the success of the individual manager depend to a large extent on the action of the planning authority. He will also have to satisfy the same authority that he has done as well as was possible.

[38]Lange and Taylor, op. cit., p. 81.

Either beforehand, or more likely retrospectively, all his calculations will have to be examined and approved by the authority. This will not be a perfunctory auditing directed to find out whether his costs have actually been what he says they have been. It will have to establish whether they have been the lowest possible ones. This means that the control will have to consider not only what he actually did but also what he might have done and ought to have done. And from the point of view of the manager it will be much more important that he should always be able to prove that in the light of the knowledge which he possessed the decision actually taken was the right one than that he should prove to be right in the end. If this must not lead to the worst forms of bureaucracy, I do not know what would.

This brings us to the general question of the responsibility of the managers. Dickinson clearly sees that "responsibility means in practice financial responsibility" and that unless the manager "bears responsibility for losses as well as for profits he will be tempted to embark upon all sorts of risky experiments on the bare chance that one of them will turn out successful".[39] This is a difficult problem with managers who have no property of their own. Dickinson hopes to solve it by a system of bonuses. This may indeed be sufficient to prevent managers from taking too great risks. But is not the real problem the opposite one, that managers will be afraid of taking risks if, when the venture does not come off, it will be somebody else who will afterwards decide whether they have been justified in embarking on it? As Dickinson himself points out, the principle would be that "although the making of profits is not necessarily a sign of success, the making of losses is a sign of failure".[40] Need one say more about the effects of such a system on all activities involving risk? It is difficult to conceive that under these circumstances any of the necessary speculative activities involving risk-bearing could be left to managerial initiative. But the alternative is to fall back for them on that system of strict central planning to avoid which the whole system has been evolved.

VIII

All this is even more true when we turn to the whole problem of new investments, that is, to all the questions which involve changes in the size (i.e., the capital) of the managerial units, whether they involve net changes in the total supply of capital or not. Up to a point it is possible to divide this problem into two parts, the decisions about the distribution of the available capital supply and the decisions about the rate at which

[39]Dickinson, op. cit., p. 214.
[40]Dickinson, ibid., p. 219.

capital is to be accumulated, although it is dangerous to carry this division too far, since the decision about how much is to be saved is necessarily also a decision about which needs for capital are to be satisfied and which are not. Both our authors agree that, as regards the problem of the distribution of capital between industries and plants, the interest mechanism should as far as possible be retained, but that the decision of how much to save and invest would necessarily have to be arbitrary.[41]

Now, however strong the desire may be to rely on the interest mechanism for the distribution of capital, it is fairly obvious that the market for capital can in no sense be a free market. And while for Lange the rate of interest is also "simply determined by the condition that the demand for capital is equal to the amount available",[42] Dickinson takes great pains to show how the SEC will, on the basis of the alternative plans of activity drawn up by the different undertakings, construct an aggregate demand schedule for capital which will enable it to determine that rate of interest at which the demand for capital will equal supply. The ingenuity and the astounding trust in the practicability of even the most complicated constructions which he displays in this connection may be illustrated by his statement that in a certain case "it will be necessary to establish a provisional rate of interest, then to allow the different organs of collective economy to re-contract with each other on the basis of this provisional rate, and so to draw up their final demand schedule for capital".[43]

All this, however, does not meet the main difficulty. If indeed it were possible to accept at their face value the statements of all the individual managers and would-be managers about how much capital they could with advantage use at various rates of interest, some such scheme as such might appear feasible. It cannot be too often repeated, however, that the planning authority cannot be conceived "simply as a kind of super-bank which lends the available funds to the highest bidder. It would lend to persons who have no property of their own. It would therefore bear all the risk and would have no claim for a definite amount of money as a bank has. It would simply have rights of ownership over all real resources. Nor can its decisions be confined to the redistribution of free capital in the form of money, and perhaps of land. It would have to decide whether a particular plant or piece of machinery should be left further to the entrepreneur who has used it in the past, at his valuation, or whether it should be transferred to another who promises a higher return for it."[44]

[41]Lange and Taylor, op. cit., p. 85; Dickinson, op. cit., pp. 80, 205.
[42]Lange and Taylor, op. cit., p. 84.
[43]Dickinson, op. cit., p. 83n.
[44]F. A. Hayek, "Present State of the Debate", in *Collectivist Economic Planning*, op. cit., pp. 232–233. [This volume, p. 109.—Ed.]

These sentences are taken from the essay where the present author discussed five years ago the "possibility of real competition under socialism".[45] At that time such systems had only been vaguely discussed and one could hope to find an answer when systematic expositions of the new ideas should become available. But it is most disappointing to find no answer whatever to these problems in the two books now under discussion. While throughout the two works claims are made about how beneficial the control of investment activity would be in many respects, no indication is given of how this control is to be exercised and of how the responsibilities are to be divided between the planning authorities and the managers of the 'competing' industrial units. Such statements as we find, as for instance that "because the managers of socialist industry will be governed in some choices by the direction laid down by the planning authority, it does not follow that they will have no choice at all",[46] are singularly unhelpful. All that seems to be fairly clear is that the planning authority will be able to exercise its function of controlling and directing investment only if it is in a position to check and repeat all the calculations of the entrepreneur.

It seems that here the two writers are unconsciously led to fall back on the earlier beliefs in the superiority of a centrally directed system over a competitive system and to console themselves with the hope that the "omnipresent, omniscient organ of the collective economy"[47] will possess at least as much knowledge as the individual entrepreneurs and will therefore be in as good if not in a better position to make the decisions as the entrepreneurs are. As I have tried to show on another occasion, it is the main merit of real competition that through it use is made of knowledge divided among many persons which, if it were to be used in a centrally directed economy, would have all to enter the single plan.[48] To assume that all this knowledge would be automatically in the possession of the planning authority seems to me to be to miss the main point. It is not quite clear whether Lange means to assert that the planning authority will have all this information when he says that "the administrators of a socialist economy will have exactly the same knowledge, or lack of knowledge, of the production functions as the capitalist entrepreneurs have".[49] If the "administrators of a socialist economy" here means merely all the managers of the units as well as of the central organization taken together, the statement can of course be readily accepted, but does in no way solve

---

[45]*Ibid.*
[46]Dickinson, op. cit., p. 217.
[47]Dickinson, *ibid.,* p. 191.
[48]See the article on "Economics and Knowledge", op. cit.
[49]Lange and Taylor, op. cit., p. 61.

the problem. But if it is intended to convey that all this knowledge can be effectively used by the planning authority in drawing up the plan, it is merely begging the whole question and seems to be based on the "fallacy of composition".[50]

On this whole all-important question of the direction of new investment and all that it involves, the two studies do not really give any new information. The problem remains where it was five years ago and I can confine myself on this point to repeating what I said then: "The decision about the amount of capital to be given to an individual entrepreneur and the decisions thereby involved concerning the size of the individual firm under a single control are in effect decisions about the most appropriate combination of resources. It will rest with the central authority to decide whether one plant located at one place should expand rather than another plant situated elsewhere. All this involves planning on the part of the central authority on much the same scale as if it were actually running the enterprise. And while the individual entrepreneur would in all probability be given some definite contractual tenure for managing the plant entrusted to him, all new investments will be necessarily centrally directed. This division in the disposition over the resources would then simply have the effect that neither the entrepreneur nor the central authority would be really in a position to plan, and that it would be impossible to assess the responsibility for mistakes. To assume that it is possible to create conditions of full competition without making those who are responsible for the decisions pay for their mistakes seems to be pure illusion. It will be at best a system of quasi-competition where the persons really responsible will not be the entrepreneur but the official who approves his decisions and where in consequence all the difficulties will arise in connection with freedom of initiative and the assessment of responsibility which are usually associated with bureaucracy."[51]

IX

The question how far a socialist system can avoid extensive central direction of economic activity is of great importance quite apart from its relation to economic efficiency: It is crucial for the question of how much

[50]Another and even worse instance of this fallacy occurs in Lippincott's introduction to the essays of Lange and Taylor, when he argues that "there can be no doubt that the Central Planning Board would exercise great power, but would it be any greater than that exercised collectively by private boards of directors? Because the decisions of private boards are made here and there, this does not mean that the consumer does not feel their collective impact, even though it may take a depression to make him aware of it." Lippincott, "Introduction", op. cit., p. 35.

[51]*Collectivist Economic Planning*, op. cit., pp. 236–237. [This volume, pp. 111–112.—Ed.]

personal and political freedom can be preserved in such a system. Both authors show a reassuring awareness of the dangers to personal freedom which a centrally planned system would involve and seem to have evolved their competitive socialism partly in order to meet this danger. Dickinson even goes so far as to say that "capitalist planning can exist only on the basis of fascism" and that in the hands of an irreponsible controller even socialist planning "*could* be made the greatest tyranny the world has ever seen".[52] But he and Lange believe that their competitive socialism will avoid this danger.

Now if competitive socialism could really rely for the direction of production largely on the effects of consumers' choice as reflected in the price system and if the cases where the authority will have to decide what is to be produced and how were made the exception rather than the rule, this claim would be to a large extent substantiated. How far is this really the case? We have already seen that with the retention of the control over investment the central authority wields most extensive powers over the direction of production, much more extensive indeed than is easily possible to show without making this discussion unduly long. To this have yet to be added, however, a further number of arbitrary elements of which Dickinson himself gives a quite substantial although by no means complete list.[53] There is in the first instance the "allocation of resources between present and future consumption" which, as we have already seen, always involves a decision about what particular needs will be satisfied and which needs will not be satisfied. There is, secondly, the need for arbitrary decision in respect to the "allocation of resources between communal and individual consumption" which, in view of the great extension of the "division of communal consumption" which he envisages means that another very large part of the resources of the society is put outside the control of the price mechanism and subject to purely authoritarian decision. Dickinson expressly adds to this only "the choice between work and leisure" and the "geographical planning and the pricing of land", but at other points of his exposition further questions emerge on which he wants effective planning in order to correct the results of the market. But although he (and still more so Lange) frequently hint at the possibilities of "correcting" the results of the price mechanism by judicious interference, this part of the programme is nowhere clearly worked out.

What our authors here have in mind perhaps comes out clearest in Dickinson's attitude towards the problem of wage changes: "If wages are too low in any one industry, it is the duty of the planning organ to adjust

[52]Dickinson, op. cit., pp. 22, 227.
[53]Dickinson, *ibid.*, p. 205.

prices and quantities produced, so as to yield equal wages to work of equal skill, responsibility, and difficulty in every industry".[54] Apparently here the price mechanism and the free choice of occupation is not to be relied upon. Later we learn that although "unemployment in any particular job affords a prima facie case for lowering the standard wage",[55] a lowering of wages is objectionable "on social grounds, because a lowering in wages. . .causes discontent; on economic grounds, because it perpetuates an uneconomic allocation of labour to different occupations". (How?) Therefore, "as invention and improved organization makes less labour necessary to satisfy human wants, society should set itself to discover new wants to satisfy".[56] "The powerful engine of propaganda and advertisement, employed by public organs of education and enlightenment instead of by the hucksters and panderers of private profitmaking industry, could divert demand into socially desirable directions while preserving the subjective impression (*sic*) of free choice".[57]

When we add to this and many other similar points where Dickinson wants his SEC to exercise a paternalistic control,[58] the fact that it will be necessary to coordinate national production "with a general plan of exports and imports",[59] since free trade "is inconsistent with the principles of collectivism",[60] it becomes fairly evident that there will be precious little economic activity which will not be more or less immediately guided by arbitrary decisions. In fact, Dickinson expressly contemplates a situation where "the state, through a definite planning organ, makes itself responsible for the consideration of economic activity as a whole" and even adds that this destroys the "illusion" maintained in a capitalist society "that the division of the product is governed by forces as impersonal and inevitable as those which govern the weather".[61] This can only mean that, with most other planners, he himself thinks of production in his system as one which is largely directed by conscious and arbitrary decisions. Yet in spite of this extensive role which arbitrary decisions are to play in his system, he is confident (and the same applies to Lange) that his system will not degenerate into an authoritarian despotism.

[54]Dickinson, *ibid.*, p. 21.
[55]Dickinson, *ibid.*, p. 127.
[56]Dickinson, *ibid.*, p. 131.
[57]Dickinson, *ibid.*, p. 32.
[58]Cf. for instance the passage in Dickinson, op. cit., p. 52, where he speaks about the "people who will not pay voluntarily beforehand for what they are only too glad to have once they have it".
[59]Dickinson, *ibid.*, p. 169.
[60]Dickinson, *ibid.*, p. 176.
[61]Dickinson, *ibid.*, p. 21.

Dickinson just mentions the argument that "even if a socialist planner wished to realize freedom he could not do so and remain a planner", yet the answer he gives makes one doubt whether he has quite seen on what considerations this argument is based. His answer is merely that "a plan can always be changed".[62] But this is not the point. The difficulty is that, in order to plan at all on an extensive scale, a much more extensive agreement among the members of the society about the relative importance of the various needs is required than will normally exist, and that in consequence this agreement will have to be brought about and a common scale of values will have to be imposed by force and propaganda. I have developed this argument at length elsewhere and I have not space here to restate it.[63] And the thesis I have developed there, that socialism is bound to become totalitarian, now seems to receive support from the most unexpected quarters. This at least appears to be the meaning when Max Eastman, in a recent book on Russia, states that "Stalinism *is* socialism, in the sense of being an inevitable, although unforeseen, political and cultural accompaniment".[64]

In fact, although he does not seem to see it, Dickinson himself, in the concluding passages of his book, makes a statement which comes very much to the same thing. "In a socialist society," he says, "the distinction, always artificial, between economics and politics will break down; the economic and the political machinery of society will fuse into one".[65] This is of course precisely the authoritarian doctrine preached by Nazis and Fascists. The distinction breaks down because in a planned system all economic questions become political questions, because it is no longer a question of reconciling as far as possible individual views and desires, but one of imposing a single scale of values, the 'social goal' of which socialists ever since the time of Saint-Simon[66] have been dreaming. In this respect

[62]Dickinson, *ibid.*, pp. 227–228.

[63]See *Freedom and the Economic System*. [This pamphlet is reprinted in this volume, chapter 9.—Ed.]

[64]Max Eastman, *Stalin's Russia and the Crisis in Socialism* (New York: Norton, 1940), p. 154. As the book is not yet available in this country, the quotation is taken from a review that appeared in the American press. [The American Max Eastman (1883–1969) was the editor and publisher of the radical organ *The Masses*. He travelled to the Soviet Union after the Revolution and married a Russian woman. By the 1930s he had become disillusioned with the Russian experiment, believing that the original purpose of Lenin's revolution had been subverted by Stalin's corrupt leadership.—Ed.]

[65]Dickinson, op. cit., p. 235.

[66][The social reformer Claude Henri de Rouvroy, Comte de Saint-Simon (1760–1825) was a founder of French socialism. In his account of the origins of Scientism and "the abuse of reason", Hayek would characterize Saint-Simon as "a megalomaniac visionary". See F. A. Hayek, "The Counter-Revolution of Science", in *The Counter-Revolution of Science: Studies in the Abuse of Reason*, op. cit., p. 222.—Ed.]

it seems that the schemes of an authoritarian socialist, from those of Hogben and Lewis Mumford,[67] whom Dickinson mentions as an example,[68] to those of Stalin and Hitler, are much more realistic and consistent than the beautiful and idyllic picture of the "libertarian socialism" in which Dickinson believes.

X

There can be no better testimony of the intellectual quality of the two books under discussion than that after having written about them at such length one is conscious of having only just scratched on the surface of the problems raised by them. But an examination in greater detail would clearly exceed the scope of an article; and since many of the doubts which are left with the reader concern points which are not answered in the two books, an adequate treatment of the subject would require another book even longer than those discussed. There are however also important problems which are discussed at some length, particularly in Dickinson's book, which we have scarcely been able to mention. This applies not only to the difficult problem of the combination of a private sector with the socialized sector, which both authors propose, but also to such important problems as the international relations of a socialist community and to the problems of monetary policy, to which Dickinson devotes a very brief, and on the whole the least satisfactory, section.

A fuller discussion would also have to point out various passages in the argument of both authors where apparently residues of earlier beliefs or views which are purely matters of political creed creep in and strike one as curiously inconsistent with the plane of the rest of the discussion. This applies for instance to Dickinson's repeated references to class conflict and exploitation or his gibes at the wastes of competition[69] and to much of Lange's interesting section on the "economist's case for socialism", where he seems to employ arguments of somewhat questionable validity.

These, however, are minor points. On the whole the books are so thoroughly unorthodox from a socialist point of view that one rather wonders whether their authors have not retained too little of the traditional trappings of socialist argument to make their proposals acceptable to socialists

---

[67][The books which Dickinson mentions are Lancelot Hogben, *Retreat from Reason* (Northampton, Mass.: The Hampshire Bookshop, and New York: The Channel Bookshop, 1937), and Lewis Mumford, *Technics and Civilization* (New York: Harcourt Brace, 1934). The English physiologist Lancelot Hogben (1895–1975) taught at Birmingham and wrote several popular books on scientific subjects; Lewis Mumford (1895–1990) was an American author, editor, and social critic.—Ed.]

[68]Dickinson, op. cit., p. 25.

[69]Dickinson, *ibid.*, pp. 22, 94.

who are not economists. As courageous attempts to face the real difficulties and completely to remould socialist doctrine to meet them they deserve our gratitude and respect. Whether the solution offered will appear
particularly practicable, even to socialists, may perhaps be doubted. To
those who, with Dickinson, wish to create "for the first time in human
history, an effective individualism",[70] a different path will probably appear more promising.

[70]Dickinson, *ibid.*, p. 26.

FOUR

THE ECONOMICS OF PLANNING[1]

What is today widely advocated as a 'planned economy' means, in so far as it means anything clearly, a centrally directed economic system—a system in which every move is determined by a unitary plan, worked out and laid down in black and white beforehand. This is the way in which we have learnt to solve most other complicated tasks which demand a rational solution. It is the way in which the engineer plans a process of production or the general plans a move of his armies. The more complicated the task, the more necessary such planning appears. It is therefore only natural that people who (with much reason) are dissatisfied with the working of our economic system should demand that it should be planned and directed like any good engineering job. To such people—and they represent today probably a majority of all educated opinion—it comes inevitably as a shock to learn that a constantly increasing number of economists not only doubt the efficacy of central planning, but even believe that it would considerably reduce economic efficiency and in addition necessarily bring about a restriction of personal freedom of exactly the kind which constitutes a totalitarian system. In this article I shall confine myself to explaining the argument which has so much shaken the belief in the efficiency and even practicability of central economic planning.

The first point which must be stressed is that it is the very complexity of the task—i.e., the very fact which usually makes comprehensive planning necessary—which renders it impracticable for the economic system as a whole. In a plan, as the engineer draws it up, all the relevant facts must enter, and to make it a coherent plan all these facts must in the last resort be commanded and mastered by a single mind. This sets a limit on the degree of complexity of the task which can be solved by completely thinking it through, because the number of variables which any mind, even with the best assistance, can manipulate is limited. But, as will presently

[1] [F. A. Hayek, "The Economics of Planning", *The Liberal Review*, vol. 1 (1941), pp. 5–11.—Ed.]

appear, the number of variables which would have to be taken into account in drawing up an economic master plan far exceeds the number which could be handled in this manner.

The second important point which is often not realized is that what is the best method of producing a given thing is not simply a technical fact. It depends on what amounts of the various skills, implements, and materials happen to be available at a given time and place. There is no unique answer to the question: What is technically the best way of supplying the people of Oxford with boots or the people of Australia with cameras? There are any number of possible combinations of resources which might produce the desired result; and even if evidently wasteful ones are ruled out there remain a very large number of ways, each of which might be best in different circumstances. The presence or absence of all the different skills, implements, and materials and all their potential uses, not only at the place in question but in every other place from which the product might be brought, as well as the expenditure of transporting them, have to be taken into account. To choose intelligently here it is not sufficient to be informed about available supplies in generic terms, as they can be easily summarized in statistics. Small differences in quality, in the state of preservation or in the location of implements or materials, or of the skill and number of the people available at the particular time and place can be of the greatest importance. All this would have to enter the master plan—as it enters into the calculations of the entrepreneurs in our present economy, or rather the pre-war economy. And all these data, not merely for a single commodity, but for all commodities, would have to be digested into a single plan, if it is to be rational. It is clear that this is a superhuman task.

The practical impossibility of solving this task by central planning becomes even more obvious when we consider how rapidly all these data change. There is probably no question of fact on which the advocates and opponents of central planning differ so much as in their (usually implicit) assumptions concerning the frequency and importance of the changes which would have to be constantly made in any comprehensive economic plan. Gigantic as the task of central planning must appear in any case, it might still seem feasible if we could conceive of the master plan being laid down in advance for a long period of years and then being adhered to. This would, however, presuppose that we could effectively control all the data, which is by no means the case. Every year, every day, the supplies of the various resources will continue to change in unpredictable ways—not only in the aggregate amounts, where these unforeseen changes are likely to some extent to offset each other—but, what is no less important, in particular places and at particular moments. And each of these changes will make extensive changes in the whole organization of production necessary. I shall later show how these changes are brought about in a competitive system. But it will be clear that it would be impossible to adjust the whole plan by central decision each time such a change occurs, and we shall also see what the consequence of this must be.

As soon as these difficulties are seriously faced, the demand for a single comprehensive plan for all production is usually abandoned and in its place appears the demand either for 'decentralized planning' or for central planning of a mere outline of operations with the details to be filled in by local decisions. The necessity for some degree of decentralization of planning is indeed usually recognized. And, in a sense, the case for competition may be summed up as an argument for making the conditions as favourable for decentralized planning as possible; while the case against central planning might be summed up in the statement that the more central planning there is, the less the individual can plan. What is usually not recognized is that any such partial or decentralized planning is something totally different from the ideal of central planning, that none of the special advantages expected from central planning can be expected from such a system, and that it raises new problems on the solution of which the functioning of the whole economic system depends and which cannot be solved by the principle of planning. In the sense in which the term 'planning' is used by the planners, 'decentralized planning' is almost a contradiction in terms. Many plans do not make a planned whole, and the problem of coordinating or correlating them raises precisely the same difficulties as centralized planning, difficulties which have to be solved by some method other than planning. There are, for instance, no rational grounds on which the desirable rate of growth of an industry can be decided, irrespective of the rate of growth of all other industries; nor grounds on which the general lines of development of all industries can be intelligently decided, apart from the sum of the particular circumstances in each place and each locality.

It is of course possible on general considerations to lay down objectives to be reached by the economic system as a whole—but that means very little, as we will have to decide which of all the desirable things can be simultaneously achieved in view of the limited means available. To lay down an absolute order of priorities irrespective of concrete possibilities would lead to appalling waste, and the very opposite of any rational husbandry of existing resources. What can be simultaneously achieved could be consciously decided only from the most complete knowledge of all detail. For what purposes and in what way particular resources are used with the greatest advantage can be intelligently decided only by the 'man on the spot'. Thus, in order to achieve the extensive division of labour on which our civilization is based, the direction of production must evidently be decentralized to a high degree, and some method must be found for coordinating these separate plans which does not depend on conscious central control. The problem is how the separate persons who have to make the decisions can be supplied with indicators of the urgency of the other needs for the resources which they want to use, so as to enable them to adjust their decisions to those of all others.

I am firmly convinced that if we had had to build up by conscious planning the modern economic system we would never have arrived anywhere near where we are but would have remained at the primitive state of production under which central direction is alone practicable.[2] That man did develop the modern industrial apparatus is due to the fact that he stumbled through a slow and gradual process of trial and error on a method which combined decentralization and coordination, a method under which nobody needs to know all the facts which a planner would have to know, and where the most essential information required for a particular decision is conveyed to those who have to make it speedily and simply by an automatic process. I mean the competitive markets and the price system. To show how the price system achieves this, it is necessary to consider somewhat more fully the problems which the central planner would have to try to solve, but cannot solve. Such a discussion of what is nothing less than *the* economic problem of society necessarily involves a brief excursion into somewhat more technical economics.

The basic fact is that the infinite variety of physical resources which we command can in no way be reduced to some common physical unit which is of any relevance for the solution of the economic problem. Although it may be possible to reduce in the last resort everything to so many units of energy, and although this has again and again led to the belief that we might use units of energy in our economic calculations, this would only

[2]That the Russians did build up a modern system of production by planning was possible because they were able to imitate the organization developed in the Western world, particularly in America; they reproduced, in other words, a system of the division of labour which had grown up under competition—in most respects without even attempting to distinguish between those aspects of the American example which were applicable to Russian conditions and those which were not.

The same applies very largely to our own war planning, where methods and techniques continue to be used because they have proved the most expedient under peacetime conditions; but with the price mechanism almost entirely suspended, there is no possibility of judging what is economic and what is not. In both cases it is, however, still possible to employ methods of division of labour developed under fairly similar conditions. What the problem of planning would really involve in the long run will be best appreciated if one tries to imagine that all the changes brought about by the industrial revolution had had to be centrally planned.

be misleading in an attempt to solve the economic problem. So long as we cannot at will convert one form of energy into another, but find that in one form it is more useful for a given purpose than in another, the ultimate composition of the different forces and materials is quite irrelevant for our task. The important points are: first, that some forms of energy are very much more useful for some purposes than others, while still others may be quite useless, and, second, that while, within limits, many of the different forms of force and matter can replace each other for a particular purpose, the degree to which they can do so is not fixed but varies with the relative quantities already in use. There is no sense in which it can be generally stated that so many loads of timber are the technical equivalent of so many tons of steel, such a quantity of starch the food equivalent of such a quantity of protein, or so many kilowatts of electricity the equivalent of so many hours of labour, etc. The situation is rather that for some purposes and in small quantities, one material or one force will be able to replace a larger quantity of another material or another force, while for another purpose, or when larger quantities are in question, the former will be capable of replacing only much less of the latter.

It will be readily seen that it would involve great waste if one industry or plant were to use two materials in such proportions that the 'marginal rate of substitution' (as the economist calls the proportion of the quantities which in given circumstances will just replace each other) is such and such, while in another industry or plant it is very different—unless this is justified by cost of transport or the like. In all such cases output in both places could evidently be increased if each plant exchanged with another plant some of the materials which render comparatively less service for some of those which render more. And the maximum increase of production which can be achieved by such exchanges will have been reached when the 'marginal rates of substitution' of the two materials in the two plants in question have become the same. But what holds true of any two plants and any two materials, implements, or forces, also holds true of all plants and all resources. Indeed, to bring production to its maximum it would be necessary that these 'marginal rates of substitution' between all the factors of production should be made the same in all plants and industries. This condition holds true whatever we want to produce.

It is evident that to bring about this state of affairs by central direction in an ever-changing world is impossible. But it is exactly the state which is at least constantly approached in a competitive system, where the entrepreneurs have to use given market prices in their calculations, and where they are forced by competition to reduce costs as low as possible. If any entrepreneur finds that in his plant the 'marginal rate of substitution' for

x for y is more favourable to x than corresponds to the relative market prices of the two factors, i..e, if he finds that the quantity of x which he can substitute for a given quantity of y and yet obtain the same product is smaller than the quantity of x which he can buy at the same price as the quantity of y displaced by it, he will take advantage of this opportunity. And the result of these efforts on the part of all entrepreneurs will be that the 'marginal rates of substitution' of the various materials will everywhere become adjusted to the proportion between their market prices and thus become the same in all plants.

Thus all that the individual entrepreneurs have to do in order to bring about that coordination of their efforts which a central planner could never achieve is to watch a few gauges, as the engineer watches a few dials, and to adjust their plans to the figures provided to them by the market. But—and this is important—this system will only function if the market is really competitive, that is, if the prices are such that demand and supply at these prices are equal, if each entrepreneur finds it in his interest to expand production till prices only just cover costs, and if no entrepreneur by his policy can appreciably affect these prices. This presupposes that the production of each article is split up between a number of independent firms which genuinely compete with each other and which cannot exclude the entry of outsiders.

The best illustration of how this automatic control of the competitive system works in comparison with a centrally planned system is perhaps provided by the effects which any sudden and unexpected change in the supply of some important and widely used material will have under either system. Assume that, for example, the current supply of some material such as tin is suddenly reduced, either absolutely or relatively, because some new and urgent demand for it has arisen. In a competitive system the consequence of this will be that the price of tin will rise till at the new price no more is demanded than can be supplied. This reduction of demand will only to some extent be brought about by the consumers having to go without the article in the production of which the tin has been used (and in the cost of which, in most cases, it will be a small item). Much more important will be the substitution of other materials for tin (or the economy of tin by the expenditure of more labour) which at the higher price of tin becomes profitable. As the price of tin rises relatively to that of other materials, the quantity of these other materials (or the amount of labour) which can be had for the price of a given quantity of tin increases, and the number of instances where it is in the interest of the entrepreneur to dispense with the use of tin increases. In this way the current supply of tin will be reserved to where it would be most difficult to do without it—and tin will even be regained from old equipment, etc., where it is now profitable to replace it.

It is clear that this could not be effected by central direction; unless, indeed, the central authority possessed all that detailed knowledge of the conditions affecting the employment of tin in every particular instance which is acquired by those who actually use it. Nor can the same effect be brought about by arbitrarily fixing some 'accounting price', because the price which will just equate demand and supply is as unknown beforehand as the quantities which will be released at each price; the only way to find it quickly is the free play of all the forces of the market where everyone concerned with it, by following his immediate interests, is contributing to the solution of the common problem. The advantage of this method is not only that it enlists the interest of all those who have concrete knowledge as to how easy or how difficult it is, in particular places, to dispense with the material in question. What is even more important is that it gives those people a measure of the urgency of the new demand—because it would be just as undesirable that it should be dispensed with where it has to be replaced by a disproportionately large quantity of other things than that it should continue to be used where it can be replaced without undue cost. Thus, in a competitive regime a thing which is urgently needed can always be had at a price, because a high enough price will bring it 'even from the moon, if necessary', as has been said with some exaggeration. A hold-up of production because of some little thing which is lacking and unobtainable is therefore practically unknown in a competitive system. But it is inevitably a constant occurrence in a planned system, whose sole resource in such a case is commandeering, which can be based only on the personal knowledge of the planner and must depend on his possessing special information as to where the thing needed can be found, and where it can be spared.

These economic considerations are as relevant in wartime as in peace, and it is to be desired that this were better understood. That in wartime we cannot rely entirely on the competitive mechanism but have to resort to a large extent to central planning is not due to any greater efficiency of such planning under ordinary conditions, but to the fact that, in wartime, political factors of all kinds inevitably interfere to such an extent with the market as almost to prevent it from functioning. But that planning thus becomes necessary as a substitute for the market in wartime is no argument for its retention in peace. But this is a problem for the further discussion of which I have no space here.

PART II

THE ECONOMICS AND POLITICS OF WAR

FIVE

PRICING VERSUS RATIONING[1]

In recent discussion of the problems of defence economics, the planners have so far been allowed to have it very much their own way. It has been taken almost for granted that the only conceivable method of allocating resources for the arms programme is by an elaborate superstructure of Government controls—control of raw materials, control of imports, control of private consumption, control of the capital market, control of this, that, and the other. For example, R. W. B. Clarke, writing in *The Banker* last month, suggested that: "Obviously the change could not be carried through without Government intervention on a huge scale".[2] My object will be to show that this is not obvious at all, that indeed the planner's method may be the very reverse of efficient, since it scarcely touches the basic economic problem, which is not simply to put all the available resources to use but to combine them and distribute them between the various possible uses in such a way as to secure the maximum effect. Rationing and Government priorities may become necessary in particular instances; but if carried too far they are more likely to hamper and disorganize industry and actually to prevent an economic use of the available resources.

When a great demand arises for new products or for additional quantities of old products, the new production will require particular materials and particular kinds of labour which will now become unusually scarce. Special alloys or highly elaborate machinery or very skilled labour which

---

[1][F. A. Hayek, "Pricing versus Rationing", *The Banker,* September 1939, pp. 242–249. The article was published with a prefatory statement: "In recent months *The Banker* has published several articles by writers who believe that it is only possible to organize a defence economy with the aid of far-reaching government intervention in the economic system. Below we have pleasure in presenting the first of three articles by Professor Hayek representing the opposite point of view. Professor Hayek advocates reliance upon the free movement in prices, even in wartime, as a guide to what is most urgently required and how it should be produced. A second article next month will deal with the problem of the rate of interest." No third article ever appeared; see the Editor's Introduction, this volume.—Ed.]

[2][This reference may be in error, as the Clarke article does not appear in *The Banker* in the month specified.—Ed.]

in the past have been used in various industries may now be urgently wanted in an industry of national importance. It will clearly be necessary that the other industries should now so far as possible dispense with their use and substitute other materials, machinery, or labour for them. But not all industries can do so with equal ease. Nor will the costs to the economic system as a whole of replacing them by some substitute necessarily depend on the national importance of the products in whose manufacture the 'scarce' factors were formerly employed.

The required quantities of the urgently needed factor of production ought to be released from those uses in which they can be dispensed with at the least sacrifice of other necessary things. But this is just what will happen if the scarce factor rises in price, since producers will dispense with it precisely for those purposes where it costs least to do without it. To say that it 'costs least' to do without it means that the least possible quantity of other resources is needed to replace the scarce material. And it must be realized that these other resources also will either be required for war purposes themselves, or can at least be used to take the place of yet other resources, which in this way will be set free to satisfy urgent demands. If the available resources are to yield the maximum result, therefore, the vital need is for some means of measuring costs. It is a common fallacy to assume that in the conduct of war everything is needed so urgently that cost does not matter. Yet, when nearly all industry, directly or indirectly, serves war purposes, no particular need (except perhaps of a purely momentary kind) can ever be so absolutely urgent and of so completely overriding a character that it will have to be satisfied 'at all costs'—because these costs mean that less will be available for other war purposes. The need of the aircraft industry for aluminum may be exceedingly urgent. But if to maintain some essential service aluminum would have to be replaced by very great quantities of magnesium metal (which, although less scarce, is also needed for war purposes), it might easily be wiser not to deprive the industry in question of the aluminum—the sort of consideration which cannot easily be fitted into a system of priorities.

The general principle which underlies all this is plain enough. If we have to husband a given supply of resources we must never use a unit of factor A if the same effect can be obtained by a quantity of factor B, which in any other employment produces less than the unit of A, which it replaces here, would do. Let us suppose that in one of two industries an additional ton of tin would contribute to the product as much as five additional tons of copper, while in the other industry a ton of tin will add to the product only as much as three tons of copper. It will clearly be possible to increase the output of both industries—without giving them any more tin or copper—merely by substituting tin for copper in the first and copper for tin in the second industry. For a ton of tin contributes relatively more to the product of the first industry than the three tons of copper which would do the same work as a ton of tin in the second industry. And it will be possible to increase output in both industries, merely by swapping tin for copper in this way, until in both industries the quantities of tin and copper which make the same contribution to the product are the same.

Now, what is true of two materials in two industries is equally true of all resources in all industries. To obtain the greatest possible output from industry as a whole, the proportions in which the different resources are used in the various industries must be so adjusted that the relative quantities of these resources which add the same amount to the product of any industry are the same in all industries. The economist expresses this by saying that the (marginal) rates of substitution between the various factors are made equal in all industries. In a competitive system with free markets this is brought about to a very high degree of perfection merely by each producer trying to reduce his costs as much as possible. If the market price of tin is five times that of copper, and if the producer can get at these prices any quantity of either metal he wants, he will never use a ton of tin if the same effect can be had by using less than five tons of copper, and vice versa. In this way the existence of free markets secures that the 'rates of substitution' are made the same in all industries and thus that waste is avoided.

A little consideration will show that a rise in price is incomparably more efficient a method of bringing forth additional supplies than alternative methods of achieving the same result. It must be admitted that if it is sought to obtain within a few days, regardless of cost, as much as possible of any given material the method of commandeering *may* be more efficient. But even in wartime it is rarely justifiable to think only of the effects in the shortest of periods without regard to the consequences. Where it is a question, not of a momentary emergency, but of obtaining the largest supplies over a period and at the least sacrifice of other production, the price mechanism is infinitely superior to any other method. A rise of prices not only forces people to use the commodity sparingly in every possible use, including myriads of uses which the cleverest planner could scarcely think of. It also encourages the use of substitutes wherever such can be found, gives people an incentive to draw on their stocks and utilize scrap, and thus draws supplies from every nook and corner, engaging the ingenuity of all who have anything to do with the commodity to find means of economizing it with a thoroughness which no central regulation could possibly imitate.[3]

---

[3]It will, of course, be clearly understood that I am not advocating a *general* rise in prices, that is, inflation. The basic assumption is that the national finances are so conducted as to

What is no less important, the rise in price will also prevent the use of the scarce resource *only* where the cost of replacing it is not too great. It will not prevent the use of the scarce commodity in question where this would have to be replaced by some other factor which was even more urgently needed or where the money which people would have spent on that product will be used instead to demand something even more urgently needed for defence.

Compare this now with the alternative method of allocating resources in wartime which is commonly believed to be preferable and more efficient. If a particular commodity or factor of production is urgently needed for war purposes, its price is not to be allowed to rise to the point at which civilian demand has been reduced by the necessary amount. Instead, a government department is to decide how much of it—if any— particular industries are to be allowed. By this arbitrary restriction of demand, the price is to be kept at a low figure at which on a free market demand would be much larger than supply.[4] Presumably industries would be classified according to the national importance of their products and after the direct government demand had been satisfied these various classes would be allocated, by some rough-and-ready method,[5] certain quotas of their normal requirements.

Such a scheme of rationing would not—and could not—take real account of the urgency of the various needs.[6] At the false prices that were being artificially maintained some 'essential' industry might continue to use nearly as much of the scarce resource as before, although it could comparatively easily substitute something else for it and would do so if it had to pay a higher price for it. On the other hand, some other industry, not classed as essential athough allowed to remain in existence, being deprived of the scarce resource entirely, might have to substitute for it very large quantities of some other material. This, in turn, although not classified as an essential material, might yet—in the larger quantities required—represent a much larger drain on the national resources than the comparatively small quantities of the carefully rationed factor.

---

set a definite limit to *total* monetary demand, on the one hand for civil consumption and on the other hand for defence purposes. The free interplay of supply and demand (within this fixed aggregate) will send up the price of those *individual* goods which are most urgently wanted. It is the effects of such changes in *relative* prices which I have been discussing.

[4]It is worth remembering that to keep down the prices of precisely those things which are needed most urgently gives producers a direct incentive to switch over from the production of essential commodities to that of the less important goods whose prices are left free. This applies with particular force if prices in general are rising as a result of inflationary finance.

[5]See Clarke's article in *The Banker* for August. [Clarke, op. cit.—Ed.]

[6]The argument which follows does not necessarily apply to the rationing of essential foodstuffs, where special considerations apply which will be discussed later.

Consider now the position of one of the firms which is allocated a given quota of an 'essential' material at a price kept artificially low. Obviously the firm cannot know whether, in using this commodity even though a comparatively cheap substitute is available, it is wastefully using a very scarce asset. Such a decision could intelligently be made only if the relative prices of the two products showed what quantities of these goods would yield an equal product in other industries. As we have seen, however, the price of the rationed commodity will be quite artificial and therefore essentially different in character from the price of the second commodity as determined in a free market.

If each firm calculates its costs in terms of the prices it actually pays, but has to use the various resources in the proportions which are allocated to it, these 'costs' mean nothing whatever from a social point of view. Since prices of the factors no longer correspond to their relative productivities, they no longer tell us what we lose by using a particular factor in one place rather than another.

Nor will the authority whose duty it is to do the rationing be in any better position. They, too, in deciding how much of one material to allow to one industry and how much to another will be deprived of all guidance, of all basis for any significant calculation. In the absence of true prices they, too, will almost certainly use the false prices which will only mislead and be worse than nothing. It must be specially emphasized that our argument in no way assumes that the rationing authority will act stupidly. Even if it does all that is humanly possible the difficulty—indeed, the impossibility—of knowing how to act so as to safeguard efficiency will be the same. To decide in any particular case whether a particular industry ought to be allowed a certain quantity of a scarce raw material it would have to know all the alternative ways in which the products of the industry might be produced, and their costs. Thus to make a sensible decision would really involve repeating and checking all the calculations of the individual entrepreneur.

It will be sufficiently evident that rationing, if it is not to lead to grave waste, would involve little less than central planning of all production *in every detail*. Not only all the 'scarce' resources but their substitutes as well would have to be planned and controlled by some central authority. If one thing has been definitely established with regard to a planned or socialist system, it is that to stop halfway will only destroy the efficiency of the competitive mechanism without realizing any of the supposed advantages of a planned system. Whatever one may think of the feasibility of a completely planned system as a long-run proposition, it seems scarcely possible to doubt that the sort of improvised planned system that would develop during an emergency could only cause an all-round decline in efficiency.

Thus it may be said with fair certainty, so far as its effect on industry is concerned, rationing and price fixing will inevitably cause inefficiency and waste of resources. It deprives industry of all basis of rational calculation. It throws the burden of securing economy on a bureaucracy which is neither equipped nor adequate in number for the task. Even worse, such a system would deprive even those in control of the whole economic machine of essential guides for their plans and reduce major decisions of policy and even strategy to little more than guesswork. So long as war claimed only a comparatively small portion of the economic resources of a country, one could more or less disregard the effect which the military demands might have on the efficiency of industry. The only effect of any disorganization caused was that the civilian population would be somewhat worse off. Under such conditions the man of single purpose who would get what he wanted and damn the consequences was the right person to look after the economic requirements of warfare. But under modern conditions, in which any increase in one kind of military supplies can be secured only at the sacrifice of some other military needs, the nicely calculated less and more of economic calculation becomes an essential condition of success. The authorities responsible for the supplies of the fighting forces must pay as close attention to relative prices and costs as industry itself. Even strategic decisions will be dependent, to an extent that is hardly yet understood, on purely economic considerations. How is the general staff to decide whether to order more tanks, or more aircraft, or more ammunition, unless it knows the relative cost of various additional quantities of these things?

Warfare has indeed become an economic problem first and foremost and like all other economic problems this can be rationally solved only if based on exact reckoning. It is, of course, true that there are also problems of equity and problems of government finance involved which have not yet been considered. Would free prices not mean that the poorer people would have to go without necessaries while others were making enormous profits? Would they not mean that the government would in some instances have to pay quite extortionate prices and that the conduct of war would become correspondingly more expensive? Such questions as these will be considered in a later article. In the meantime, however, we must turn to yet another problem: the problem of the rate of interest in war and near-war conditions. This will be dealt with in the next article in this series.[7]

[7]["The Economy of Capital", reprinted in this volume as chapter 6.—Ed.]

SIX

THE ECONOMY OF CAPITAL[1]

In discussions of war economics it is generally taken for granted that the monetary authorities should always employ all the means at their disposal to keep rates of interest as low as possible. That it is possible to postpone a threatened rise of interest rates for a long time cannot be doubted. The real problem is whether it is desirable to do so. For nearly two hundred years economists fought fairly consistently against the popular argument in favour of such a policy; and until two or three years ago, when these old arguments experienced a sudden recrudescence, it was commonly regarded as highly dangerous. For the time being the prompt rise of the Bank Rate at the outbreak of war has provided a temporary answer. But with the infinitely greater demands for capital during actual warfare the problem is bound to return in much more acute and pressing form.

Basically, the question at issue is the same as that discussed in the article on pricing versus rationing in the last issue of *The Banker*.[2] Should we rely on the price mechanism to provide us with an indicator of the relative scarcity of the various factors of production? Or should we deliberately make this price mechanism inoperative and try to substitute for it a detailed regulation of all productive activity by a central authority? And the argument that the rate of interest should be allowed to express the real scarcity of capital is fundamentally the same as that with respect to any other price. But this similarity was never easy to see, since in the case of capital we have not to deal with a single concrete resource but with a somewhat abstract concept. And the more recent discussions, confining themselves entirely to the monetary influences at work, can hardly have increased the understanding of this problem.

---

[1][F. A. Hayek, "The Economy of Capital", *The Banker,* October 1939, pp. 38–42. The magazine's editors noted, "This is the second article by Professor Hayek on the economic problems of war. The first article, on "Pricing versus Rationing", appeared in the September issue."—Ed.]

[2]["Pricing versus Rationing" is reprinted in this volume as chapter 5.—Ed.]

It is often believed, and has been explicitly argued by J. M. Keynes,[3] that if the use of all real resources, raw materials as well as labour and machinery, is effectively controlled, there is no further problem of the economy of capital. Given the relative value of these various concrete resources, this is supposed to be all we need to know in deciding on their best use. This, however, is not so. It will often be possible by installing some machinery to dispense with labour costing much more than that machinery. Yet it may not be advantageous to do so, simply because the whole cost of the machine will have to be laid out now, whereas the saving of labour will accrue only over a prolonged period of time. To install the machinery is not simply to substitute the product of one kind of labour for labour of another kind. It also means spreading the return from the former over a long period of time, or 'investing' it. Investment always means sacrificing something in the near future to gain something at a more distant time. Hence the extent to which we can invest is limited and must be treated as a separate scarce factor. It may be that in one case the investment of a certain amount of steel in a machine will release ten workmen per year for a period of five years. In another case the present expenditure of labour and some other very scarce material may set free twenty workmen, but for two years only. The steel needed in the one case and the labour and material needed in the other may have the same value in current production; that is, the sacrifice of current production involved in using either in investment is the same. But which of these alternative methods of investing present resources is the more advantageous cannot be decided unless we know how great is the supply of capital on which we must base our plans, and what is the minimum return we must obtain from the capital if it is to be used economically.

These considerations are particularly important when we have to prepare for a war which may last years. If it were a question of a few months the problem of husbanding our capital resources would be of minor importance and we could largely disregard the needs of next year. But if we are basing our policy on the assumption of a three years' war, no opportunity must be lost of using our capital resources so as to make the greatest possible contribution to output throughout the whole duration of the war. This means that we have to use our capital so as to give the highest

---

[3][Throughout much of the 1930s, J. M. Keynes had argued for a policy of low long-term interest rates. In his article "Borrowing by the State", which appeared in *The Times* on July 24 and 25, 1939, and is reprinted in *Activities 1931–1939: World Crises and Policies in Britain and America*, ed. Donald Moggridge, vol. 21 (1982) of *The Collected Writings of John Maynard Keynes*, op. cit., pp. 551–564, he continued to advocate this policy even in the face of a fully employed workforce as the nation prepared for war. The newspaper article is probably the source of Hayek's reference.—Ed.]

possible rate of return within this period. Investments which return the initial amount plus eight per cent after one year must be given precedence over others which will return the original value plus fourteen per cent only after two years. The latter will in turn take precedence over one year investments which bring a surplus of only six per cent.

It was explained last month that, to maximize production, no material or other resource must be employed in a use where it will add less to output than it could do elsewhere. In the same way, present resources devoted to increasing future output must be used where they will bring the highest return. And the available supply of capital can be reserved for the most urgent needs only if the price charged for it, that is the rate of interest, expresses its true scarcity.

That the true scarcity of capital will be very much greater and therefore the true rate of interest very much higher in war than in peace cannot be doubted. Not only must there be an enormous increase in the production of armaments, involving the production of new capital equipment on a large scale. The mere fact that for the duration of the war current needs will be so very much more important than those of the more remote future would in itself be sufficient cause for a considerable rise in interest rates.

It is a widely prevalent misconception that the main function of the rate of interest is to bring forth the supply of savings needed. If this were true, its importance under present conditions would indeed be small. In war time the current supply of savings required for war purposes can most effectively be increased by taxation. But it is doubtful whether the rate of interest is ever very important in this respect. Its main importance is always to regulate the allocation of the limited supply of capital to the purpose for which it can be used with the greatest advantage. This function is, of course, particularly important when new and urgent needs suddenly arise. Only very limited supplies of capital can be obtained by cutting down current consumption—and it must be remembered that current output is required for war purposes just as much as for the needs of the civil population. The only other source of capital is the stock of productive equipment which we have been able to accumulate in peacetime. Most of this cannot be directly turned to war purposes; and a considerable part of it will have to be maintained or replaced in some way or other even in wartime. But just as when we were accumulating capital we were constantly 'putting in' more into the productive process than we were taking out, so we can release capital by 'putting in' less than its current output. This can be done by cutting down amortisation, by replacing existing capital equipment, if at all, by less costly, less durable, or less labour-saving equipment.

By reverting in this way to what in a sense are more primitive methods of production, appropriate to a state of greater scarcity of capital, we can for a long time take out of the normal productive process more than we currently put in; and what we save here in labour and materials becomes available for the creation of new equipment of the kind now most urgently needed. At the same time, it would not be economical either to cease replacement altogether or to enforce some proportional curtailment all round. Every production manager must be able to decide on the basis of all his special knowledge whether, at a rate of interest which expresses the true scarcity of capital, it is still advantageous to use a given amount of capital or whether direct labour should be used instead. A false rate of interest which does not express the true scarcity of capital will mislead private entrepreneurs just as much as the controlling authority. To keep the rate of interest artificially low cannot alter the fact that in wartime the urgency of present needs and the scarcity of resources available for investment will be greatly intensified. It can only have the effect that the limitations on the supply of capital will be disregarded and valuable resources wasted. All this is, of course, only one aspect of the problem of interest rates, but it is an aspect which is commonly neglected and which therefore most urgently needs to be emphasized.

SEVEN

DOCUMENTS RELATING TO THE WAR

1. Control of Armaments[1]

It is probably safe to say that Germany will never submit to a scheme of control of armaments which appears to be specially designed to allay the suspicions entertained against her by some of her neighbours. And it must be admitted that any scheme that is to be effective and that is drawn up at the present time with a view to immediate application to Germany, even if intended to apply in the same way to all other nations, is liable to be interpreted in this way. But why not, once we know that full success will not be achieved immediately and that we shall have to work for a more distant goal, begin with putting a detailed scheme of mutual control in operation between some other great Powers between whom no such suspicions exist? This would not only give an opportunity to test its efficacy and to make it more effective where it is found wanting, but also remove the main difficulty to later general application. Surely Germany could not refuse to accept a scheme of mutual control to which, say, France and Great Britain had voluntarily submitted and which had for some time been in operation between these and, perhaps, some other great Powers.

2. War Aims[2]

Sir, Sir Norman Angell in his article on war aims last week has at last expressed what I know many feel is one of the most urgent tasks of the moment; "to begin, now, to build up a real federal unity with France: to make of the French and British Empires a unit, not merely for war purposes, but as a beginning of the permanent reconstruction of Europe and the world on new lines".[3] No doubt nothing could be more effective in

---

[1][F. A. Hayek, "Control of Armaments", letter to *The Times*, December 28, 1933.—Ed.]

[2][F. A. Hayek, "War Aims", letter to *The Spectator*, November 17, 1939, p. 716.—Ed.]

[3][Sir Norman Angell, "What Collective Security Means", *The Spectator*, August 11, 1939, p. 220. Sir Norman Angell (1873–1967) received the Nobel Prize for Peace in 1933. A journalist, editor, and author, his most influential work was *The Great Illusion: A Study of the Rela-*

proving to the world that the two countries are sincerely striving for a new and better world order, and that they are ready to shed ancient prejudices to achieve it. Even more important at this moment, however, is the fact that real political and economic union with France is perhaps the most important step towards winning this war which could now be taken. Is it not too absurd for words that in the present circumstances each of the two countries should continue to buy dear at home what it might get more cheaply from its partner, that we now should even go to the length of using inferior substitutes rather than what our friends can give us, and that each of the two countries should husband its supply of the currency of the other, not merely as we must husband all our resources, but as if for us the resources of France and for France the resources of Great Britain were as difficult to obtain as those of any other country? Can there be any doubt that this state of affairs must keep the productive capacity of each of the two countries considerably below what it might be? How long are we to go on, not merely to maintain all the expensive controls of the commerce between the two countries, but to pile up new ones with all the delay and disorganization which they cause merely to make our common productive machine less efficient than it might be? Surely there is not even a good reason why, so long as we are still able to afford any luxuries, British demand should not help the French luxury trade and French demand the corresponding trade in this country, which are both particularly hard hit and whose resources are on the whole of little use for war purposes. There will, inevitably, be increased difficulties of cross-channel transport. But beyond this there appears to be no conceivable reason why extra war restrictions should be placed on the trade between the two countries and every reason for removing those which existed before the outbreak of war.

3. An Anglo-French Federation[4]

Sir, As Mr. J. Roger Carter[5] seems to feel so superior to the "typical Western European mind", perhaps one who can hardly be suspected of this

---

tion of Military Power to National Advantage (London: Heinemann, 1912), in which he argued that wars harm both victor and vanquished. His book is credited for stimulating interest in the formation of a League of Nations.—Ed.]

[4][F. A. Hayek, "An Anglo-French Federation", letter to *The Spectator*, December 15, 1939, p. 866.—Ed.]

[5][J. Roger Carter's letter appeared in *The Spectator*, December 8, 1939, pp. 819–820. Taking a pacifist line, he argued that Robbins and others calling for federation were attempting to impose democracy by force on Central Europeans. He wrote in part that " . . . 'they that live by the sword shall perish by the sword' is an epigram worth noting by those who hope, even in this War, to preserve by violence the democratic spirit which we ever hope will make

particular disability may venture to reply to his strictures on Professor Robbins's proposals.[6] If ever hard facts have suggested to many people independently the same remedy, it is precisely the "polyglot, multinational, heterogeneous aspect of Central Europe" which has again and again impressed on its best minds the necessity of a federal organization. The necessity of this solution, which Professor Robbins, like many others, has advocated long before Mr. Streit,[7] is perhaps more fully realized in those parts of Europe than in the rest. The experience of the last twenty years in particular has shown that in a region where any state, whatever its borders, will always include large racial minorities, the existence of many sovereign national states will for ever remain a serious danger to peace. If the case of Czecho-Slovakia proves anything, it is that even a democratic people cannot be trusted not to abuse the weapon of modern economic policy—against which no minority statute can protect—for the oppression of racial minorities. Of this thousands of German-speaking Jews from the Sudetenland, who cannot be suspected of Nazi sympathies, are ready to testify. And in Austria-Hungary, where, whatever we may have thought at the time, racial minorities have enjoyed greater freedom than has existed in those parts ever since, the nature of the problem of nationalities was guiding developments decidedly in the direction of federalism. If federation were not desirable for other reasons, it would have to be invented for Central Europe; and I have yet to find the person who has studied her problems and who does not regard some sort of federation as the only way of securing lasting peace and economic improvement in that part of the world.

From the point of view of the Western Powers, however, the difficulty is that any federation confined to Central Europe, with the inevitable preponderance the Germans would have in it, would in effect strengthen German influence and, for that reason, would be intolerable for France. Even with France and perhaps the North European countries inside the Continental Federation, the danger of German hegemony would still be great enough to make such a scheme unacceptable to France. From her point of view, with the memory of the defection by her allies after 1919 fresh in her mind, it is only wise to hold aloof from any such scheme till

---

the world safe for democracy, for it is in this realm that the ideal of democracy belongs. Persuasion, conversion, example, these are the only instruments we can cherish".—Ed.]

[6][Lionel Robbins had argued for federation in his article "An Anglo-French Federation?", *The Spectator,* November 24, 1939, pp. 739–740.—Ed.]

[7][The American journalist and author Clarence K. Streit (1896–1986) was the author of *Union Now: A Proposal for a Federal Union of the Democracies of the North Atlantic,* op. cit. Robbins had earlier advocated federation in his book *Economic Planning and International Order* (London: Macmillan, 1937).—Ed.]

it is certain beyond human doubt that in any future order Great Britain will stand by her. For France only a federation with Great Britain as a member can offer the security which otherwise she would seek—and for a time might obtain—by the dismemberment of her enemy. But it is not for her at this stage to show undue enthusiasm for a plan which can have attraction to her only if she is assured that Great Britain will permanently take her place in the new order of Europe. If such an order is to be achieved, it is this country which must take the lead, and which can make such an order possible by merely showing its willingness to enter such a federation. Is there a better way in which this essential assurance can be given to France than by concluding a federation with her now?

It is clearly unreasonable to expect the Government to announce now what it will do after the War. But it is a different thing for the people of this country to show that they are no longer prevented by false pride to submit to those restrictions of national sovereignty which a real rule of law in international affairs implies. Where the creation of the new order appears to involve sacrifices of national pride, it is the strong who must lead the way. Far from threatening to impose the new order by force, as Mr. Carter suggests, to begin federation by Great Britain and France voluntarily submitting to the restrictions of their sovereignty which federation involves, and then to offer entry on equal terms to others, seems to be the only way to allay the supicion that the new order is only a new device to keep a particular country down. When victory comes, almost any restrictions will be accepted by the defeated nation without causing resentment if the victors have themselves submitted to the same restrictions—and almost any restriction of the liberty of the defeated will be a lasting grievance, and the cause of future conflict, if it is imposed on the defeated only.

4. Mr. Keynes and War Costs[8]

The outstanding topic in financial circles in the past week has been the ingenious proposal which we owe to the most fertile mind among living economists.[9] That is not surprising, for if the proposal were adopted it would go far to solve one of the most difficult and pressing economic problems of the war, and immediately affect the position of the great ma-

[8][F. A. Hayek, "Mr. Keynes and War Costs", *The Spectator*, November 24, 1939, pp. 740–741. This short article appeared in the "Middles" (as opposed to the "Leading Articles") section of *The Spectator*.—Ed.]

[9][Keynes's proposal, "Paying for the War", first appeared as two articles published in *The Times*, November 14 and 15, 1939. It is reprinted in *Activities 1939–1945: Internal War Finance*, ed. Donald Moggridge, vol. 22 (1978) of *The Collected Writings of John Maynard Keynes*, op. cit., pp. 41–51.—Ed.]

jority of the population. As Mr. J. M. Keynes in the past has often expressed views which were peculiarly his own, it may be said at once that
the main features of his present proposal, and particularly those which
concern the financial problems arising from the war, will probably be accepted by most economists—certainly by some who in other respects have
been regarded as his scientific antipodes.

The essential features of Mr. Keynes's proposal are fairly simple and by
now probably generally familiar. It will be recalled that he suggests that
in addition to ordinary income tax a further substantial part of current
incomes should be retained by the Government in the form of blocked
savings accounts. This would apply particularly to the lower income
groups, now largely or entirely exempt from direct taxation. People in
this class are to be made to contribute some part of their income, and in
particular any increase in their real income due to a rise in wages, to the
costs of the war, not as a permanent but as a merely temporary contribution, since at the end of the war they would be in possession of saving
deposits of a corresponding amount. They would, in other words, merely
be forced to save part of their income for a time, during which it would
help to finance the war.

I cannot attempt to restate here at length all the arguments which so
strongly recommend this proposal to the economist. But since the gravity
of the problem to which Mr. Keynes addresses himself does not yet appear to be generally apprehended, at least the main considerations on
which his proposal is based must be briefly summarized. Although we
have unquestionably still unused reserves of *some* kinds of productive resources, this is true only of some and not of all, and we shall consequently
only be able to satisfy the material requirements of war if we curtail the
current production for civilian needs. The difficulty of bringing about the
required reduction in civilian demand lies in the fact that, as Mr. Keynes
points out, "three-fifths of the net expenditure on consumption is by
those whose incomes are less than £250 a year".[10] This difficulty is increased by the fact that money-wages have already begun to rise in what,
from this point of view, must appear an alarming degree, and are likely
to continue to rise. Mr. Keynes cautiously suggests that the working
classes "must not, at the best, consume any more than they did";[11] it is
more likely, at least if the war lasts long, that they too will have to reduce
their consumption. And this will be the case whatever financial policy is
adopted. But if the working class are left free to spend their increased
earnings to the full, we shall soon be in the vicious spiral of rising wages

[10]["Paying for the War", op. cit., p. 44.—Ed.]
[11][*Ibid.*, p. 42.—Ed.]

leading to rising prices and rising prices bringing about a further rise in wages. But this inflationary method, while ultimately it will also bring about the necessary reduction of consumption, since the rise of wages will lag more and more behind prices, is indescribably wasteful. It disorganizes production, upsets all calculations, creates additional injustice and is apt to cause a destruction of capital.

It is this kind of development, which in the end would harm everybody, which must be avoided at all costs. But if it is to be avoided, action will have to be taken very soon. And if outright taxation of the lower incomes to the required extent is impracticable, or, what amounts to the same thing, is generally regarded as unjust, Mr. Keynes's proposal, or something very like it, appears to be the only real solution. What it in effect amounts to is that the contribution of the people in the lower income categories is made a temporary contribution, to be repaid later out of increased taxation of the people in the higher income groups, since it will be out of ordinary taxation that the funds for interest and repayments from these forced savings will have to come.

It is true that Mr. Keynes does not envisage this sort of long- term effect. He contemplates that the deposits accumulated during the war should be released in cash "probably in a series of installments, at some date after the war".[12] It is only at this stage that the details of his proposal are closely connected with his particular views about the nature of depressions. Mr. Keynes believes that the release of these deposits "would help us through the first postwar slump" and that "the appropriate date for the release would have arrived when the resources of the community were no longer fully engaged".[13] Now there are reasons which make it at least doubtful whether such a wholesale increase of expenditure is really a safe cure for slumps. However that may be, it is certain that to leave this sort of decision in the balance would create very serious political problems. If the question whether to release or not to release these balances is left to political decision it would be bound to become the subject of popular agitation. We should, at the end of the war, be left with a sort of "soldiers' bonus" problem of gigantic dimensions. And when we remember that in many countries, including Great Britain, the greater part of the inflation occurred not during, but immediately after, the last war, it does not seem improbable that such pressure for the release of these funds might come at a time when to release them would be particularly dangerous.

Any scheme which required Parliament to come to a decision about the method of repayment in the years immediately following the war would

[12][*Ibid.*, p. 49.—Ed.]
[13][*Ibid.*—Ed.]

create really grave political danger. And it must seem doubtful whether such repayment in cash of the "forced savings", otherwise than by ordinary sinking-fund methods, should be contemplated at all. There might, however, be a strong case for a capital levy on old wealth, payable partly in shares of the industrial capital of the country, to create a trust fund, a kind of giant holding company, which would give the holders of the war savings, instead of a claim against the government, an equity in the industrial capital of the country. The ordinary objection to a capital levy, that it means using capital resources for current expenditure, would of course not hold in this case. Nor need the use of this technique increase the burden on the capitalists. It would merely avoid carrying indefinitely the burden of a deadweight debt in the budget and thus to some extent reduce future budget problems.

There is one special feature of Mr. Keynes's proposals on which he only just touches, but which is of some importance even independently of his main scheme. He assumes that all income tax, and particularly income tax on wages and salaries, should be deducted at the source. In so far as income payments are made monthly or weekly this would mean that tax payments would come in, on the average, three months earlier than they do now. This would be of considerable assistance in solving one of the most difficult problems, that of catching up with the rapidly mounting expenditure. And, irrational though it may be, many a harassed taxpayer would probably welcome an arrangement with a sense of relief which, instead of forcing him to accumulate the tax over a period of six months, gave him his monthly income already reduced by income tax.

5. Hayek's Review of How to Pay for the War[14]

The main features and probably even the detail of Mr. Keynes's plan for war finance will now be familiar to the readers of this journal. It can indeed be said that his scheme, already after its first sketch was published in *The Times* last November,[15] and still more after the appearance of the present pamphlet, was received with more than sympathetic interest by economists in this country. After Mr. Keynes had acknowledged that "in war we move back from the Age of Plenty to the Age of Scarcity"[16] and

[14][F. A. Hayek, "Book Review: John Maynard Keynes, *How to Pay for the War*", *Economic Journal*, vol. 50, June—September 1940, pp. 321–326.—Ed.]

[15][*How to Pay for the War* is a revised and expanded version of "Paying for the War". It is reprinted in *Essays in Persuasion*, vol. 9 (1972) of *The Collected Writings of John Maynard Keynes*, op. cit., pp. 367–439.—Ed.]

[16][Keynes, *How to Pay for the War*, op. cit., p. 384. The "Age of Plenty" was Keynes's whimsical term for the slump: What was plentiful were resources. His point is that in an age of plenty, scarcity no longer is operative, so that the conclusions of standard economic analysis (which takes scarcity as a fundamental starting point) need not hold.—Ed.]

that "the Age of Scarcity has arrived before the whole available labour has been employed",[17] the difference which had so long separated him from the more 'orthodox' economists had disappeared and any contribution to the burning problem coming from him was certain of the closest attention. Even so, however, the unanimity with which his proposal was approved by economists and the fact that neither serious criticism of the basic idea nor a real alternative was offered are a remarkable tribute paid to the author by his colleagues. It is unfortunate that in the existing conditions this practical unanimity of the experts could not find adequate expression. With so large a proportion of the economists of the country in Government service, and thus prevented from publicly expressing opinions on questions of policy, it may not be out of place for the reviewer here to record his personal impression that, so far as the main outline of Mr. Keynes's proposal is concerned, this unanimity was almost complete.

Well known as the leading ideas of the proposal are by now, it may not be altogether unnecessary briefly to re-state the reasoning which leads to it in a way slightly different from that employed by Mr. Keynes. Excluding inflation as an instrument of deliberate financial policy, the amounts required for the finance of the war must be raised by taxation and genuine borrowing. To obtain them entirely from the rich is literally impossible. As Mr. Keynes shows, even if their incomes were levelled down to that of the lower middle class (more precisely to £500 a year), the result would provide only two-thirds of Mr. Keynes's modest estimate of Government requirements of five months ago—quite apart from the resulting "widespread breaches of existing contracts and commitments which would considerably reduce taxable income".[18] Even a flat reduction of all incomes to £250 a year would only just suffice to produce the approximately £1000 million of revenue for which Mr. Keynes was then seeking.[19] It is clear, therefore, that a substantial contribution must come not only from the income groups under £500 a year, but also from those under £250. To obtain this by taxation is regarded as politically impossible. Nor would it necessarily be equitable. While it is inevitable that the lower-income groups should make some contribution now, it is not necessary that they should sacrifice once and for all the part of their income they must at the moment give up. Hence the plan for "deferred pay". What it amounts to in effect is that the poorer classes should merely advance what cannot be raised now from the wealthier classes, the sums so advanced to be repaid out of continued higher taxation of the latter after the war. That the comparatively poor must make their contribution to the material costs of the

[17][*Ibid.*, p. 385.—Ed.]
[18][*Ibid.*, p. 389.—Ed.]
[19][*Ibid.*, pp. 389–390.—Ed.]

168

war is not a matter on which we can choose. Whatever plan we adopt, it cannot be avoided. If we let matters drift, inflation will hit them even harder, and the poorest hardest of all. The only choice we have is whether or not the inevitable sacrifice of the poor shall at least give them a share in our future income.

In view of these considerations, it is somewhat surprising that the proposal has not been more enthusiastically received by the representatives of the working class. Here the explanation probably is that although fairly simple, and explained by Mr. Keynes with the lucidity of which he is capable as so few others, the dilemma which we have to face is still too complicated to be easily grasped by the man in the street. More surprising, however, must appear the objections, raised from different quarters, against the compulsory character of the savings imposed by the scheme. They seem to overlook that the 'deferred pay' is a substitute for taxation which must bring in the sums required, even if it means a drastic reduction in standards of living, and that to leave this to the voluntary decisions of the individual is about as reasonable as to substitute voluntary contributions for taxation.[20] It seems that Mr. Keynes is unquestionably right when he writes that to say "We shall depend on the voluntary system" is another way of saying "We shall depend on inflation to the extent that is necessary".[21]

In the full exposition of his plan in the present pamphlet Mr. Keynes combines his original proposal with a scheme for family allowances and a qualified support of a system of "iron rations".[22] Although the former may superficially appear as a suggestion for social reform at a time when we can least afford it, and while it would actually add to budget totals, it may in fact prove an important instrument in war finance. When it becomes essential that even people in very low income groups should curtail their consumption, and when this is brought about partly by a rise in the cost of living, any measure which relieves those who would suffer more than the average will decrease the pressure for higher money wages, and thus ease the position.

At the time of writing the pamphlet, Mr. Keynes, as most other people, was still comparatively optimistic about the extent to which such a reduction of consumption would become necessary and even hoped that for

---

[20]When Sir John Simon in his budget speech explained that "the reason why taxation is put on a compulsory basis is that so few people make taxation contribution voluntarily", this in no way proves that we can rely on voluntary savings so long as the number of savers is large! [The British politician Sir John Simon (1873–1954) was Chancellor of the Exchequer from 1937 to 1940 and Lord Chancellor for the rest of the war.—Ed.]

[21][Keynes, *How to Pay for the War*, op. cit., p. 422.]

[22]["Iron rations" refers to a minimum ration of consumption goods that would be made available at a low fixed price.—Ed.]

the class with incomes under £250 a year no serious reduction of *aggregate* consumption would be required. His main concern was still to prevent an increase of private consumption, so that at least all the increase of output could serve for war purposes. Retrospectively all the concrete figures mentioned by him appear extraordinarily mild; and what we have learned since makes, as Mr. Keynes himself says in comparing his suggestions with what had been done in France, his "careful and humanitarian arguments and apologetically mild proposals sound pitiful and weak".[23] Considering the state of public opinion at the time, they were, however, bold—unfortunately too bold to be accepted. It is instructive to compare Mr. Keynes's figures with those of the lamentable budget presented by Sir John Simon a few weeks later.[24] Mr. Keynes contemplated an additional war expenditure (taking £900 million as peacetime expenditure) of £1950 millions,[25] of which only £900 million was to be raised by borrowing—a sum which his careful estimates of voluntary savings, of proceeds from the realization of foreign assets, and of depreciation funds, makes appear just feasible without inflation. Sir John Simon in his budget visualized additional war expenditure of only about £1770 million, and left £1432 million to be raised by borrowing. The difference between this latter figure and Mr. Keynes's corresponding £900 million is almost the whole £600 million which Mr. Keynes had proposed to raise in the form of "deferred pay". And since there is little reason to suppose that, without inflation, voluntary savings can be increased to anything like that amount, the adoption of Mr. Keynes's plan would have solved the main problem which the budget left open.

What is its significance now, when we are faced with an annual expenditure probably 50 per cent higher than that contemplated by Mr. Keynes, and a gap between expenditure and revenue increased by about £1000 million? It is probably clear that by itself it can no longer solve our financial problem, as it might have done on the scale of expenditure of three months ago. Even if we take into account the increase in money incomes which has already taken place, and contemplate higher scales than those proposed by Mr. Keynes, it can scarcely be made to yield more than 10 or 20 per cent above the estimate given by him. It remains, however, one of the most potent weapons which we possess when it has become doubly necessary to curtail consumption of all classes. Mr. Keynes

[23][Keynes, *How to Pay for the War,* op. cit., p. 428.—Ed.]
[24][Keynes's pamphlet was published on February 27, 1940, and Sir John Simon's budget appeared on April 23. Keynes's reaction to the budget may be found in Keynes, *Activities 1939–1945: Internal War Finance,* op. cit., pp. 132–142.—Ed.]
[25]Including £100 million for the family allowances.

has never claimed that there were no alternatives—only that they were even less pleasant. He mentions that "for example, a retail sales tax of 50 per cent, or a wage tax of 20 per cent"[26] or a correspondingly heavier income tax would be no less drastic and no less effective. In the present situation these are probably no longer alternatives. We shall probably have to employ all, or at least most, of these methods simultaneously.

There are many other things in this little volume which would deserve special attention, or rather which, if attention had been paid to them in the proper quarters, might have spared us many difficulties and prevented much groping in the dark. Among them is the discussion of the relation between borrowing and inflation which one hopes will be read and re-read, the considerations on rationing, and some such brief but pregnant remarks as that a 100 per cent excess profits duty "is not advisable in practice because it would deprive those, who would nevertheless remain in control of their businesses, of any incentive toward economy".[27]

There remains one point where the reviewer wishes to add a word of explanation on his own behalf. Mr. Keynes has incorporated in the present exposition of his plan the proposal of a capital levy as a means of repaying the "deferred pay" after the war, and he mentions that the reviewer was the first to suggest it in this connection. What I wish to point out is that the purpose for which I proposed it was very different from that to which Mr. Keynes intends to put it. I was, and still am, afraid of the consequences of such large amounts suddenly (or even, as Mr. Keynes now proposes, in a series of installments) released in cash, and particularly so when the decision as to the time and form of this release is likely to become the subject of political agitation. I suggested, therefore, that, in order to avoid cash repayments on a large scale, the holders of the blocked balances should be given equity titles in the productive capital of the country, and that the capital levy should be used to transfer an appropriate portion of these titles to a kind of giant holding company, who would in turn issue shares to the holders of the blocked balances.

Mr. Keynes wants to use the capital levy to finance the cash repayment. His view about the desirability of such cash repayments as a means to combat a postwar depression, as well as my belief that they are undesirable, are both based on the assumption that in the conditions after the war the receivers will be likely to spend most of the money soon after they receive it. In this we may, of course, both be wrong. But if we are both right in this common assumption, there remains a fundamental difference with regard to the purpose of the capital levy. This difference

[26][Keynes, *How to Pay for the War*, op. cit., p. 413.—Ed.]
[27][*Ibid.*, p. 408.—Ed.]

can, however, be left over till Mr. Keynes feels that we have returned to the Age of Plenty.

6. How We Can Do It[28]

Here is a really important book, small and readable, that should make layman and expert understand this war better. The record of the Editor of the *Economist*[29] for enlightening public opinion on some of the crucial problems of the war is already distinguished. By this book he places us under a further debt.

As a sane and balanced picture of the relative economic strength of the belligerents, and of what we may and what we may not expect from the blockade, the first part of the book could hardly be bettered. With a few well-chosen figures, which give the little book the value of a work of reference, it provides a comprehensive picture of the position as it has arisen since the collapse of France. And although it hides from us none of the more unpleasant results of this—or rather because it faces the hard realities—the outcome is definitely encouraging. While Germany is now more or less adequately supplied with steel, coal, and timber, she suffers from a greater or lesser shortage of most of the other essential raw materials, and has only just enough food, provided harvests are not seriously deficient. Thus, while "those who expect the blockade to lead to a German collapse are deluding themselves", the importance of the blockade is "that it will set limits to the economic efforts Germany can make".[30]

Even more remarkable as a piece of exposition is the discussion of the difficult problems of our economic policy. Particularly interesting to the general reader will be the explanation how wide is the range of possibilities within which we can choose, how we can really get nearly every thing we want, but not all things at the same time, and how the various shortages are, or ought to be, the result of deliberate decision. At the same time, and that is one of the greatest merits of the book, it makes plain "what a very long way we have to go till we have done all that a war economy requires".[31] Mr. Crowther shows as clearly as anyone has yet done how much more of our private needs will have to go unsatisfied and how far short of the necessary effort is the mobilization of our resources for war purposes. If there is any ground for doubt, it is that Mr. Crowther

---

[28][F. A. Hayek, "How We Can Do It", review of Geoffrey Crowther, *Ways and Means of War, The Spectator*, September 6, 1940, pp. 247–248.—Ed.]

[29][The economist, journalist, and businessman Baron Geoffrey Crowther (1907–1972) served as Editor of the *Economist* from 1938 to 1956.—Ed.]

[30][Crowther, op. cit., pp. 73–74.—Ed.]

[31][*Ibid.*, p. 121.—Ed.]

seems to place too much faith in rationing. And many economists will probably feel that his vision of the postwar world is too optimistic. But on the whole the book is remarkably free from any contentions with which many of his fellow economists are likely to disagree.

The explanation of the relations between the financial and monetary mechanism and the disposition of the real resources is brilliant. But is it not placing too little confidence in the people to suggest that the necessary process of reducing private consumption "is necessarily so painful that it cannot be openly faced, but must be accomplished by the device that 'works silently and imperceptibly and irresistibly'"? [32] Surely if the people were told as definitely and lucidly as Mr. Crowther tells us why we need more "plain honest taxes that hurt plain honest people",[33] and what the alternative, inflation, would mean, the people would prefer the plain honest method. The trouble is that in the economic sphere—at least so far as the concerns of the people as a whole are affected—we still lack the intelligent and inspiring leadership which we now have in the political sphere. But the knowledge which such leadership would require is unfortunately not common. It is for this reason that it is so refreshing to find a book which shows so plainly and convincingly what is required and which tells us not merely that we shall and must win, but how we can win, and what the effort is that is required. It is a book which should be read by the few really busy people in the country even more than by everybody else.

7. Nazi Order[34]

Recent controversy between the authors of these books might have led one to expect irreconcilable differences of opinion. In fact, since each writer confines himself to the field in which he is a recognized authority, though they aim at amending the popular view of Nazi policy in opposite directions, the corrections which they provide are equally needed and

---

[32][*Ibid.*, pp. 146–147.—Ed.]

[33][*Ibid.*, p. 157.—Ed.]

[34][F. A. Hayek, "Nazi Order", Review of Paul Einzig, *Hitler's 'New Order' in Europe* (London: Macmillan, 1941), and C. W. Guillebaud, *The Social Policy of Nazi Germany* (Cambridge: Cambridge University Press, 1941). Hayek's review appeared in *The Spectator,* April 14, 1941, p. 372. Einzig (1897–1973) served as foreign editor and, during the war, political correspondent for the *Financial News* of London. He was a prolific writer on monetary and financial arrangements, as well as on political affairs. Claude William Guillebaud (1890–1971) was educated and later taught at St. John's College, Cambridge, and saw more good early on in Hitler's policies than did many of his contemporaries. A nephew of Mary Paley Marshall, he is best remembered as editor of the 9th *variorum* edition of Alfred Marshall's *Principles of Economics*, 2 vols (London: Macmillan, 1961).—Ed.]

equally important. And in their different ways they achieve their objects with the same success. Even the utter difference in tone between the two books helps in their respective tasks. Dr. Einzig's passionate pamphlet most effectively debunks the German 'New Order' in Europe which, incredible as it may sound, seems to exercise its intended propaganda effect even in this country. Mr. Guillebaud's admirably detached and scholarly evaluation of German social policy corrects perhaps even more widely held misconceptions about the nature of the activities of the Nazis in this field, and goes far to explain the hold which National Socialism undoubtedly still has on the great mass of German workers. If Dr. Einzig uses vivid colours and a lively imagination, the picture which he presents of the probable shape of the New Order is, I believe, as correct as one can make it at the moment, and exactly what is needed to disillusion the naive and gullible who allow themselves to be beguiled by German promises. And if Mr. Guillebaud presents a painstaking and balanced account of German policy with the result that it appears in a considerably less unfavourable light than that in which it is commonly seen, this is certainly the right way to make the public recognize this less palatable but no less important truth. It is true that in reading it one feels at times apprehensive about the effect this objective account will have on some readers to whom official propaganda (if the BBC may be thus described) has represented Hitler as the very antithesis of socialism and as the servant of capitalist interests. But this is not Mr. Guillebaud's fault. It is surely more important to know the sources of Nazi strength than to cherish illusions on this score—even if to some the Nazis may in consequence appear less odious than they nevertheless are. And Mr. Guillebaud cannot be accused of suppressing the discreditable aspects of the regime where they come into his field.

If the two books have a real fault it is a common one, and one which is characteristic of the attitude of most of our contemporaries towards the phenomenon of the Totalitarian State. Both authors are inclined to approve many of the methods and means used by the Nazis, but deplore the ends for which they are employed. It does not seem to occur to them that the two things may be connected. It is unnecessary to conclude, as Dr. Einzig seems to, that the results are so obviously bad, the intentions must have been entirely bad; or, as Mr. Guillebaud's reader will sometimes feel, that something good at least must come from measures which in themselves are so similar to what has long been advocated by social reformers elsewhere. Is it not possible that all that planning and direction, which in Germany longer than elsewhere has been universally demanded, necessarily require a "totalitarian" regime, arbitrary preferences, the use of force, and the institution of a new hierarchical order of society, and that only the most ruthless and unscrupulous are capable of satisfying the clamour of the masses for 'action', while the decent falter and fail when faced with the concrete task? Is not the truest explanation of developments in Germany still that given by the poet Hölderin[35] more than a hundred years ago that "what has always made the State a hell on earth has been that man has tried to make it his heaven"?

8. Knowledge of Germany[36]

If any further illustration had been needed of how uncertain and unsettled are the opinions about the characteristic features of German thought, recent controversies would have provided it. But they really are no more than an illustration of a historic fact of considerable importance—the extraordinary vicissitudes, the violent fluctuations between extremes, which views about the German people have undergone in the past hundred years. No other nation in modern times has experienced such ups and downs in its reputation, at one moment exercising so profound an influence on all other peoples, to be held up shortly afterwards as the embodiment of everything that is detestable. It is not enough that every time we change our views about the Germans we resolve that we are not going to change them again. There is something more deeply wrong with our opinions if from time to time they need such complete revision. If the source of this instability of the views about Germany is not removed, we shall continue to fly from one extreme to another. However convinced the present generation may remain that the Germans are thoroughly bad, another generation will once more discover that they have also other qualities which do not fit into the picture presented by their elders, and in the enthusiasm of that discovery will once more build up a new and equally one-sided picture. The serious consequence is that these vacillations in British views about Germany have led to similar vacillations of British policy. There will be no stable policy towards Germany till a stable view of her has been achieved, which must be a view that suppresses neither the bad nor the good side, but combines them into a coherent picture. The fact that German thought itself is highly unstable and full of conflicting elements is no reason why we should not form a stable picture of the causes of this situation.

In the years between the two wars knowledge of Germany in this country, never very great, has further decreased. This may at first sound sur-

---

[35][The German lyric poet Johann Christian Friedrich Hölderin (1770–1843) joined classical and Christian themes in his work. The editor was unable to locate the source of this quote.—Ed.]

[36][F. A. Hayek, "Knowledge of Germany", *The Spectator*, December 26, 1941, p. 595.—Ed.]

prising, because there were probably never before in this country so many people who had been to Germany and therefore thought that they knew her. But such visits to Germany, or other occasional contacts, produced either lovers of Germany, because they had seen one side of her, or—till comparatively recently these were very few—haters of Germany, because they had seen another side of her. But an understanding of those intellectual currents in Germany which ultimately determine evolution and policy was scarcely to be found in this country. So far as the views of the general public about any other country are concerned, this is, of course, true of most people. What was lacking in England, however, was any body of professional students of other countries who were capable of interpreting these currents, of correcting one-sided impressions, and who could act as expert advisers when the need arose. I doubt whether there was in 1939 anyone in this country who knew Germany as Elie Halévy, or even Dibelius, knew England, or as Andler or Vermeil in France knew Germany, or Curtius in Germany knew France.[37]

This is not a matter of merely academic or long-range importance. Never shall we need knowledge of Germany so much as during and immediately after the war. It has been well said that the first step to victory is a complete and thorough understanding of the enemy's ideas. This step has yet to be taken. Whether we like it or not, we need people who know Germany not merely in an amateurish way, who devote the whole of their time to the study of German ideas, and who approach them not merely with a literary interest but with genuine political and historical understanding. To understand is in such a case by no means necessarily to forgive or to condone. But it is an essential basis for any intelligent action. The none-too-glorious history of the efforts of British propaganda towards Germany during the last two years is only the most recent, but not the most important, instance of the defects of our knowledge of Germany telling heavily against us. There will be any number of opportunities for further mistakes of this kind during the next few years if we do not succeed in remedying this defect. If, as the experience of the last few years strongly suggests, people who have the required knowledge do not exist,

[37][French historian Elie Halévy (1870–1937) was a professor of political science at Paris and author of *Histoire du Peuple anglais au XIXe siècle*, 6 vols (Paris: Hachette, 1926). The German historian Wilhelm Dibelius (1876–1931) was author of numerous books on Britain, including *England* (London: Jonathan Cape, 1922). The French historian Charles Andler (1866–1933) was author of *Origines du socialisme d'Etat en Allemagne* (Paris: F. Alcan, 1897). Edmond Vermeil (1878–1964) also wrote on Germany; his books included *L'Allemagne contemporaine: 1919–1924* (Paris: F. Alcan, 1925). Ernst Robert Curtius (1886–1956) wrote a number of books on France, among them *Die französische Kultur: eine Einführung* (Stuttgart, Berlin: Deutsche Verlag, 1930; 2nd ed., Bern: Francke, 1975).—Ed.]

it is important that we train them now as part of our war effort. Here is a splendid opportunity for the universities to provide expert knowledge which is urgently needed but which existing courses do not provide. While the numerous German exiles in this country, with their inevitably somewhat biased outlook, can never replace British experts, they could be of much use in helping to train them.

It would be a mistake to contend that too much occupation with German thought is dangerous and should not be encouraged. Here, as elsewhere, it is only partial knowledge that is dangerous. It is undoubtedly true, much more than is commonly realized, that during the past fifty years English people have constantly taken over from Germany bits of ideas without regard for whether these could be properly separated from the whole German system of thought, so much so that they have even to some extent lost the sense of what is characteristically English and what German. Twenty-five years ago the English people in general had probably a clearer conception of these national differences than they have now, and at the present moment the intelligent German is perhaps more aware of these differences than the Englishman. The extent to which during the last twenty-five years German ideas have penetrated into this country is indeed a strong reason for a fuller knowledge of the whole system of thought, in order that we may learn to understand what part of it can and what part cannot be separated from the features which we loathe.

Still more important is the fact that German ideas have made even greater progress in other parts of the world than in this country, and that we shall not be able to counter them without really understanding them. There can be no doubt, for example, that, as I am afraid we shall learn to our embarrassment, most of the Central European nations, including some of our present allies, have derived their thought on social and political matters largely from German sources, and that even after such ideas have disappeared in Germany they will continue to operate there. And we should never forget that German views about the origins of the last war have exercised a profound influence on the teaching of some of the most distinguished American historians; it would not be difficult to point to instances where disregard of this has deprived presentations of the British view of their effect.

Instead of our improving our dangerously defective knowledge of Germany, our ignorance of current German thought is at present rapidly increasing. It is an error to believe that even in wartime dictatorial control has succeeded in completely stifling the development of thought. But we know almost nothing about what is happening. In this respect the situation is very different from what it was during the last war. A glance through the files of any scientific or technical periodical from 1914 to

1918 will show that the more important German books and reviews continued to arrive in this country and to be reviewed regularly. Now even the specialist, if he is not in an official position, has no means of informing himself about what is happening in his field in Germany. This may become the cause of serious difficulties when we have once again to deal with the Germans by methods other than the sword. It is not enough that the German literary output should be watched, as it presumably is, by some official organization. The hurried and overworked civil servant can hardly pay attention to anything except what is of immediate importance. If we are to understand and appreciate the significance of tendencies in the intellectual life of a big country it is essential that its literary output should be accessible to the corresponding specialists here. There are, of course, numerous and compelling reasons why German books and periodicals should not be obtainable as freely and profusely as in peacetime. But there seems to be no reason why one copy of each important publication should not be made available in one place, where all competent people with a legitimate interest would have access to it. Many a scholar or literary man who has few other ways of contributing to the war effort might thereby be enabled to make a most useful contribution by watching developments in Germany in his own field and drawing attention to them whenever they appear significant.

PART III

PLANNING, FREEDOM, AND THE POLITICS OF SOCIALISM

EIGHT

FREEDOM AND THE ECONOMIC SYSTEM[1]

The link between classical liberalism and present-day socialism—often still misnamed liberalism—is undoubtedly the belief that the consummation of individual freedom requires relief from the most pressing economic cares. If this seems attainable only at the price of restricting freedom of economic activity, then that price must be paid; and it may be conceded that most of those who want to restrict private initiative in economic life do so in the hope of creating more freedom in spheres which they value higher. So successfully has "the socialist ideal of freedom—social, economic, and political"[2]—been preached that the old cry of the opponents that socialism means slavery has been completely silenced. Probably the great majority of the socialist intellectuals regard themselves as the true upholders of the great tradition of intellectual and cultural liberty against the threatening monster, the authoritarian Leviathan.

Yet here and there, in the writings of some of the more independent minds of our time, who have generally welcomed the universal trend towards collectivism, a note of disquiet can be discerned. The question has forced itself upon them whether some of the shocking developments of the past decades may not be the necessary outcome of the tendencies which they had themselves favoured. There are some elements in the present situation which strongly suggest that this may be so, such as the intellectual past of the authoritarian leaders, and the fact that many of the more advanced socialists openly admit that the attainment of their ends is not possible without a thorough curtailment of individual liberty. The similarity between many of the most characteristic features of the 'fascist' and the 'communist' regimes becomes steadily more obvious. Nor is it an accident that in the fascist states a socialist is often regarded as a

---

[1][F. A. Hayek, "Freedom and the Economic System", *Contemporary Review*, April 1938, pp. 434–442. A slightly revised version was reprinted as "What Price a Planned Economy?", *American Affairs*, July 1945, pp. 178–181. The article formed the basis for the pamphlet *Freedom and the Economic System* that is reprinted in chapter 9 of this volume.—Ed.]

[2]*The Times* (London) of July 16, 1936, in a review of Jawaharlal Nehru, *India and the World: Essays* (London: Allen and Unwin, 1936).

potential recruit, while the liberal of the old school is recognized as the arch-enemy. And, above all, the effects of the gradual advance towards collectivism in the countries which still cherish the tradition of liberty on social and political institutions provide ample food for thought. Anyone who has had an opportunity to watch at close range the intellectual evolution of the peoples who eventually succumbed to authoritarianism cannot fail to observe a very similar chain of cause and effect in a much less advanced state proceeding in the countries which are yet free.

Are we certain that we know exactly where the danger to liberty lies? Was the rise of the fascist regimes really simply an intellectual reaction fomented by those whose privileges were abolished by social progress? Of course the direction of affairs in those countries has been taken out of the hands of the working classes and has been placed in those of a more efficient oligarchy. But have the new rulers not taken over the fundamental ideas and methods and simply turned them to their own ends?

It is astounding that these fateful possibilities which suggest themselves have not yet received more attention. If the suspicion of such a connection should prove right, it would mean that we are witnessing one of the great tragedies in human history: more and more people being driven by their indignation about the suppression of political and intellectual freedom in some countries to join the forces which make its ultimate suppression inevitable. It would mean that many of the most active and sincere advocates of intellectual freedom are in effect its worst enemies, much more dangerous than its avowed opponents, because they bring the support of those who would recoil in horror if they understood the ultimate consequences.

An attempt will be made here to show why this connection, which experience suggests must be regarded as of a necessary character—as dictated by the inherent logic of things. The main point is very simple. It is that the central economic planning, which is regarded as necessary to organize economic activity on more rational and efficient lines, presupposes a much more complete agreement on the relative importance of the different ends than actually exists, and that, in consequence, in order to be able to plan, the planning authority must impose upon the people that detailed code of values which is lacking. And imposing here means more than merely reading such a detailed code of values into the vague general formulae on which alone the people are able to agree. The people must be made to believe in this particular code of values, since the success or failure of the planning authority will in two different ways depend on whether it succeeds in creating that belief. On the one hand it will only secure the necessary enthusiastic support if the people believe in the ends which the plan serves; and on the other hand the outcome will only be regarded as successful if the ends served are generally regarded as the right ones.

A fuller exposition must begin with the problems which arise when a democracy begins to plan. Planning must be understood here in the wide sense of any deliberate attempt at central direction of economic activity which goes beyond mere general rules that apply equally to all persons, and which tells different people individually what to do and what not to do. The demand for such planning arises because people are promised a greater measure of welfare if industry is consciously organized on rational lines, and because it seems obvious that those particular ends which each individual most desires can be achieved by means of planning. But the agreement about the ends of planning is, in the first instance, necessarily confined to some blanket formula like the general welfare, greater equality or justice, etc.

Agreement on such a general formula is, however, not sufficient to determine a concrete plan, even if we take all the technical means as given. Planning always involves a sacrifice of some ends in favour of others, a balancing of costs and results, and this presupposes a complete ranging of the different ends in the order of their importance. To agree on a particular plan requires much more than agreement on some general ethical rule; it requires much more than general adherence to any of the ethical codes which have ever existed; it requires that sort of complete quantitative scale of values which manifests itself in the actual decisions of every individual but on which, in an individualist society, agreement is neither necessary nor present.

This fact—that a measure of agreement which does not exist is required in order to translate the apparent agreement on the desirability to plan into concrete action—has two important consequences. In the first instance, it is responsible for the conspicuous inability of democratic assemblies to carry out what is apparently the expressed will of the people, because it is only when it comes to translate the vague instructions into action that the lack of real agreement manifests itself. Hence the growing dissatisfaction with the 'talking shops' which fail to carry out what to the man in the street seems a clear mandate.

The second effect of the same cause, which appears wherever a democracy attempts to plan, is the general recognition that if efficient planning is to be done in a particular field, the direction of affairs must be 'taken out of politics' and placed in the hands of independent autonomous bodies. This is usually justified by the technical character of the decisions to be made, for which the members of a democratic assembly are not qualified. But this excuse does not go to the root of the matter. Alterations in the structure of the civil law are no less technical and no more difficult to appreciate in all their implications; yet nobody would seriously suggest that legislation should here be delegated to a body of experts. The fact is that in these fields legislation will be carried no further than true agreement between a majority exists. But in the direction of economic activity, say of transport, or industrial planning, the interests to be reconciled are so divergent that no true agreement on a single plan could be reached in a democratic assembly. Hence, in order to be able to extend action beyond the questions on which agreement exists, the decisions are reserved to a few representatives of the most powerful 'interests'.

But this expedient is not effective enough to placate the dissatisfaction which the impotence of the democracy must create among all friends of extensive planning. The delegation of special decisions to many independent bodies presents in itself a new obstacle to proper coordination of State action in different fields. The legislature is naturally reluctant to delegate decisions on really vital questions. And the agreement that planning is necessary, together with the inability to agree on a particular plan, must tend to strengthen the demand that the government, or some single person, should be given power to act on their own responsibility. It becomes more and more the accepted belief that if one wants to get things done the responsible director of affairs must be freed from the fetters of democratic procedure.

That the increasing discredit into which democratic government has fallen is due to democracy having been burdened with tasks for which it is not suited is a fact of the greatest importance which has not yet received adequate recognition. Yet the fundamental position is simply that the probability of agreement of a substantial portion of the population upon a particular course of action decreases as the scope of State activity expands. There are certain functions of the State on the exercise of which there will be practical unanimity. There will be others on which there will be agreement among a substantial majority. And so on until we come to fields where, although every individual might wish the government to intervene in some direction, there will be almost as many views about how the government should act as there are different persons.

Democratic government worked successfully so long as, by a widely accepted creed, the functions of the State were limited to fields where real agreement among a majority could be achieved. The price we have to pay for a democratic system is the restriction of State action to those fields where agreement can be obtained; and it is the great merit of a liberal society that it reduces the necessity of agreement to a minimum compatible with the diversity of individual opinions which will exist in a free society. It is often said that democracy will not tolerate capitalism. But if here "capitalism" means a competitive society based on free disposal over private property, the much more important fact is that only capitalism makes democracy possible. And if a democratic people comes under the sway of an anti-capitalistic creed, this means that democracy will inevitably destroy itself.

But if democracy had to abdicate only from the control of economic life, this might still be regarded as a minor evil compared with the advantages expected from planning. Indeed, many of the advocates of planning fully realize—and have resigned themselves to the fact—that if planning is to be effective, democracy in the economic sphere has to go by the board.[3] But it is a fatal delusion to believe that authoritarian government can be confined to economic matters. The tragic fact is that dictatorial direction cannot remain confined to economic matters but is bound to expand and to become 'totalitarian' in the strict sense of the word. The economic dictator will soon find himself forced, even against his wishes, to assume dictatorship over the whole of the political and cultural life of the people. We have already seen that the planner must not only impose a concrete and detailed scale of values into the vague and general instructions given by popular clamour, but must also, if he wants to act at all, make the people believe that this imposed code of values is the right one. He is forced to create that unity of purpose which—apart from national crises like war—is absent in a free society. Even more, if he is to be allowed to carry out the plan which he thinks to be the right one, he must retain the popular support, that is, he must at all costs appear successful.

The decision on the relative importance of conflicting aims is necessarily a decision about the relative merits of different groups and individuals. Planning becomes necessarily a planning in favour of some and against others.[4] The problem here is, of course, not that the different people concerned have not the most decided opinions on the relative

[3]Cf. Mr. Stuart Chase's statement that "political democracy can remain if it confines itself to all but economic matters". Quoted by Walter Lippmann, "The Collectivist Movement in Practice", *Atlantic Monthly*, December 1936, p. 729. [Accountant, freelance writer, and author Stuart Chase (1888–1985), whom Lippmann quotes, was a popular writer in the interwar years. Among his many books on economics were *The Tragedy of Waste* (New York: Macmillan, 1925) and *A New Deal* (New York: Macmillan, 1934). He also provided the foreword to Thorstein Veblen, *The Theory of the Leisure Class* (New York: Modern Library, 1934).The American journalist, author, and social commentator Walter Lippmann (1889–1974) wrote for the *New York Herald Tribune*. He won the Pulitzer Prize for international reporting in 1962.—Ed.]

[4]This is freely admitted by all the authoritarian governments when they insist on the predominance of politics over economics and has been clearly formulated by one of the sociologists of present-day Germany, Professor Hans Freyer in *Herrschaft und Planung* (Hamburg: Hanseatische Verlagsanstalt, 1933). [The German philosopher and sociologist Hans Freyer (1887–1969) taught at Kiel, Leipzig, and Münster in Germany and Ankara, Turkey.—Ed.]

merits of their respective wishes; it is rather that these opinions are irreconcilable. But the ground on which the more or less arbitrary decision of the authority rests must be made to appear just, to be based on some ultimate ideal in which everybody is supposed to believe. The inevitable distinction between persons must be made a distinction of rank, most conveniently and naturally based on the degree to which people share and loyally support the creed of the ruler. And it further clarifies the position if to the aristocracy of creed at one end of the scale there corresponds a class of outcasts at the other, whose interests can in all cases be sacrificed to those of the privileged classes.

But conformity to the guiding ideas cannot be regarded as a special merit, although those who excel by their devotion to the creed will be rewarded. It must be exacted from everybody. Every doubt in the rightness of the ends aimed at or the methods adopted is apt to diminish loyalty and enthusiasm and must therefore be treated as sabotage. The creation and enforcement of the common creed and of the belief in the supreme wisdom of the ruler becomes an indispensable instrument for the success of the planned system. The ruthless use of all potential instruments of propaganda and the suppression of every expression of dissent is not an accidental accompaniment of a centrally directed system—it is an essential part of it.

Nor can moral coercion be confined to the acceptance of the ethical code underlying the whole plan. It is in the nature of things that many parts of this code, many parts of the scale of values underlying the plan, can never be explicitly stated. They exist only implicitly in the plan. But this means that every part of the plan, in fact every action of the government or its agencies, becomes sacrosanct and exempt from criticism.

It is, however, only the expression of criticism that can be forcibly suppressed. But doubts that are never uttered and hesitation that is never voiced have equally insidious effects if they dwell only in the minds of the people. Everything which might induce discontent must therefore be kept from them. The basis for comparison with conditions elsewhere, the knowledge of possible alternatives to the course taken, information which might suggest failure on the part of the government to live up to its promises or to take advantage of opportunities to improve the lot of the people—all these must be suppressed. Indeed, there is no subject that has not some possible bearing on the estimation in which the government will be held. There is consequently no field where the systematic control of information will not be practiced. That the government which claims to plan economic life soon asserts its totalitarian character is no accident—it can do nothing less if it wants to remain true to the intention of planning. Economic life is not a sector of human life which can be separated from the rest; it is the administration of the means for all our different ends. Whoever takes charge of these means must determine which ends shall be served, which values are to be rated higher and which lower—in short, what men should believe and strive for. And man himself becomes little more than a means for the realization of the ideals which may guide the dictator.

It is to be feared that to a great many of our contemporaries this picture, even should they recognize it as true, has lost most of the terror which it would have inspired in our fathers. There were, of course, always many to whom intellectual coercion was only objectionable if it was exercised by others, and who regarded it as beneficial if it was exercised for ends of which they approved. How many of the exiled intellectuals from the authoritarian countries would be only too ready to apply the intellectual coercion which they condemn in their opponents in order to make the people believe in their own ideals—incidentally another illustration for the close kinship of the fundamental principles of fascism and communism!

But, although the liberal age was probably freer from intellectual coercion than any other, the desire to force upon people a creed which is regarded as salutary for them is not a new phenomenon. What is new is the attempt to justify it on the part of the socialist intellectuals of our time. There is no real freedom of thought in a capitalist society, so it is said, because the opinions and tastes of the masses are inevitably shaped by propaganda, by advertising, by the example of the upper classes, and by other environmental factors which relentlessly force the thinking of the people into well-worn grooves. But if, the argument proceeds, the ideals and tastes of the great majority are formed by environmental factors which are under human control, we might as well use this power to turn their thoughts in what we think a desirable direction. That is, from the fact that the great majority have not learned to think independently but accept the ideas which they find readymade, the conclusion is drawn that a particular group of people—of course, those who advocate this— are justified in assuming to themselves the exclusive power to determine what the people should believe.

It is not my intention to deny that for the great majority of individuals the existence or non-existence of intellectual freedom makes little difference to their personal happiness; nor to deny that they will be equally happy if born or coaxed into one set of beliefs rather than another, and whether they have grown accustomed to one kind of amusement or another. That in any society it will be only the comparatively few for whom freedom of thought is of any significance or exists in any real sense is probably only too true. But to deprecate the value of intellectual freedom because it will never give everybody the same opportunity of independent thought is completely to miss the reasons which give intellectual freedom its value. What is essential to make it serve its function as the prime mover of intellectual progress is not that everybody may think or write everything, but that any cause or any idea may be argued by somebody. So long as dissent is not actually prevented there will always be some who will query the ideas ruling their contemporaries and put new ideas to the test of argument and propaganda. The social process which we call human reason and which consists of the interaction of individuals possessing different information and different views, sometimes consistent and sometimes conflicting, goes on. Once given the possibility of dissent there will be dissenters, however small the proportion of people who are capable of independent thought. Only the imposition of an official doctrine which must be accepted and which nobody dare question can stop intellectual progress.

How completely the imposition of a comprehensive authoritarian creed stifles all spirit of independent inquiry, how it destroys the sense for any other meaning of truth than that of conformity with the official doctrine, how differences of opinion in every branch of knowledge become political issues, one must have seen in one of the totalitarian countries to appreciate. One must hope that those in the Western world who seem to be ready to sacrifice intellectual freedom because it does not mean the same opportunity for all do not yet realize what is at stake. Indeed, the great danger comes from the fact that we take so much of the inheritance of the liberal age for granted—have come to regard it as the inalienable property of our civilization—that we cannot fully conceive what it would mean if we lost it. Yet freedom and democracy are not free gifts which will remain with us if we only wish. The time seems to have come when it is once again necessary to become fully conscious of the conditions which make them possible, and to defend these conditions even if they seem to block the path to the achievement of other ideals.

NINE

FREEDOM AND THE ECONOMIC SYSTEM
[1939][1]

I

'Freedom' and 'liberalism' have become terms that are used to describe the exact opposite of their historic meaning. In a recent article in *Harper's Magazine,* an author managed to speak quite innocently about "united action of all liberal groups under the leadership of the Communists". The editor of an American 'liberal' weekly actually wrote in support of "taking communism away from the communists",[2] but while these are striking examples, it is perhaps more characteristic of the collectivists of the left to camouflage under the time-honoured liberal label.

The intellectual transition from nineteenth-century liberalism to present-day socialism, its extreme opposite, was made possible by one idea they had in common: the belief that the consummation of individual freedom can only be achieved if we break the "despotism of physical want".[3] If free competition from time to time inevitably endangers the livelihood of some, and if security to all could be attained only by restricting the freedom of economic activity, then that price did not appear too high. It would be unfair to deny that most of those who want to restrict private initiative in economic matters do so in the hope of creating greater freedom in spheres which they value higher. So successfully has the world been taught to believe that "the socialist ideal of freedom, social, economic, and political"[4] can be realized simultaneously in all these respects, that the old cry of the opponents that socialism means slavery has been completely silenced. The great majority of the socialist intellectuals of our time sincerely believe that they are the true upholders of the great tradi-

---

[1][F. A. Hayek, *Freedom and the Economic System* (Chicago: University of Chicago Press, 1939), Public Policy Pamphlet No. 29 in the series edited by Harry D. Gideonse. This is an expanded version of Hayek's 1938 article from *Contemporary Review,* reprinted as chapter 8 of this volume.—Ed.]

[2][The Editor was unable to locate either of these quotations.—Ed.]

[3]Cf. W. S. Jevons, *The State in Relation to Labour* (London: Macmillan, 1887; 4th ed., 1910; reprinted, New York: Kelley, 1968), pp. 14–15.

[4]*The Times* (London) of July 16, 1936, in a review of Jawaharlal Nehru, *India and the World: Essays,* op. cit.

tion of intellectual and cultural liberty against the threatening monster of the authoritarian Leviathan.

Yet here and there in the writings of some of the more independent minds of our time, men who have in general supported the universal trend towards collectivism, a note of disquiet can be discerned. The question has forced itself upon them whether some of the shocking developments of the past decades may not be the necessary outcome of the tendencies which they had themselves favoured. Is it mere accident that the continuous expansion of the powers of the state, which they had welcomed as an instrument to bring about greater justice, has in so many countries brought the disappearance of all personal freedom and the end of all justice? Is it mere chance that the very countries which until comparatively recently were regarded as socially most advanced and as examples worthy of imitation were the first to succumb to real despotism? Or is this development not, perhaps, the unforeseen but inevitable outcome of those very efforts to make the fate of the individual less dependent on impersonal and perhaps accidental forces and more subject to conscious human control?

There are many features of our situation which strongly suggest that this may be so and that the attempt to realize some of the most cherished and widely held ambitions of our time has led us along a path which is fatal to the preservation of greater achievements of the past. The similarity of many of the most characteristic features of the 'fascist' and 'communist' regimes is becoming steadily more obvious. Not a few of the more advanced intellectual leaders of socialism have openly admitted that the attainment of their ends is not possible without a thorough curtailment of individual liberty. The intellectual past of the authoritarian leaders as well as the fact that in the fascist states a socialist is often regarded as a potential recruit, while the liberal of the old school is recognized as the arch-enemy, point to a filiation of ideas which is very different from that commonly assumed.

Above all, however, the effects of the gradual advance towards collectivism in the countries which still cherish the tradition of liberty in their social and political institutions provide ample food for thought. The complaint about the 'new despotism' of bureaucracy may have been exaggerated and premature. But anyone who has had an opportunity to watch at close range the intellectual evolution of the countries which eventually succumbed to authoritarianism cannot fail to observe a very similar development in a much less advanced stage in the countries which are yet free. And many changes, which in themselves look innocent enough, assume an entirely different aspect if seen in that setting.

There is much talk about the 'dangers to liberty', and professed readiness to 'defend' it against the wicked designs of sinister interests. But are we certain that we know exactly where the danger to liberty lies? Ought we not at least to pause and ask whether the menace may not have its roots in our own ambitions and endeavours? Is it as evident as many believe that the rise of the fascist regimes was simply an intellectual reaction fomented by those whose privileges were threatened by social progress? It is, of course, true that the direction of affairs in those countries has been taken out of the hands of the working classes and has been placed in those of a more efficient oligarchy. But have the new rulers not taken over the fundamental ideas and methods of their socialist and communist opponents, and simply turned them to their own ends?[5]

The fateful possibilities which such analysis suggests deserve further attention. If the suspicion should prove right that the expansion of state control over economic life, which is so generally wanted, should necessarily lead to the suppression of intellectual and cultural freedom, it would mean that we are witnessing one of the greatest tragedies in the history of the human race: More and more people are being driven by their indignation about the suppression of political and intellectual freedom in some countries to join the very forces which make the ultimate suppression of their own freedom inevitable. It would mean that many of the most active and sincere advocates of intellectual freedom are in effect its worst enemies, much more dangerous than its avowed opponents, because they bring to the collectivist movement which will ultimately destroy intellectual as well as economic freedom the support of those who would recoil in horror if they understood these consequences.

It is, of course, not a new idea that the central direction of economic activity might involve the destruction of freedom and of democratic insti-

---

[5]Long before the rise of fascism, Marxist socialism made politics a question of *Weltanschauung*. Long before they were imitated by their opponents, socialists attempted to penetrate every department of life with their political organizations and to make arts and sports, no less than the forms of personal intercourse, a question of political doctrine. It was they who began to organize children of the tenderest age in political clubs, and who made sure that the people enjoyed their football and hiking no less than their theater and music only in socialist organizations. The armed political troops for the 'protection of their meetings' no less than the specific methods of greeting among the comrades were first developed by them. *Balilla* and *Hitler Jugend*, *Dopolavoro* and *Kraft durch Freude*, and even the fascist militia and the S.A., are direct descendants of their socialist prototypes. [*Balilla* was the Italian Fascist organization for boys, named after the boy who started the insurrection which drove the Austrians out of Genoa in 1746. The *Hitler Jugend*, or Hitler Youth, was the organization for the indoctrination of the young within Germany. *Dopolavoro* (from *dopo lavoro*, Italian for "after work") was the Italian Fascist recreational program, which included sports, cultural, and tourist events. Begun in 1925, by 1939 it had over five million members in 24,500 groups. Its German counterpart was *Kraft durch Freude* (Strength through Joy). Founded in 1933 within the German Labour Front and modeled after *Dopolavoro*, it was designed to win the working classes to National Socialism, which was particularly important after the trade unions were abolished.—Ed.]

191

tutions. This has often been dogmatically asserted and even more often been vehemently denied. In a recent symposium on 'planned society', we find author after author concerned about this problem, either repeating the charge or attempting to refute it.[6] Indeed, Professor Gustav Cassel states his apprehension there with a clarity which leaves nothing to be desired. He writes:

> Planned Economy will always tend to develop into Dictatorship . . . [because] experience has shown that representative bodies are unable to fulfill all the multitudinous functions connected with economic leadership without becoming more and more involved in the struggle between competing interests with the consequence of a moral decay ending in party—if not individual—corruption. The parliamentary system can be saved only by wise and deliberate restrictions of the functions of parliament. Economic dictatorship is much more dangerous than people believe. Once authoritative control has been established, it will not always be possible to limit it to the economic domain.[7]

It will be useful to inquire whether this must necessarily be so or whether, as even Professor Cassel half suggests, the coincidence is accidental.

A careful examination of the transition undergone by countries which only recently seemed the most 'advanced' in the social and political sphere and which have now passed into a stage which we are inclined to associate with the distant past, actually reveals a pattern of development which suggests that these were not unfortunate historical accidents but that a similarity of methods applied to achieve ideal ends, which were

---

[6]Findlay MacKenzie, ed., *Planned Society: Yesterday, Today, Tomorrow, A Symposium by Thirty-Five Economists, Sociologists and Statesmen* (New York: Prentice Hall, 1937). See particularly the articles by H. D. Laswell, D. Mitrany, and Sidney Hook in Part 4 and the editor's prefatory note to Professor Lasswell's article which concludes that "freedom can never have the same meaning in a planned society that it once had or pretended to have in an automatic economy" (p. 629). [Harold D. Lasswell (1902–1978) was an associate professor of political science at the University of Chicago when this book was published; after the war, he became a professor of law at Yale. Author and educator David Mitrany (1888–1975) was born in Romania, educated at the London School of Economics, and became known as a specialist in international affairs. The American philosopher Sidney Hook (1902–1989) taught at New York University from 1932 to 1972 and was known for his brilliant expositions and critiques of the ideas of Marx and John Dewey. For Hayek's review of this book, see the Appendix, this volume.—Ed.]

[7]Gustav Cassel, "From Protectionism through Planned Economy to Dictatorship", Cobden Memorial Lecture delivered in London, May 10, 1934, and reprinted in *Planned Society*, op. cit., pp. 775–798, particularly pp. 797–798. [For more on Cassel, see chapter 1, note 13.—Ed.]

approved by almost all men of good will, was bound to produce entirely unanticipated consequences. An attempt will be made here to bring out these connections which can be traced between economic planning and dictatorship and to show why they must be regarded as a more or less inevitable pattern, dictated by characteristics that are interwoven with the very idea of a planned society.

The main point is very simple. It is that comprehensive economic planning, which is regarded as necessary to organize economic activity on more rational and efficient lines, presupposes a much more complete agreement on the relative importance of the different social ends than actually exists, and that in consequence, in order to be able to plan, the planning authority must impose upon the people the detailed code of values that is lacking. To impose such detail means more than merely reading such a detailed code into the vague general formulas which people are sometimes willing to accept fairly easily. The people must be made to believe in the particularized code of values, because the success or failure of the planning authority will in two different ways depend on whether it succeeds in creating that belief. On the one hand, it will only secure the necessary enthusiastic support if the people believe in the ends which the plan serves; and, on the other hand, the outcome will only be regarded as successful if the ends achieved are generally regarded as the right ones.

II

A fuller exposition must begin with the problems which arise when a democracy embarks upon a course of economic planning. Although the full political consequences of planning will generally only reveal themselves after it has led to the destruction of democracy, it is during that process of transition that it can best be seen why personal freedom and central direction of economic affairs are irreconcilable and where the conflict arises.

Before we can turn to that task it is, however, necessary to clear away the mist of confusion and ambiguity which enshrouds the term 'planning'. Unless we are very careful in this respect there is great danger that the vagueness of the term will lead to argument at cross-purposes and that the real source of the danger we are facing will be misunderstood. Incidentally, these reflections will also enable us to draw a somewhat sharper distinction between the true liberalism which, it will be argued, is alone compatible with freedom, and socialism and collectivism in all their forms which—as the argument will show—cannot be reconciled with free and democratic institutions.

The confusion about which we speak is particularly dangerous because planning in the strict sense, about which the whole controversy turns, owes its wide appeal largely to the fact that the same word, 'planning', is also applied to describe the application of reason to social problems in general—which is, of course, indispensable if we want to deal with these matters intelligently and to which it is impossible to object on rational grounds. The appeal to reason which the word 'planning' carries with it because of this second connotation probably accounts for a good deal of its popularity when it is used loosely. Yet there is a world of difference between economic planning in the narrow sense of the term and the application of reason to social problems in general.

We can 'plan' a system of general rules, equally applicable to all people and intended to be permanent (even if subject to revision with the growth of knowledge), which provides an institutional framework within which the decisions as to what to do and how to earn a living are left to the individuals. In other words, we can plan a system in which individual initiative is given the widest possible scope and the best opportunity to bring about effective coordination of individual effort.[8] Or we can 'plan' in the sense that the concrete action of the different individuals, the part each person is to play in the social process of production—what he is to do and how he is to do it—is decided by the planning agency. Planning in the first sense means that the direction of production is brought about by the free combination of the knowledge of all participants, with prices conveying to each the information which helps him to bring his actions in relation to those of others.[9] The planning of the planners of our time, however—the central direction according to some preconceived social blueprint—involves the idea that some body of people, in the last instance some individual mind, decides for the people what they have to do at each moment.

While this distinction between the construction of a rational system of law, under the rule of which people are free to follow their preferences, and a system of specific orders and prohibitions is clear enough as a general principle, it is not easy to define it exactly and sometimes even very difficult to apply it to a concrete case.[10] This difficulty has undoubtedly contributed further to confuse the distinction between planning for free-

[8]On the liberal 'plan', see in particular Lionel Robbins, *Economic Planning and International Order*, op. cit., passim.

[9]On the whole question of the 'combination of knowledge' in a competitive system and the significance of competitive equilibrium I may, perhaps, be allowed to refer to my own article on "Economics and Knowledge", op. cit.

[10]Cf. Walter Lippmann, *An Inquiry into the Principles of the Good Society* (New York: Grosset and Dunlap, 1937), passim. [See chapter 8, note 3, for more on Lippmann.—Ed.]

dom and planning for constant interference. And while an attempt to provide a satisfactory discussion of this question would clearly exceed the limits of the present sketch, it is essential to develop this crucial distinction somewhat farther.

By the construction of a rational framework of general and permanent rules, a mechanism is created through which production is to be directed, but no decision is consciously made about the ends to which it is directed. The rules aim mainly at the elimination of avoidable uncertainty[11] by establishing principles from which it can be ascertained who at any moment has the disposition over particular resources, and of unnecessary error by the prevention of deception and fraud. These rules are not made, however, in the expectation that A will be benefitted and that B will be harmed by them. Both will be able to choose their position under the law and both will find themselves in a better position than would be the case if no law existed. These rules (of civil and criminal law) are general not only in the sense that they apply equally to all people, but also in the sense that they are instrumental in helping people to achieve their various individual ends, so that in the long run everybody has a chance to profit from their existence. The very fact that the incidence of their effects on different individuals cannot be foreseen, because these effects are spread far too widely and the rules themselves are intended to remain in force for a very long period, implies that in the formulation of such rules no deliberate choice between the relative need of different individuals or different groups need or can be made, and that the same set of rules is compatible with the most varied individual views about the relative importance of different things.

Now it must be admitted that this task of creating a rational framework of law has by no means been carried through consistently by the early liberals. After vindicating on utilitarian grounds the general principles of private property and freedom of contract, they have stopped short of applying the same criterion of social expediency to the specific historic forms of the law of property and of contract. Yet it should have been obvious that the question of the exact content and the specific limitations of property rights, and how and when the state will enforce the fulfillment of contracts, require as much consideration on utilitarian grounds as the general principle. Unfortunately, however, many of the nineteenth-

---

[11]The stress is here on *avoidable uncertainty,* such as that by deliberate deception and willful nonfulfillment of contracts. The elimination of such uncertainty must not be confused with the attempts to make changes like advances of knowledge, which have actually occurred and altered the existing opportunities, ineffective by preventing people from adjusting themselves to them. Although this is often regarded as a task of planning, it is certainly a bad argument in favour of planning.

century liberals, after they had satisfied themselves about the justification of the general principle which they had rightly refused to accept as a dictate of the law of nature, were on the whole content to accept the law in its existing formulation, as if this was the only conceivable and natural one. A certain dogmatism in this respect, which often had the appearance of an unwillingness to reason on these problems, brought the development of this kind of planning to an early standstill and has tended to throw the whole liberal doctrine into discredit.

'Planning' in the second, narrower sense, which is the only subject of discussion in our days, would be more accurately described, following the French term *économie dirigée*, as a system of 'directed economy'. Its essence is that the central authority undertakes to decide the concrete use of the available resources, that the views and the information of the central authority govern the selection of the needs that are to be satisfied and the methods of their satisfaction. Here planning is no longer confined to the creation of conditions which have their effect because they are known in advance and are taken into account in the decision of individuals. Regulations and orders are made with the intention of review, and change in connection with a change in circumstances, which, under the first type of planning, would simply have led to a changed response of the producers concerned. The foresight of the individuals is here no longer used to get every change in circumstances registered in the price structure as soon as anyone notices or expects such a change. The knowledge which guides production is no longer combined knowledge of the people who are in immediate charge of the various operations—it is the knowledge of the few directing minds which participate in the formulation and execution of a consciously thought-out plan. The only known mechanism by which the knowledge of all can be utilized, the price mechanism, is discarded in favour of a method by which the knowledge and the views of a few are consistently and exclusively utilized. It is planning in this sense which is today increasingly used when one industry is told not to exceed a certain limit of output or not to increase its equipment, when another is prevented from selling below (or above) a certain price, when the owner is forbidden to exploit a particular mine or to farm a specified acreage, when the number of shops in a particular branch is restricted or a producer is subsidized to produce in one place rather than in another, and in the infinite number of measures of a similar kind. And it is in particular planning in this sense which, as we shall see, every reorganization of society along socialist lines involves.

Now it is not intended to deny here that some amount of central planning of this kind will always be necessary. There are unquestionably fields, like the fight against contagious diseases, where the price mechanism is not applicable, either because some services cannot be priced, or because a clear object desired by an overwhelming majority can only be achieved if a small dissenting minority is coerced. The problem we are discussing is not, however, whether the price system must be supplemented, whether a substitute must be found where in the nature of the case it is inapplicable, but whether it ought to be supplanted where the conditions for its working exist or can be created. The question is whether we can do better than by the spontaneous collaboration secured by the market, and not whether needed services, which cannot be priced and therefore will not be obtainable on the market, have to be provided in some other way.

The belief that central planning in this sense is necessary to secure a more 'rational' conduct of production in general—that is, to secure greater general productivity in some technical sense so that everybody would be better off—is, however, only one of the roots of the demand for such planning. It would be interesting, but it is not possible within the space available, to show how this belief is largely due to the intrusion into the discussion of social problems of the preconceptions of the pure scientist and the engineer, which have dominated the outlook of the educated man during the past hundred years. To a generation brought up in these views any suggestion that an order and purposeful reaction could exist which was not due to the conscious action of a directing mind was in itself 'medieval rubbish'[12], a piece of ridiculous theology which vitiated and discredited all conclusions based on such arguments. Yet it can be shown, in a manner which nobody who has understood the argument has ever contradicted, that the unconscious collaboration of individuals in the market leads to the solution of problems which, although no individual mind has even formulated these problems in a market economy, would have to be consciously solved on the same principle in a planned system.[13]

[12][Lancelot Hogben, *Education for an Age of Plenty* (London: British Institute of Adult Education, Life and Leisure Pamphlet No. 7, 1937), p. 10. For the complete phrase see chapter 10, this volume. For more on Hogben, see chapter 3, note 67, this volume.—Ed.]

[13]A beautiful specimen of this 'scientific' prejudice occurs in the Foreword to *Planned Society*, op. cit., where Mr. Lewis Mumford speaks of the "sublime and now incredible theology: the conception that order is so far preordained in human affairs that a multitude of blind actions and reactions will bring it to pass" (p. v). Yet while this is still the attitude of those brought up on popular science, it is essentially the more rigid 'mechanist' view of the nineteenth century—there must be few eminent scientists now who are guilty of this dogmatism. At least in so far as biology and psychology are concerned even an outstanding 'positivist' and eminent student of the methods of pure science like the late Professor Schlick recognizes a "general principle" that "frequently proves to be valid in psychology and biology; namely that the result of organic, unconscious or instinctive processes is frequently the same as what would have resulted from rational calculation" (*Fragen der Ethik* [Vienna: J. Springer, 1930], translated as *Problems of Ethics* [New York: Prentice Hall, 1939], p. 98). Vilfredo Pareto, in an interesting and little-noticed passage in his *Manuel d'économie*

Under the price system the solution of these problems is impersonal and social in the strict sense of the term and we can only just indicate in passing the curious intellectual somersault by which so many thinkers, after extolling society as a whole as infinitely superior and insisting that it is in some sense more than a mere collection of individuals, all end up by demanding that it must not be left to be guided by its own impersonal social forces, but must be made subject to the control of a directing mind—that is, of course, in the last analysis, the mind of an individual.

It is also not possible within the limits of this essay to show why this belief in the greater efficiency of a planned economy cannot any longer be defended on economic grounds. At any rate, recent discussion of these problems has at least thrown much doubt on this belief, and many advocates of planning are now content to hope that they will succeed in making such a planned system, in so far as formal rationality is concerned, come very near to the results of a competitive system. But it can be rightly said that this is not the decisive question. Many planners would be willing to put up with a considerable decrease of efficiency if at that price greater distributive justice could be achieved. And this, indeed, brings us to the crucial question. The ultimate decision for and against socialism cannot rest on purely economic grounds, and cannot be based merely on the determination of whether a greater or smaller output of society is likely to be obtained under the alternative systems in question. The aims of socialism as well as the costs of its achievement are mainly in the moral sphere. The conflict is one of ideals other than merely material welfare, and the difficulty is that these conflicting ideals still live together in the breasts of most people without their being aware of the conflict. It is on considerations like those discussed here that we shall have to base our final choice.

It is undeniably true that planning in the specific sense, while it is not required to make production more rational in any formal sense, is required if the relative well-being of different people is to be made to conform to some preconceived order, and that a distribution of incomes which corresponds to some absolute conception of the merits of different people can only be achieved by planning. In fact, it is only this argument of justice and not the argument of greater rationality which can be legiti-

---

politique, op. cit., p. 234, spoke of the equations which determine equilibrium in a market, and concluded that "if one really knew all these equations, the only means available to human powers to solve them would be to observe the solution given in practice by the market". [Moritz Schlick (1882–1936) was the founder of the Vienna Circle (the *Wiener Kreis* was also sometimes called the *Schlick Kreis*) of logical positivism; he was murdered by an insane student on the steps of the university library. For more on Pareto, see chapter 1, note 13; and on Mumford, see chapter 3, note 67.—Ed.]

mately advanced in favour of planning. It is for this reason also that *all* forms of socialism involve planning in this specific sense. 'Society' cannot take possession of all the material instruments of production without taking upon itself the decision of the purpose for which and the manner in which they are to be used. This is no less true under the systems of 'socialist competition' which have been recently proposed as a solution of the difficulties of calculation under a more centralized system than under the older schemes of socialist planning.[14]

It must also be added here that planning of this kind, if it is to be done rationally and consistently, cannot long be confined to partial or local interference with the working of the price system. So long as state action is confined to supplement the operation of the price system by providing for certain collective wants, or be giving all the same security against violence or infectious diseases, this leaves the price system in its sphere intact. But once the state attempts to correct the results of the market and to control prices and quantities produced in order to benefit particular classes or groups, it will be difficult to stop halfway. It is not necessary to review the familiar economic arguments which show why mere 'interven-

[14]I have no doubt that this statement will be violently contradicted, since many of my socialist friends believe, and have publicly asserted, that they have found a method by which collective ownership of the material resources and the impersonal direction of production can be combined. I have here neither space, nor is this the proper place, to explain in detail why I think that this belief is erroneous. It must suffice here to point out that even if the socialist managers of production were given the greatest amount of discretion compatible with the end that the income derived from the material resources should go to society, the decision as to the amount of equipment to be entrusted to a particular manager, as to the risks he should be allowed to take, and as to the directions in which he should be allowed to test the wishes of the consumers, must be reserved to the central authority. This means that the decision about the size and number of the separate enterprises, as well as the nature of the industries to be established and the goods to be produced, will be taken centrally. Even if in this decision the planning authority would attempt to follow only economic considerations, it will in last analysis be this authority which decides the nature and the quantity of the goods that are to be produced, and, therefore, the nature of the needs that are to be satisfied. And, although I have carefully studied all the proposals for socialist systems which professedly avoid central direction, I have failed to find one where the ultimate decision about the use to be made of the available resources is not left to the essentially arbitrary decision of some central authority. The contrary impression derived from a cursory reading of these proposals is due to the fact that the crucial question of how it is decided what resources are to be given to an individual producer is usually left obscure or treated as if it were an insignificant administrative detail. Dr. O. Lange's recent study, *On the Economic Theory of Socialism*, op. cit., which has been acclaimed by some of the younger socialists as a real solution of the difficulty, amounts to nothing but an elaborate system of price fixing in spite of an impressive scientific nomenclature. All the important questions remain unanswered (who is to do the price fixing, at what intervals prices are to be fixed or revised, how the action of the managers is to be controlled, etc.). A more detailed examination of such proposals must, however, be reserved for another occasion.

199

tionism' is self-defeating and self-contradictory, and how, if the central purpose of intervention is to be achieved, intervention must expand until it becomes a comprehensive system of planning.[15]

But it is relevant in this connection to underline certain sociological factors which operate in the same direction. Inequality is undoubtedly more readily borne if it is due to accident, or at least to impersonal forces, than when it is due to design. People will submit to misfortune which may hit anyone, but not as easily to suffering which is the result of arbitrary decision of authority. Dissatisfaction with one's lot will inevitably grow with the consciousness that it is the result of human decision. Once government has embarked upon planning for justice's sake, it cannot refuse responsibility for anybody's fate. In particular it will not be able to refuse protection against the consequences of any change which are regarded as undeserved. But so long as there is any remainder of a free market every single change will always be to the detriment of some, although the result of progress will in the long run benefit all. There is, therefore, no progress which somebody with an equity in the received ways of doing things would not have the interest to stop. The great advantage of the competitive system, however, lies exactly in the fact that it offers a premium on foresight and adaptability, and on the fact that one has to pay for it if one wishes to stay in an occupation which has become less needed. Any attempt to indemnify people against the consequences of changes which they have not foreseen makes the forces of the market inoperative and makes it necessary to put central direction in their place.

III

The wide popularity which the idea of central direction of all economic activity enjoys today is easily explained by the two facts that, on the one hand, people are promised by experts a greater amount of welfare if industry is 'organized' along rational lines, and, on the other, that it is so obvious that those particular ends which each individual most desires can be achieved by planning. But if people agree about the desirability of planning in general, their agreements about the ends which planning is to serve will in the first instance necessarily be confined to some general formula like 'social welfare', the 'general interest', the 'common good', greater equality or justice, etc. Agreement on such a general formula is, however, not sufficient to determine a concrete plan, even if we take all the technical means as given. The sad but undeniable fact is that all these formulas which are so freely used prove empty of content as soon as we attempt to use them as guides in any concrete decision as to economic

[15]Cf. L. von Mises, *Kritik des Interventionismus*, op. cit.

planning. Economic planning always involves the sacrifice of some ends in favour of others, a balancing of costs and results, a choice between alternative possibilities; and the decision always presupposes that all the different ends are ranged in a definite order according to their importance, an order which assigns to each objective a quantitative importance which tells us at what sacrifices of other ends it is still worth pursuing and what price would be too high.

We only need to visualize for a moment the type of specific questions the planning authority will have to decide in order to see the ultimate issues involved. The planning authority would not only have to decide between, say, electric light for the farmer or bathrooms for the industrial worker in town, but it would also have to decide whether, if the installation of electric light in a hundred farms is regarded as more important than the provision of bathrooms for fifty working-class families, they ought still to give preference to the claims of the farmers if instead they might have provided sixty working-class families with baths. The planner will not only have to know whether an additional doctor or an additional schoolteacher is more urgently needed, but he will have to know how to choose if, at the cost of training three doctors, he can train five teachers, and how if at the same cost he can train six teachers and so on. A decision whether a housing scheme in one town or another ought to be started first, or whether the greater costs of building in the one place are more than offset by the greater urgency of the needs there, a decision whether the cost of dispersing population to a certain extent is greater or smaller than the aesthetic and cultural advantages thereby obtained, can only be arbitrary—that is, there are within wide limits no grounds on which one person could convince another that the one decision is more reasonable than the other. Yet in making his decision the planner must give a preference, he must create distinctions of value or merit, and in a plan as a whole there is inevitably implied a whole scale of values. Agreement on a particular plan requires, therefore, much more than agreement on some general ethical rule; it requires much more than adherence to any of the ethical codes which have ever existed; it requires for society as a whole the same kind of complete quantitative scale of values as that which manifests itself in the decision of every individual, but on which, in an individualist society, agreement between the individuals is neither necessary nor present.

The idea that a completely planned or directed economic system could and would be used to bring about distributive justice presupposes, in fact, the existence of something which does not exist and has never existed: a complete moral code in which the relative values of all human ends, the relative importance of all the needs of all the different people, are assigned a definite place and a definite quantitative significance.[16] If such a complete code, which it is difficult even to conceive, were in existence, then planning would indeed raise few political difficulties. But no single mind is comprehensive enough to form even an individual conception of such a comprehensive scale of human aims and desires. And still less has there ever been or can there ever be agreement on such a code between a number of individuals, not to speak of agreement between a majority of all. But only to the extent that such agreement exists can we speak of the existence of such ethical code. Such a complete code as would be required in a completely directed economy would in effect have to decide for every human action how it was to be taken. No known religious or moral code—at least among civilized people with a high degree of dif-ferentiation between individuals—has even to any limited extent ap-proached such a system.

This idea of a complete ethical code—indeed, the idea of any differ-ences in comprehensiveness of different moral codes—is somewhat unfa-miliar.[17] That there are questions which when they are raised are 'moral' questions, but to which 'morality' has no answer, where there are no given values on the basis of which to decide, and where such values would

---

[16]To this statement only egalitarianism, in its strictest and most mechanical interpreta-tion, constitutes an exception. If we could agree that all persons, old or young, healthy or sick, men or women, industrious or idle, were to be given the same money income to be spent as they please—it would probably have to be the same income in terms of commodi-ties—we would have a definite rule to guide us. But the mere wish to approach greater equality provides no serviceable guide. Even if we agree that everything which we take from the rich to give to the poor means a social gain, we have not yet decided to whom the spoils are to go. The formula of the approach to equality is as empty as that of the 'common welfare', the 'social good', etc.

[17]The ideal of a complete moral code which comprehends all the needs of all people and gives them their definite value helps, incidentally, to clear up an old confusion about the meaning of 'self-interest' and 'egotism' in economic analysis. All that is presupposed in the 'individualist' approach is that in the scale of values only a limited number of objectives and only some needs of some other people will and can have a definite place, and that a comprehensive scale does nowhere exist. It makes no difference for analytical purposes whether in the scale of values of an individual only his own physical needs or also those of a number of other people have a definite place. It may also be pointed out that what is commonly called 'egotism' and 'altruism' does by no means correspond with the nar-rowness or comprehensiveness of the individual scales of values. The 'altruist' is very fre-quently the person who feels the distress which he sees so much more than that of which he only knows intellectually that he is very willing to sacrifice those of whose needs he only knows by hearsay to those whose suffering he has under his eyes. *Ce qu'on voit et ce qu'on ne voit pas* has its moral side, and those whose vivid sensation of the suffering they see makes them impatient to relieve it by any means may often be much more egotistic (in the sense of narrowness of their scale of values) than the cool reasoner who takes the indirect effects of a particular measure into account.

202

therefore have to be deliberately created if the question were to be answered, is an idea to which we have yet to accustom ourselves. Yet it is the problem which is inevitably raised by the suggestion that unified direction of individual activity should be used in the service of social justice, and we must beware of minimizing a difficulty because it is of a character with which we are not familiar. The fact is that on questions of this sort, because they have so far not constituted a problem for anyone, there has been no occasion to seek an answer, and still less has there been occasion for a common opinion to arise concerning them. Only when we try to make explicit in deliberate discussion and decision that which formerly was decided by chance, or at least by impersonal market forces, can these questions be rationally answered, and all the actions of the members of the planned society will have to be guided by the answer.

Before leaving this subject it should at least be indicated that the development of human civilization in the past has been accompanied by a movement from (in this sense) more to less comprehensive moral systems. From the member of the primitive tribe, whose daily life is a succession of acts regulated by a firmly established ritual, to the individual in the feudal society, whose fixed status determines the claims on life to which he is entitled, down to our own times, development has been towards a life in which a constantly widening area was governed by individual taste and preference. The change made necessary by central planning would require a complete reversal of this tendency by which moral—and legal—rules have for centuries tended to become more formal and general, and less specific.[18]

But our question here is not whether we ought or ought not to have such a complete and comprehensive moral code which would provide a generally acceptable basis of planning for social justice. The question is whether anything approaching such a complete code exists—that is, whether most people, or even only those who are regarded as the best and wisest by the others, agree at least on the major problems of value which an attempt to plan would raise. And there can be no doubt that the answer to this is negative, that where such moral rules will be needed they cannot be found but will have to be created.

IV

These excursions in what may seem remote speculations on questions of moral philosophy are not without relevance to our concrete problem. We

[18]This is not to say that a somewhat too rapid emancipation from traditional moral and religious belief may not be partly responsible for the mental instability of our generation. There can be little doubt that the existence of firm tradition has materially helped to pre-

can now return to the question of what happens when a democracy begins to plan, and shall find that these general considerations find an immediate application here. The fact that a measure of agreement, which does not exist in a free society, is required in order to translate the apparent agreement on the desirability of planning into concrete action has two important consequences. In the first instance, it is responsible for the conspicuous inability of democratic assemblies to carry out what is apparently the expressed will of the people, because it is only when the vague instructions have to be translated into specific action that the lack of real agreement manifests itself. The second effect of the same cause, which appears wherever a democracy attempts to plan, is the recognition that if efficient planning is to be done in a particular field the direction of affairs must be 'taken out of politics' and placed in the hands of permanent officials or independent autonomous bodies. This is usually justified by the 'technical' character of the decision to be made, for which the members of a democratic assembly are not qualified. But this excuse does not go to the root of the matter. Alterations in the structure of civil law are no less technical and no more difficult to appreciate in all their implications; yet nobody has as yet seriously suggested that legislation should here be delegated to a body of experts. The fact is that in these fields legislation will be carried no farther than the general rules on which true majority agreement can be achieved. But in the direction of economic activity—say of transport, or of industrial planning—the interests to be reconciled are so divergent that no true agreement on a single plan can be reached in a democratic assembly. Any decision here involves the direct and conscious choice between the satisfaction of particular needs of one group of people and that of another. There will often be a great many slightly affected in one way, and a few affected in another. If action were dependent on the agreement of a numerical majority, no action could be taken. But, in order to be able to extend action beyond the questions on which true agreement exists, the decisions are reserved to a few representatives of the most powerful 'interests'.

But this expedient of 'delegation' is not effective enough to placate the dissatisfaction which the impotence of the democracy must create among all friends of extensive planning. The delegation of special decisions to numerous separate organizations presents in itself a new obstacle to proper coordination of the plans in different fields. Even if, by this expe-

---

serve free institutions in the Western world, just as its absence has contributed to their downfall in Central Europe. But the essential point here is probably that the coercive apparatus of law should cover a narrower field than the rules of morals and tradition, and that great caution should be exercised in going beyond it.

dient, democracy succeeded in planning every sector of economic life separately, it would still remain impotent with regard to the larger task of a comprehensive plan for all the sectors taken together. Many special plans do not yet make a planned whole; in fact, as the planners ought to be the first to admit, they may be worse than no plan. But the legislature will be naturally reluctant to delegate decisions on really vital issues. In the end agreement that planning is necessary, together with the inability of the democratic assembly to agree on a particular plan, must strengthen the demand that the government, or some single individual, should be given powers to act on their own responsibility. It becomes more and more the accepted belief that, if one wants to get things done, the responsible director of affairs must be freed from the fetters of democratic procedure.

That the increasing discredit into which democratic government has fallen is due to democracy having been burdened with tasks for which it is not suited is a fact of the greatest importance. It has not yet received adequate recognition. Government by agreement is possible only if government action is confined to subjects on which people have common views. If we decide first that it must act on a certain question and inquire only afterward whether agreement exists on how it should act, we may find that we shall either have to coerce people to agree, or to abandon government by agreement, or both. And the farther the scope of government action extends, the greater the likelihood that this situation will arise. The fundamental position is simply that the probability of agreement of a substantial portion of the population upon a particular course of action decreases as the scope of state activity expands. There are certain functions of the state on the exercise of which there will be practical unanimity; there will be others on which there will be agreement of a substantial majority—and so on until we come to fields where, although every individual might wish the state to intervene in some direction, there will be almost as many views about how the government should act as there are different persons.

Democratic government worked successfully as long as, by a widely accepted creed, the functions of the state were limited to fields where real agreement among a majority could be achieved. The price we have to pay for a democratic system is the restriction of state action to those fields where agreement can be obtained; and it is the great merit of the liberal creed that it reduces the necessity of agreement to a minimum compatible with the diversity of individual opinions which will exist in a free society. It is often said that democracy will not tolerate capitalism. If 'capitalism' here means a competitive society based on free disposal over private property, it is far more important to observe that only capitalism makes

205

democracy possible. And if a democratic people comes under the sway of an anti-capitalistic creed, this means that democracy will inevitably destroy itself.

If democracy had to abdicate its control over economic life, this might still be regarded as a minor evil compared with the advantages expected from planning. Indeed, many of the advocates of planning fully realize—and have resigned themselves to the fact—that if planning is to be effective democracy, in so far as economic legislation is concerned, has to go by the board. Mr. Stuart Chase believes that he can reassure us that "political democracy can remain if it confines itself to all but economic matters".[19] It is, however, a fatal delusion to believe that authoritarian government can be confined to economic matters. The tragic fact is that authoritarian direction cannot be restricted to economic life, but is bound to expand and to become 'totalitarian' in the strictest sense of the word. The economic dictator will soon find himself forced, even against his wishes, to assume dictatorship over the whole of the political and cultural life of the people. We have already seen that the planner must not only translate the vague and general 'ends' that command popular approval into a concrete and detailed scale of values, but he must also, if he wants to act at all, make the people believe that the particular detailed code of value which he imposes is the right one. He is forced to create that singleness of purpose which—apart from national crises like war—is absent in a free society. Even more, if he is to be allowed to carry out the plan which he thinks the right one, he must retain the popular support—that is, he must at all costs appear successful.

It is in vain to blame the dictator who has been carried into power by the universal wish for consistent and energetic use of the powers of the state if he uses this power to make the people's wishes and ambitions fit into his plans. 'Rational' action is only possible in the service of a given system of ends, and if society as a whole is to act rationally it must be given such a common scale of values. The dictator will find at a very early stage that if he wants to carry out the will of the people he will have to tell them what to want. We need not go to authoritarian countries to find instances of this tendency. Not very long ago Mr. Henry A. Wallace found it necessary to warn the American people "that a steadfast national allegiance to any fixed course, international or intermediate, also requires a certain degree of regimented opinion".[20] What can we expect from a man who has to organize a nation for the execution of one gigantic plan if this

[19]Quoted by Walter Lippmann, "The Collectivist Movement in Practice", *Atlantic Monthly*, op. cit., p. 729. [See chapter 8, note 3, for more on Chase and Lippmann.—Ed.]

[20]Henry Wallace, *America Must Choose: The Advantages and Disadvantages of Nationalism, of World Trade, and of a Planned Middle Course* (New York and Boston: Foreign Policy Association; World Peace Foundation, 1934), quoted by Lawrence Sullivan, "Government by Mim-

is the lesson which a responsible statesman draws from the comparatively moderate experiments in planning made by the United States? If there is no activity and no human relation which is not regulated by the state, how can opinion about these things be left free?

The decision of the planner about the relative importance of conflicting aims is necessarily a decision about the relative merits of different groups and individuals. Planning necessarily becomes planning in favour of some and against others. This is in effect admitted by all the authoritarian governments when they insist upon the predominance of politics over economics; and it has been explicitly stated by one of the leading sociologists of present-day Germany. He writes:

> Planning means the highest degree of taking sides for and against the various forces and interests, a long-run commitment in favour of one side or the other. . . . The fact that planning means taking sides in the struggle of interests is only obscured by representing particular individual interests as the interest of the whole. . . .[21]

The problem here, of course, is not that the different people concerned have not the most decided opinions about the relative merits of their respective wishes; it is rather that these opinions are irreconcilable. But the ground on which the more or less arbitrary decision of the authority rests must seem to be just, it must appear to be based on some ultimate ideal in which everybody is supposed to believe.[22] The inevitable distinction between persons must be made a distinction of rank, most conveniently and naturally based on the degree to which people share and

---

eograph", *Atlantic Monthly*, March 1938, pp. 306–307. [As Secretary of Agriculture during the New Deal, Henry Agard Wallace (1888–1965) was the sponsor of the Agricultural Adjustment Act, which brought a price support system to American agriculture. He served as Vice President during President Franklin Roosevelt's third term.—Ed.]

[21]Hans Freyer, *Herrschaft und Planung*, op. cit., p. 19. [See chapter 8, note 4, for more on Freyer.—Ed.]

[22]This is the real function of the 'political myths' which the unwitting pupils of Sorel are so fertile in inventing. The myth of '*Blut und Boden*' is the basis of a whole system of agricultural policy and the myth of the 'corporative state' a most convenient cloak to impose a new hierarchical order upon society. [*Blut und Boden* (Blood and Soil), a term first introduced by the historian Oswald Spengler, was the doctrine that the state rightly consists of people of a uniform race on their own land. The Nazis used it to justify a number of changes in agricultural policy, including the seizure of the land of non-Germans and the institution of the Hereditary Farm Law, which was meant to preserve an exclusively German peasantry as a source of bloodlines for the German *Volk*. The French philosopher Georges Sorel (1847–1922) argued that political opposition must make use of violence; 'social myths' would need to be invoked in order to inspire collective action.—Ed.]

loyally support the creed of the ruler. And it further clarifies the position if to the aristocracy of creed on the one end of the scale there corresponds a class of outcasts on the other, whose interests can in all cases be sacrificed to those of the privileged classes.[23]

Conformity to the guiding ideas cannot, however, be regarded as a special merit—although those who excel by their devotion to the creed will be rewarded. It must be exacted from everybody. Every doubt cast upon the rightness of the ends sought or the means chosen is apt to diminish loyalty and enthusiasm, and must therefore be treated as sabotage. The creation and enforcement of the common creed and of the belief in the supreme wisdom of the ruler becomes an indispensable instrument for the success of the planned system. The ruthless use of all possible instruments of propaganda, and the suppression of every expression of dissent, are not accidental accompaniments of a centrally directed system—they are essential parts of it. Nor can moral coercion be confined to the acceptance of the ethical code underlying the whole plan. It is in the nature of things that many parts of this code, many parts of the scale of values underlying the plan, can never be explicitly stated. They exist only implicitly in the plan. But this means that every part of the plan, in fact every action of the government or its agencies, must become sacrosanct and exempt from criticism.

It is, however, only the public expression of criticism that can be forcibly suppressed. But doubts that are never uttered and hesitation that is never voiced have equally insidious effects if they dwell only in the minds of the people. Everything which might induce discontent must therefore be kept from them.[24] The basis for comparisons with conditions elsewhere, the knowledge of possible alternatives to the course taken, information which might suggest failure on the part of the government to live up to its promises or to take advantage of opportunities to improve the lot of the people, all these must be suppressed. There is consequently no field where the systematic control of information will not be practiced. That the government which claims to plan economic life soon asserts its

---

[23]The suffering of the racial or national minorities does not begin with the totalitarian regimes. How completely in the modern interventionist state the idea of equality before the law has lost its meaning could be easily shown by a discussion of the treatment of minorities in various democratic European states since the war. It has been amply demonstrated that it is possible to wage incessant economic warfare against a particular group and completely to destroy the basis of its economic life without in the least infringing the letter of the laws or treaties guaranteeing the rights of minorities.

[24]"Whilst the work is in progress, any public expression of doubt, or even of fear, that the plan will not be successful, is an act of disloyalty, and even of treachery, because of its possible effect on the wills and on the efforts of the rest of the staff" (Sidney and Beatrice Webb, *Soviet Communism*, op. cit., p. 1038).

totalitarian character is no accident—it can do nothing less if it wants to remain true to the intention of planning. Economic activity is not a sector of human life which can be separated from the rest; it is the administration of the means with which we seek to accomplish all our different ends. Whoever takes charge of these means must determine which ends shall be served, which values are to be rated higher and which lower—in short, what men should believe and strive for. And man himself becomes little more than a means for the realization of the ideas which may guide the dictator.

Perhaps it is not unnecessary to add here that this suppression of individual freedom is not so much the result of the transition from democracy to dictatorship as both are the result of the enormous expansion of the scope of government. While undoubtedly democracy is to some extent a safeguard of personal freedom, and while its decline is due to the very fact that it makes the suppression of freedom more difficult, our problem is not mainly one of constitutional change in the strictly political sense. There can be no doubt that in history there has often been much more cultural and political freedom under an autocratic rule than under some democracies—and it is at least conceivable that under the government of a very homogeneous and doctrinaire majority democratic government might be as oppressive as the worst dictatorship. The point is not that any dictatorship must inevitably eradicate freedom, but that planning leads to dictatorship because dictatorship is the most effective instrument of coercion and enforcement of ideals, and as such is essential to make central planning on a large scale possible. A true 'dictatorship of the proletariat', even if democratic in form, if it undertook to direct economic activity would probably destroy the last vestiges of personal freedom as completely as any autocracy.

VI

It is to be feared that to a great many of our contemporaries this picture, even if it should be recognized as true, has lost most of the terror which it would have inspired in our fathers. There have always been many, of course, to whom intellectual coercion was only objectionable if it was exercised by others, and who regarded it as beneficial if it was exercised for ends of which they approved. How many of the exiled intellectuals from the authoritarian countries would be only too ready to apply the intellectual coercion which they condemn in their opponents in order to make people believe in their own ideals—incidentally furnishing another illustration for the close kinship of the fundamental principles of fascism and communism? But, although the liberal age was probably freer from intellectual coercion than any other age, the desire to force upon people a creed which is regarded as salutary for them is certainly not a phenomenon that is new or peculiar to our time. What is new is the attempt on the part of our socialist intellectuals to justify it. There is no real freedom of thought, so it is said, because the opinions and the tastes of the masses are inevitably shaped by propaganda, by advertising, by the example of the upper classes, and by other environmental factors which relentlessly force the thinking of the people into well-worn grooves. But if, the argument proceeds, the ideals and tastes of the great majority are determined by factors which are under human control, we might as well use this power to turn their thoughts into what we think a desirable direction. That is, from the fact that the great majority have not learned to think independently but accept ideas which they find readymade, the conclusion is drawn that a particular group of people—of course those who advocate this—are justified in assuming for themselves the exclusive power to determine what people should believe.

It is not my intention to deny that for the great majority the existence or nonexistence of intellectual freedom makes little difference to their personal happiness; nor to deny that they will be equally happy if born or coaxed into one set of beliefs rather than another, and whether they have grown accustomed to one kind of amusement or another. It is probably only too true that in any society freedom of thought will be of direct significance or will exist in any real sense for only a small minority. But to deprecate the value of intellectual freedom because it will never give everybody the same opportunity of independent thought is completely to miss the reasons which give intellectual freedom its value. What is essential to make it serve its function as the prime mover of intellectual progress is not that everybody may think or write anything, but that any cause or any idea may be argued by somebody. So long as dissent is not actually suppressed, there will always be some who will query the ideas ruling their contemporaries and put new ideas to the test of argument and propaganda. The social process which we call human reason and which consists of the interaction of individuals, possessing different information and different views, sometimes consistent and sometimes conflicting, goes on. Once given the possibility of dissent, there will be dissenters, however small the proportion of people who are capable of independent thought. Only the imposition of an official doctrine which must be accepted and which nobody dares to question can stop intellectual progress.

Perhaps it must actually be seen and appreciated in one of the totalitarian countries to fathom how completely the imposition of a comprehensive authoritarian creed stifles all spirit of independent inquiry, how it destroys the sense for any meaning of truth other than that of conformity with the official doctrine, and how differences of opinion in every branch of knowledge become political issues to be decided by the intervention of authority. Experience indicates, however, that there are still many who are ready to sacrifice intellectual freedom because it does not mean the same opportunity for all. Surely they do not realize what is at stake. Indeed, the great danger comes from the fact that we take the inheritance of the liberal age for granted, and have come to regard it so confidently as the inalienable property of our civilization that we cannot fully conceive what it would mean if we lost it. Yet freedom and democracy are not free gifts which will remain with us if only we wish it. The time seems to have come when it is once again necessary to become fully conscious of the conditions which make them possible, and to defend these conditions—even if they should block the path to the achievement of competing ideals.

The danger which our generation faces is not merely that the process of experimentation—to which we owe all progress in the social sphere as elsewhere—should lead us into error. The danger is rather that by error we may bring the process of experimentation itself to an end. If the experiment of planning leads to the disappearance of free institutions, there will be no opportunity for the correction of that mistake. Once the only method of peaceful change yet invented, democracy (that admirable convention of 'counting heads in order to save the trouble of breaking them'), has gone, the way for a peaceful correction of an error once committed is blocked. Those in power, who owe not only their position but also—and more significantly—the opportunity to realize their ideals to this error, will not recognize it as such and will therefore not correct it; and nobody else will have a chance. With an altogether unwarranted optimism a recent writer predicted that, within a generation, the 'planners' and all their works will be swept away by a violent revulsion of feeling if the material stability they promise has to be bought at the price of intellectual and spiritual oppression.[25] It must appear highly doubtful, in view of the unprecedented power over the minds of the people which the modern techniques of propaganda give to the state, whether a reversal of intellectual tendencies through forces from inside the organized group will still be possible once the machinery for control has been firmly established. It is more likely that the struggle for the survival of ideas will then take the form of a war of ideologies between nations, which, even if it should lead to the survival of the most efficiently organized group, may well mean the destruction of everything which to us represents the greatness of humanity.

[25]D. Mitrany, in *Planned Society*, op. cit., p. 662.

TEN

PLANNING, SCIENCE, AND FREEDOM[1]

The last ten years have witnessed in Great Britain a strong revival of a movement that for at least three generations has been a decisive force in the formation of opinion and the trend of social affairs in Europe: the movement for 'economic planning'. As in other countries—first in France and then particularly in Germany—this movement has been strongly supported and even led by men of science and engineers. It has now so far succeeded in capturing public opinion that what little opposition there is comes almost solely from a small group of economists. To these economists this movement seems not only to propose unsuitable means for the ends at which it aims; it also appears to them as the main cause of that destruction of individual liberty and spiritual freedom which is the great threat of our age. If these economists are right, a large number of men of science are unwittingly striving to create a state of affairs which they have most reason to fear. It is the purpose of the following sketch to outline the argument on which that view is based.

Any brief discussion of 'economic planning' is handicapped by the necessity of first explaining what precisely is meant by 'planning'. If the term were taken in its most general sense of a rational design of human institutions, there could be no room for argument about its desirability. But although the popularity of 'planning' is at least partly due to this wider connotation of the word, it is now generally used in a narrower, more specific sense. It describes one only among the different principles which might be deliberately chosen for the organization of economic life: that of central direction of all economic effort as against its direction by competition. Planning, in other words, now means that not only the kind of economic system which we want to adopt should be rationally chosen, but that we should choose one that rests on 'conscious' or central control of all economic activity. It is evidently in this sense that, for example,

[1][F. A. Hayek, "Planning, Science, and Freedom", *Nature*, vol. 143, November 15, 1941, pp. 580–584. Reprinted by permission from *Nature*, ©1941, Macmillan Magazines Ltd.— Ed.]

Professor P. M. S. Blackett uses the term when he explains that "the object of planning is largely to overcome the results of competition".[2] This narrow use of the term is of course meant to suggest that only this kind of economic organization is rational, and that therefore it alone deserves to be called planning. It is this contention which economists deny.

The full argument which leads to the conclusion that planning in the sense of central direction is in fact an inefficient system cannot be reproduced in a few sentences. But the gist of it is simple enough. It is that the competitive or price system makes possible the utilization of an amount of concrete knowledge which could never be achieved or approached without it. It is true, of course, that the director of any centrally planned system is likely to know more than any single entrepreneur under competition. But the former could not possibly use in his single plan all the combined knowledge of all the individual entrepreneurs that is used under competition. The knowledge which is significant here is not so much knowledge of general laws, but knowledge of particular facts and the ever-changing circumstances of the moment—a knowledge which only the man on the spot can possess. The problem of the maximum utilization of knowledge can therefore be solved only by some system which decentralizes the decisions. There is no possibility of a division between the general outline of the plan and the detail of the execution—or at least no way for such a division has yet been shown. The reason for this is that the general features are just the result of an infinity of detail, and there are no principles which, without harm, can be laid down irrespective of the detail. Yet, in order that in a decentralized system the individual decisions should be mutually adjusted to each other, it is of course essential that the individual entrepreneur should learn as promptly as possible about any relevant change in the conditions affecting the factors of production and the commodities with which he is concerned. Now this is precisely what the price system brings about *if* competition is functioning. It is in effect a system under which every change in conditions and opportunities is promptly and automatically registered so that the individual entrepreneur can read off, as it were, from a few gauges and in simple figures, the relevant results of everything which happens anywhere in the system with respect to the factors and commodities with which he is concerned.

This method of solving by an automatic decentralization a task which, if it had to be solved consciously, would exceed the powers of any human mind, would have been hailed as one of the most marvellous inventions—if it has been invented deliberately. Compared with it the more obvious

---

[2] P. M. S. Blackett, "The Frustration of Science", in Sir Daniel Hall and others, *The Frustration of Science,* op. cit., p. 142. [See chapter 3, note 14 for more on Blackett.—Ed.]

method of solving the problem by central direction appears incredibly clumsy, primitive, and limited in scope. It is very significant that those socialist economists who have most carefully studied the practical problems of a socialist economy have more than once re-discovered competition and the price system as the best solution—only that unfortunately this system cannot work without private property.[3] For the general attitude towards the price system it has, however, been most unfortunate that it has not been deliberately invented, but that it has spontaneously grown up long before we had learnt to understand its operation. It seems to offend a deep instinct of the man of science and particularly the engineer to be asked to believe that anything which has not been deliberately constructed but is the result of a more or less accidental historical growth should be the best method for a human end. Yet the contention is of course not that by some miracle just that system has spontaneously developed which is best suited to modern civilization, but rather that the division of labour, which forms the basis of modern civilization, has been able to develop on a large scale only because man happened to stumble on the method which made this possible.

It is now sometimes argued—often by the same type of people who by their propaganda against competition have contributed largely towards its progressive suppression—that although all this is quite true, and although it would be desirable to have competition if it were still possible, technological facts prevent this, and that therefore central planning has become inevitable. This, however, is just one of the many myths which, like that of the 'potential plenty', are taken over by one propagandist work from another until they come to be regarded as established facts, although they have little relation to reality. There is no space here to discuss this point at any length, and it must suffice to quote the conclusion at which the most comprehensive recent investigation of the facts has arrived. This is what the final report of the investigation on the "Concentration of Economic Power", by the American Temporary National Economic Committee, has to say on the point: "It is sometimes asserted, or assumed, that large scale production, under the conditions of modern technology, is so much more efficient than small-scale production that competition must inevitably give way to monopoly as large establishments drive their smaller rivals from the field. But such generalization finds scant support in any evidence that is now at hand".[4] Indeed few people who have watched economic development during the last twenty years or

[3][H. D. Dickinson, *Economics of Socialism*, op. cit.; Oscar Lange and F. M. Taylor, *On the Economic Theory of Socialism*, op. cit.; F. A. Hayek, "Socialist Calculation: The Competitive 'Solution'", op. cit., reprinted as chapter 3 of this volume.—Ed.]

[4]Final Report of the Temporary National Economic Committee, United States of America, 77th Congress, 1st Session, Senate Document No. 35, p. 89.

so can have much doubt that the progressive tendency towards monopoly is not the result of any spontaneous or inevitable force, but the effect of a deliberate policy of the governments, inspired by the ideology of 'planning'. The really remarkable fact is the vitality of competition, which in spite of the persistent attempts towards its suppression is ever again raising its head—only to encounter new measures designed to stifle it.

It is a serious thing that in this situation men of science and engineers should so frequently be found leading a movement which in effect merely serves to support the unholy alliance between the monopolistic organizations of capital and labour, and that for a hundred men of science who attack competition and 'capitalism' scarcely one can be found who criticizes the restrictionist and protectionist policies which masquerade as 'planning' and which are the true cause of the 'frustration of science'. That this attitude should be so common among natural scientists can scarcely be fully explained by that characteristic bias for anything consciously constructed and against anything which has merely grown up, to which I have already alluded. It is at least as much due to the antagonism of so many natural scientists towards the teaching of economics, whose methods appear to them unfamiliar and strange, and whose results they often either disregard or, like Prof. L. Hogben, even violently attack as "the medieval rubbish taught as economics at our Universities".[5] This conflict over the methods proper to the pursuit of the study of society is an old one and raises exceedingly complex and difficult problems. But as the prestige which the natural scientists enjoy with the public is so often used to discredit the results of the only systematic and sustained effort to increase our understanding of social phenomena, this dispute is a matter of sufficient importance to make in this context a few words of comment necessary.

If there were reason to suspect that the economists persist in their ways merely from the force of habit and in ignorance of the methods and techniques which in other fields have proved so eminently successful, there could indeed be grave doubt about the validity of their arguments. The attempts to advance the social sciences by a more or less close imitation of the methods of the natural sciences, far from being new, have been a constant feature for more than a century. The same objections against 'deductive' economics, the same proposals to make it at last 'scientific', and it must be added, the same characteristic errors and primitive mistakes to which the natural scientists approaching this field seem to be prone, have been repeated and discussed over and over again by successive generations of economists and sociologists and have led precisely no-

---

[5]Lancelot Hogben, op. cit., p. 10. [See chapter 3, note 23 for more on Hogben.—Ed.]

216

where. All the progress in the understanding of the phenomena which has been achieved has come from the economists patiently developing the technique which has grown out of their peculiar problems. But in their efforts they have constantly been embarrassed by famous physicists or biologists pronouncing in the name of science in favour of schemes or proposals which do not deserve serious consideration. It was expressing a common experience of all students of social problems when an American sociologist recently complained that "one of the most terrible examples of unscientific mindedness is frequently an eminent natural, i.e., physical or biological, scientist speaking on societal matters".[6]

As the dispute on central planning has become so closely connected with the dispute on the scientific validity of economics, it has been necessary briefly to refer to these matters. But this must not draw us away from our main theme. The technical inferiority or superiority of central planning over competition is not the sole or even the main problem. If the degree of economic efficiency were all that is at stake in this controversy, the dangers of a mistake would still be small compared with what they really are. But just as the alleged greater efficiency of central planning is not the only argument used in its favour, so the objections do not rest solely on its real inefficiency. It must indeed be admitted that if we wanted to make the distribution of incomes between individuals and groups conform to any predetermined absolute standard, central planning would be the only way in which this could be achieved. It could be argued—and has been argued—that it would be worth putting up with less efficiency if thereby greater distributive justice could be obtained. But unfortunately the same factors which make it possible in such a system to control the distribution of income also make it necessary to impose an arbitrary hierarchical order comprising the status of every individual and the place of practically all values of human life. In short, as is now being more and more generally recognized, economic planning inevitably leads to, and is the cause of, the suppression of individual liberty and spiritual freedom which we know as the 'totalitarian' system. As has recently been said in *Nature* by two eminent American engineers, "the State founded on dictatorial authority. . .and the planned economy are essentially one and the same thing".[7]

---

[6]Read Bain, "Freedom, Law, and Rational Social Control", *Social Philosophy*, vol. 230, April 1939, p. 230. [The American sociologist Read Bain (1892–1979) taught principally at Miami University in Ohio.—Ed.]

[7]Frank B. Jewett and Robert King, "Engineering Progress and the Social Order", *Nature*, vol. 146, December 28, 1940, p. 826. [Electrical engineer Frank B. Jewett (1879–1949) was President of Bell Telephone Laboratories from 1925 to 1940 and Chairman of the Board from 1940 to 1944. Their article carries the following note: "Substance of an address deliv-

The reasons why the adoption of a system of central planning necessarily produces a totalitarian system are fairly simple. Whoever controls the means must decide which ends they are to serve. As under modern conditions control of economic activity means control of the material means for practically all our ends, it means control over nearly all our activities. The nature of the detailed scale of values which must guide the planning makes it impossible that it should be determined by anything like democratic means. The director of the planned system would have to impose his scale of values, his hierarchy of ends, which, if it is to be sufficient to determine the plan, must include a definite order of rank in which the status of each person is laid down. If the plan is to succeed or the planner to appear successful, the people must be made to believe that the objectives chosen are the right ones. Every criticism of the plan or the ideology underlying it must be treated as sabotage. There can be no freedom of thought, no freedom of the press, where it is necessary that everything should be governed by a single system of thought. In theory socialism may wish to enhance freedom, but in practice every kind of collectivism consistently carried through must produce the characteristic features which Fascism, Nazism, and Communism have in common. Totalitarianism is nothing but consistent collectivism, the ruthless execution of the principle that 'the whole comes before the individual' and the direction of all members of society by a single will supposed to represent the 'whole'.

It would need much more space than can be given to it here to show in detail how such a system produces a despotic control in every sphere of life, and how in particular in Germany two generations of planners have prepared the soil for Nazism. This has been demonstrated elsewhere.[8] Nor is it possible here to show why planning tends to produce intense nationalism and international conflict,[9] or why, as the editors of one of the most ambitious cooperative volumes on planning discovered to his sorrow, "most 'planners' are militant nationalists".[10] We must turn

---

ered September 18 before the Section on Natural Sciences of the University of Pennsylvania Bicentennial Conference".—Ed.]

[8]Walter Lippmann, *The Good Society*, op. cit.; M. Polanyi, *The Contempt of Freedom: The Russian Experiment and After*, op. cit.; Walter Sulzbach, "Tolerance and the Economic System", *Ethics*, vol. 50, April 1940, pp. 290–313; F. A. Hayek, "Freedom and the Economic System", op. cit., reprinted as chapter 9 of this volume. [See chapter 8, note 3 for more on Walter Lippmann. Michael Polanyi (1891–1976), born in Hungary, was from 1933 to 1948 a professor of physical chemistry at Manchester, then from 1948 to 1958 a professor of social studies there. His best known book is *Personal Knowledge* (Chicago: University of Chicago Press, 1958). Walter Sulzbach (1888–) taught in the United States and was author of *Capitalist Warmongers: A Modern Superstition* (Chicago: University of Chicago Press, 1942), Public Policy Pamphlet No. 35 in the series edited by Harry D. Gideonse.—Ed.]

[9]Lionel Robbins, *Economic Planning and International Order*, op. cit.

[10]Findlay MacKensie, ed., *Planned Society*, op. cit., p. xx.

218

here to a more immediate danger which the present trend in Great Britain creates. It is that of a growing divergence between the economic systems here and in the United States which threatens to make impossible any real economic collaboration between the two countries after the war. In the United States the present development is well described by the programme for restoring competition developed by President Roosevelt in the message to Congress of April 1938, which, in the President's words, is based on the thesis "not that the system of free private enterprise for profit has failed in this generation, but that it has not yet been tried".[11] Of Great Britain, on the other hand, it could be rightly said about the same time that "there are many signs that British leaders are growing accustomed to thinking in terms of national development by controlled monopolies".[12] This means that we are following the paths on which Germany has led and which the United States is abandoning because, as states the report on the "Concentration of Economic Power" to which the President's message gave rise, "the rise of political centralism is largely the result of economic centralism".[13] The alternative is, of course, not laissez faire, as this misleading and vague term is usually understood. Much needs to be done to ensure the effectiveness of competition; and a great deal can be done *outside* the market to supplement the results. But by the attempts to supplant it we deprive ourselves not only of an instrument which we cannot replace, but also of an institution without which there can be no freedom for the individual.

Nothing in this situation deserves to be studied and pondered so much as the intellectual history of Germany during the last two generations. What has to be realized is that the features which made her what she is are largely the same as those which made her admired and which still exert their fascination; and that the corruption of the German mind came largely from the top, the intellectual and scientific leaders. Men, undoubtedly great in their way, made Germany an artificially constructed State—'organized through and through', as the Germans prided themselves. This provided the soil in which Nazism grew and in which representatives of State-organized science were found among its most enthusiastic supporters. It was the 'scientific' organization of industry which deliberately created the giant monopolies and represented them as inevitable growths fifty years before it happened in Great Britain. The very type of social doctrine which is now so popular among some British men of science began to be preached by their German counterparts in the seventies and eighties of the last century. The subservience of the men of

[11]Final Report of the Temporary National Economic Committee, op. cit., p. 20.

[12]"The Government as Business Partner", unsigned editorial, *The Spectator,* March 3, 1939, p. 337.

[13]Final Report of the Temporary National Economic Committee, op. cit., p. 5.

science to whatever became official doctrine began with the great development of State-organized science which is the subject of so much eulogy in Great Britain. It was the State in which everyone tended to become a State employee and in which all pursuits for profit were held in contempt which produced the disregard and final destruction of liberty which we now witness.

I shall conclude with an illustration of what I have said about the role of some of the great men of science of Imperial Germany. The famous physiologist Emil du Bois-Reymond was one of the leaders of the movement anxious to extend the methods of natural sciences to social phenomena and one of the first and most effective advocates of the now so fashionable view that "the history of natural science is the real history of mankind".[14] It was also he who uttered what is perhaps the most shameful statement ever made by a man of science on behalf of his fellows. "We, the University of Berlin," he proclaimed in 1870 in a public oration as rector of the university, "quartered opposite the King's palace, are, by the deed of our foundation, the intellectual bodyguard of the house of Hohenzollern".[15] The allegiance of the German scientist-politicians has since changed, but their respect for freedom has not increased. And the phenomenon is not confined to Germany. Has not Mr. J. G. Crowther recently, in a book which develops views so similar to du Bois-Reymond's, undertaken to defend even inquisition because, in his view, it "is beneficial to science when it protects a rising class"?[16] On this view clearly all the persecutions of men of science by the Nazis after they came to power could be justified—for were not the latter then a "rising class"?

[14]Emil du Bois-Reymond, *Kulturgeschichte und Naturwissenschaft* (Leipzig: Verlag von Veit, 1878). [The German physiologist Emil du Bois-Reymond (1818–1896) was a student of Johannes Müller's and succeeded to Müller's chair at the University of Berlin.—Ed.]

[15]Emil du Bois-Reymond, *A Speech on the German War* (London: Richard Bentley, 1870), p. 31. [The speech was delivered on August 3, 1870, before the University of Berlin, where du Bois-Reymond was at that time Rector.—Ed.]

[16]J. G. Crowther, *The Social Relations of Science*, op. cit., p. 333. [British journalist and author James Gerald Crowther (1899–) was the science correspondent for the *Manchester Guardian* from 1928 to 1948 and a prolific popular science author.—Ed.]

ELEVEN

THE INTELLECTUALS AND SOCIALISM[1]

I

In all democratic countries, in the United States even more than elsewhere, a strong belief prevails that the influence of the intellectuals on politics is negligible. This is no doubt true of the power of intellectuals to make their peculiar opinions of the moment influence decisions, of the extent to which they can sway the popular vote on questions on which they differ from the current views of the masses. Yet over somewhat longer periods they have probably never exercised so great an influence as they do today in those countries. This power they wield by shaping public opinion.

In the light of recent history it is somewhat curious that this decisive power of the professional secondhand dealers in ideas should not yet be more generally recognized. The political development of the Western World during the last hundred years furnishes the clearest demonstration. Socialism has never and nowhere been at first a working class movement. It is by no means an obvious remedy for an obvious evil which the interests of that class will necessarily demand. It is a construction of theorists, deriving from certain tendencies of abstract thought with which for a long time only the intellectuals were familiar; and it required long efforts by the intellectuals before the working classes could be persuaded to adopt it as their program.

In every country that has moved towards socialism the phase of the development in which socialism becomes a determining influence on politics has been preceded for many years by a period during which socialist ideals governed the thinking of the more active intellectuals. In Germany this stage had been reached towards the end of the last century; in England and France, about the time of the first World War. To the casual observer it would seem as if the United States had reached this phase after World War II and that the attraction of a planned and directed economic system is now as strong among the American intellectuals as it

---

[1][F. A. Hayek, "The Intellectuals and Socialism", *University of Chicago Law Review*, vol. 16, Spring 1949, pp. 417–433.—Ed.]

ever was among their German or English fellows. Experience suggests that once this phase has been reached it is merely a question of time until the views now held by the intellectuals become the governing force of politics.

The character of the process by which the views of the intellectuals influence the politics of tomorrow is therefore of much more than academic interest. Whether we merely wish to foresee or attempt to influence the course of events, it is a factor of much greater importance than is generally understood. What to the contemporary observer appears as the battle of conflicting interests has indeed often been decided long before in a clash of ideas confined to narrow circles. Paradoxically enough, however, in general only the parties of the left have done most to spread the belief that it was the numerical strength of the opposing material interests which decided political issues, whereas in practice these same parties have regularly and successfully acted as if they understood the key position of the intellectuals. Whether by design or driven by the force of circumstances, they have always directed their main effort towards gaining the support of this 'elite', while the more conservative groups have acted, as regularly but unsuccessfully, on a more naive view of mass democracy and have usually vainly tried directly to reach and to persuade the individual voter.

II

The term intellectuals, however, does not at once convey a true picture of the large class to which we refer, and the fact that we have no better name by which to describe what we have called the 'secondhand dealers in ideas' is not the least of the reasons why their power is not better understood. Even persons who use the word 'intellectual' mainly as a term of abuse are still inclined to withhold it from many who undoubtedly perform that characteristic function. This is neither that of the original thinker nor that of the scholar or expert in a particular field of thought. The typical intellectual need be neither: He need not possess special knowledge of anything in particular, nor need he even be particularly intelligent, to perform his role as intermediary in the spreading of ideas. What qualifies him for his job is the wide range of subjects on which he can readily talk and write, and a position or habits through which he becomes acquainted with new ideas sooner than those to whom he addresses himself.

Until one begins to list all the professions and activities which belong to this class, it is difficult to realize how numerous it is, how the scope for its activities constantly increases in modern society, and how dependent on it we all have become. The class does not consist only of journalists, teachers, ministers, lecturers, publicists, radio commentators, writers of fiction, cartoonists, and artists—all of whom may be masters of the technique of conveying ideas but are usually amateurs so far as the substance of what they convey is concerned. The class also includes many professional men and technicians, such as scientists and doctors, who through their habitual intercourse with the printed word become carriers of new ideas outside their own fields and who, because of their expert knowledge on their own subjects, are listened to with respect on most others. There is little that the ordinary man of today learns about events or ideas except through the medium of this class; and outside our special fields of work we are in this respect almost all ordinary men, dependent for our information and instruction on those who make it their job to keep abreast of opinion. It is the intellectuals in this sense who decide what views and opinions are to reach us, which facts are important enough to be told to us and in what form and from what angle they are to be presented. Whether we shall ever learn of the results of the work of the expert and the original thinker depends mainly on their decision.

The layman, perhaps, is not fully aware to what extent even the popular reputations of scientists and scholars are made by that class and are inevitably affected by its views on subjects which have little to do with the merits of the real achievements. And it is specially significant for our problem that every scholar can probably name several instances from his field of men who have undeservedly achieved a popular reputation as great scientists solely because they hold what the intellectuals regard as 'progressive' political views; but I have yet to come across a single instance where such a scientific pseudo-reputation has been bestowed for political reason on a scholar of more conservative leanings. This creation of reputations by the intellectuals is particularly important in the fields where the results of expert studies are not used by other specialists but depend on the political decision of the public at large. There is indeed scarcely a better illustration of this than the attitude which professional economists have taken to the growth of such doctrines as socialism or protectionism. There was probably at no time a majority of economists, who were recognized as such by their peers, favourable to socialism (or, for that matter, to protection). In all probability it is even true to say that no other similar group of students contains so high a proportion of its members decidedly opposed to socialism (or protection). This is the more significant as in recent times it is as likely as not that it was an early interest in socialist schemes for reform which led a man to choose economics for his profession. Yet it is not the predominant views of the experts but the views of a minority, mostly of rather doubtful standing in their profession, which are taken up and spread by the intellectuals.

The all-pervasive influence of the intellectuals in contemporary society is still further strengthened by the growing importance of 'organization'. It is a common but probably mistaken belief that the increase of organization increases the influence of the expert or specialist. This may be true of the expert administrator and organizer, if there are such people, but hardly of the expert in any particular field of knowledge. It is rather the person whose general knowledge is supposed to qualify him to appreciate expert testimony, and to judge between the experts from different fields, whose power is enhanced. The point which is important for us, however, is that the scholar who becomes a university president, the scientist who takes charge of an institute or foundation, the scholar who becomes an editor or the active promoter of an organization serving a particular cause, all rapidly cease to be scholars or experts and become intellectuals in our sense, people who judge all issues not by their specific merits but, in the characteristic manner of intellectuals, solely in the light of certain fashionable general ideas. The number of such institutions which breed intellectuals and increase their number and powers grows every day. Almost all the 'experts' in the mere technique of getting knowledge over are, with respect to the subject matter which they handle, intellectuals and not experts.

In the sense in which we are using the term, the intellectuals are in fact a fairly new phenomenon of history. Though nobody will regret that education has ceased to be a privilege of the propertied classes, the fact that the propertied classes are no longer the best educated, and the fact that the large number of people who owe their position solely to their general education do not possess that experience of the working of the economic system which the administration of property gives are important to understanding the role of the intellectual. Professor Schumpeter, who has devoted an illuminating chapter of his *Capitalism, Socialism and Democracy* to some aspects of our problem,[2] has not unfairly stressed that it is the absence of direct responsibility for practical affairs and the consequent absence of firsthand knowledge of them which distinguishes the typical intellectual from other people who also wield the power of the spoken and written word. It would lead too far, however, to examine here further the development of this class and the curious claim which has

---

[2][Joseph Schumpeter, *Capitalism, Socialism and Democracy* (New York: Harper and Row, 1942; 3rd ed., 1950). Hayek is probably referring to the section of Schumpeter's book entitled "The Sociology of the Intellectual", pp. 145–155. See F. A. Hayek, *The Fortunes of Liberalism*, op. cit., chapter 5, for Hayek's views on Schumpeter.—Ed.]

recently been advanced by one of its theorists that it was the only one whose views were not decidedly influenced by its own economic interests. One of the important points that would have to be examined in such a discussion would be how far the growth of this class has been artificially stimulated by the law of copyright.[3]

III

It is not surprising that the real scholar or expert and the practical man of affairs often feel contemptuous about the intellectual, are disinclined to recognize his power, and are resentful when they discover it. Individually they find the intellectuals mostly to be people who understand nothing in particular especially well, and whose judgement on matters they themselves understand shows little sign of special wisdom. But it would be a fatal mistake to underestimate their power for this reason. Even though their knowledge may be often superficial and their intelligence limited, this does not alter the fact that it is their judgement which mainly determines the views on which society will act in the not too distant future. It is no exaggeration to say that once the more active part of the intellectuals have been converted to a set of beliefs, the process by which these become generally accepted is almost automatic and irresistible. They are the organs which modern society has developed for spreading knowledge and ideas, and it is their convictions and opinions which operate as the sieve through which all new conceptions must pass before they can reach the masses.

It is of the nature of the intellectual's job that he must use his own knowledge and convictions in performing his daily task. He occupies his position because he possesses, or has had to deal from day to day with, knowledge which his employer in general does not possess, and his activities can therefore be directed by others only to a limited extent. And just because the intellectuals are mostly intellectually honest it is inevitable that they should follow their own convictions whenever they have discretion and that they should give a corresponding slant to everything that passes through their hands. Even where the direction of policy is in the hand of men of affairs of different views, the execution of policy will in general be in the hand of intellectuals, and it is frequently the decision on the detail which determines the net effect. We find this illustrated in

---

[3]It would be interesting to discover how far a seriously critical view of the benefits to society of the law of copyright or the expression of doubts about the public interest in the existence of a class which makes its living from the writing of books would have a chance of being publicly stated in a society in which the channels of expression are so largely controlled by people who have a vested interest in the existing situation.

almost all fields of contemporary society. Newspapers in 'capitalist' own-ership, universities presided over by 'reactionary' governing bodies, broadcasting systems owned by conservative governments have all been known to influence public opinion in the direction of socialism, because this was the conviction of the personnel. This has often happened not only in spite of but perhaps even because of the attempts of those at the top to control opinion and to impose principles of orthodoxy.

The effect of this filtering of ideas through the convictions of a class which is constitutionally disposed to certain views is by no means con-fined to the masses. Outside his special field the expert is generally no less dependent on this class and scarcely less influenced by their selection. The result of this is that today in most parts of the Western world even the most determined opponents of socialism derive from socialist sources their knowledge on most subjects on which they have no firsthand in-formation. With many of the more general preconceptions of socialist thought the connection of their more practical proposals is by no means at once obvious, and in consequence many men who believe themselves to be determined opponents of that system of thought become in fact effective spreaders of its ideas. Who does not know the practical man who in his own field denounces socialism as 'pernicious rot' but when he steps outside his subject spouts socialism like any left journalist?

In no other field has the predominant influence of the socialist intellec-tuals been felt more strongly during the last hundred years than in the contacts between different national civilizations. It would go far beyond the limits of this article to trace the causes and significance of the highly important fact that in the modern world the intellectuals provide almost the only approach to an international community. It is this which mainly accounts for the extraordinary spectacle that for generations the suppos-edly 'capitalist' West has been lending its moral and material support almost exclusively to those ideological movements in the countries farther east which aimed at undermining Western civilization; and that at the same time the information which the Western public has obtained about events in Central and Eastern Europe has almost inevitably been col-oured by a socialist bias. Many of the 'educational' activities of the Ameri-can forces of occupation in Germany have furnished clear and recent examples of this tendency.

IV

A proper understanding of the reasons which tend to incline so many of the intellectuals towards socialism is thus most important. The first point here which those who do not share this bias ought to face frankly is that it is neither selfish interests nor evil intentions but mostly honest convictions and good intentions which determine the intellectuals' views. In fact, it is necessary to recognize that on the whole the typical intellectual is today more likely to be a socialist the more he is guided by good will and intelligence and that on the plane of purely intellectual argument he will generally be able to make out a better case than the majority of his opponents within his class. If we still think him wrong we must recognize that it may be genuine error which leads the well-meaning and intelligent people who occupy those key positions in our society to spread views which to us appear a threat to our civilization.[4] Nothing could be more important than to try and understand the sources of this error in order that we should be able to counter it. Yet those who are generally regarded as the representatives of the existing order and who believe that they comprehend the dangers of socialism are usually very far from such understanding. They tend to regard the socialist intellectuals as nothing more than a pernicious bunch of highbrow radicals without appreciating their influence, and, by their whole attitude to them, tend to drive them even further into opposition to the existing order.

If we are to understand this peculiar bias of a large section of the intellectuals we must be clear about two points. The first is that they generally judge all particular issues exclusively in the light of certain general ideas; the second that the characteristic errors of any age are frequently derived from some genuine new truths it has discovered, and they are erroneous applications of new generalizations which have proved their value in other fields. The conclusion to which we shall be led by a full consideration of these facts will be that the effective refutation of such errors will frequently require further intellectual advance, and often advance on points which are very abstract and may seem very remote from the practical issues.

It is perhaps the most characteristic feature of the intellectual that he judges new ideas not by their specific merits but by the readiness with which they fit into his general conceptions, into the picture of the world which he regards as modern or advanced. It is through their influence on him and on his choice of opinions on particular issues that the power of ideas for good and evil grows in proportion with their generality, abstractness, and even vagueness. As he knows little about the particular issues, his criterion must be consistency with his other views, suitability

---

[4]It was therefore not (as has been suggested by one reviewer of *The Road to Serfdom*, Professor J. Schumpeter), "politeness to a fault" but profound conviction of the importance of this which made me, in Professor Schumpeter's words, "hardly ever attribute to opponents anything beyond intellectual error". [Schumpeter's review appeared in the *Journal of Political Economy*, vol. 54, June 1946, pp. 269–270.—Ed.]

to combine them into a coherent picture of the world. Yet this selection from the multitude of new ideas presenting themselves at every moment creates the characteristic climate of opinion, the dominant *Weltanschauung* of a period which will be favourable to the reception of some opinions and unfavourable to others, and which will make the intellectual readily accept one conclusion and reject another without a real understanding of the issues.

In some respects the intellectual is indeed closer to the philosopher than to any specialist, and the philosopher is in more than one sense a sort of prince among the intellectuals. Although his influence is farther removed from practical affairs and correspondingly slower and more difficult to trace than that of the ordinary intellectual, it is of the same kind and in the long run even more powerful than that of the latter. It is the same endeavour towards a synthesis, pursued more methodically, the same judgement of particular views in so far as they fit into a general system of thought rather than by their specific merits, the same striving after a consistent world view, which for both forms the main basis for accepting or rejecting ideas. For this reason the philosopher has probably a greater influence over the intellectuals than any other scholar or scientist, and more than anyone else determines the manner in which the intellectuals exercise their censorship function. The popular influence of the scientific specialist begins to rival that of the philosopher only when he ceases to be a specialist and commences to philosophize about the progress of his subject—and usually only after he has been taken up by the intellectuals for reasons which have little to do with his scientific eminence.

The "climate of opinion" of any period is thus essentially a set of very general preconceptions by which the intellectual judges the importance of new facts and opinions. These preconceptions are mainly applications to what seem to him the most significant aspects of scientific achievements, a transfer to other fields of what has particularly impressed him in the work of the specialists. One could give a long list of such intellectual fashions and catchwords which in the course of two or three generations have in turn dominated the thinking of the intellectuals. Whether it was the "historical approach" or the theory of evolution, nineteenth-century determinism and the belief in the predominant influence of environment as against heredity, the theory of relativity or the belief in the power of the unconscious—every one of these general conceptions has been made the touchstone by which innovations in different fields have been tested. It seems as if the less specific or precise (or the less understood) these ideas are, the wider may be their influence. Sometimes it is no more than a vague impression rarely put into words which thus wields a profound

influence. Such beliefs as that deliberate control or conscious organization is also in social affairs always superior to the results of spontaneous
processes which are not directed by a human mind, or that any order
based on a plan laid down beforehand must be better than one formed
by the balancing of opposing forces, have in this way profoundly affected
political development.

Only apparently different is the role of the intellectuals where the development of more properly social ideals is concerned. Here their peculiar propensities manifest themselves in making shibboleths of abstractions, in rationalizing and carrying to extremes certain ambitions which
spring from the normal intercourse of men. Since democracy is a good
thing, the further the democratic principle can be carried, the better it
appears to them. The most powerful of these general ideas which have
shaped political development in recent times is of course the ideal of material equality. It is, characteristically, not one of the spontaneously grown
moral convictions, first applied in the relations between particular individuals, but an intellectual construction originally conceived in the abstract and of doubtful meaning or application in particular instances.
Nevertheless, it has operated strongly as a principle of selection among
the alternative courses of social policy, exercising a persistent pressure
towards an arrangement of social affairs which nobody clearly conceives.
That a particular measure tends to bring about greater equality has come
to be regarded as so strong a recommendation that little else will be considered. Since on each particular issue it is this one aspect on which those
who guide opinion have a definite conviction, equality has determined
social change even more strongly than its advocates intended.

Not only moral ideals act in this manner, however. Sometimes the atti-
tudes of the intellectuals towards the problems of social order may be the
consequence of advances in purely scientific knowledge and it is in these
instances that their erroneous views on particular issues may for a time
seem to have all the prestige of the latest scientific achievements behind
them. It is not in itself surprising that a genuine advance of knowledge
should in this manner become on occasion a source of new error. If no
false conclusions followed from new generalizations they would be final
truths which would never need revision. Although as a rule such a new
generalization will merely share the false consequences which can be
drawn from it with the views which were held before, and thus not lead
to *new* error, it is quite likely that a new theory, just as its value is shown
by the valid new conclusions to which it leads, will produce other new
conclusions which further advance will show to have been erroneous. But
in such an instance a false belief will appear with all the prestige of the
latest scientific knowledge supporting it. Although in the particular field

to which this belief applies all the scientific evidence may be against it, it will nevertheless, before the tribunal of the intellectuals and in the light of the ideas which govern their thinking, be selected as the view which is best in accord with the spirit of the time. The specialists who will thus achieve public fame and wide influence will thus not be those who have gained recognition by their peers but will often be men whom the other experts regard as cranks, amateurs, or even frauds, but who in the eyes of the general public nevertheless become the best known exponents of their subject.

In particular, there can be little doubt that the manner in which during the last hundred years man has learned to organize the forces of nature has contributed a great deal towards the creation of the belief that a similar control of the forces of society would bring comparable improvements in human conditions. That, with the application of engineering techniques, the direction of all forms of human activity according to a single coherent plan, should prove to be as successful in society as it has been in innumerable engineering tasks is too plausible a conclusion not to seduce most of those who are elated by the achievement of the natural sciences. It must indeed be admitted both that it would require powerful arguments to counter the strong presumption in favour of such a conclusion and that these arguments have not yet been adequately stated. It is not sufficient to point out the defects of particular proposals based on this kind of reasoning. The argument will not lose its force until it has been conclusively shown why what has proved so eminently successful in producing advances in so many fields should have limits to its usefulness and become positively harmful if extended beyond these limits. This is a task which has not yet been satisfactorily performed and which will have to be achieved before this particular impulse towards socialism can be removed.

This, of course, is only one of the many instances where further intellectual advance is needed if the harmful ideas at present current are to be refuted, and where the course which we shall travel will ultimately be decided by the discussion of very abstract issues. It is not enough for the man of affairs to be sure, from his intimate knowledge of a particular field, that the theories of socialism which are derived from more general ideas will prove impracticable. He may be perfectly right, and yet his resistance will be overwhelmed and all the sorry consequences which he foresees will follow if he is not supported by an effective refutation of the *idées mères*. So long as the intellectual gets the better of the general argument, the most valid objections of the specific issue will be brushed aside.

V

This is not the whole story, however. The forces which influence recruitment to the ranks of the intellectuals operate in the same direction and help to explain why so many of the most able among them lean towards socialism. There are of course as many differences of opinion among intellectuals as among other groups of people; but it seems to be true that it is on the whole the more active, intelligent, and original men among the intellectuals who most frequently incline towards socialism, while its opponents are often of an inferior caliber. This is true particularly during the early stages of the infiltration of socialist ideas; later, although outside intellectual circles it may still be an act of courage to profess socialist convictions, the pressure of opinion among intellectuals will often be so strongly in favour of socialism that it requires more strength and independence for a man to resist it than to join in what his fellows regard as modern views. Nobody, for instance, who is familiar with large numbers of university faculties (and from this point of view the majority of university teachers probably have to be classed as intellectuals rather than as experts) can remain oblivious to the fact that the most brilliant and successful teachers are today more likely than not to be socialists, while those who hold more conservative political views are as frequently mediocrities. This is of course by itself an important factor leading the younger generation into the socialist camp.

The socialist will, of course, see in this merely a proof that the more intelligent person is today bound to become a socialist. But this is far from being the necessary or even the most likely explanation. The main reason for this state of affairs is probably that, for the exceptionally able man who accepts the present order of society, a multitude of other avenues to influence and power are open, while to the disaffected and dissatisfied an intellectual career is the most promising path to both influence and the power to contribute to the achievement of his ideals. Even more than that: The more conservatively inclined man of first-class ability will in general choose intellectual work (and the sacrifice in material reward which this choice usually entails) only if he enjoys it for its own sake. He is in consequence more likely to become an expert scholar rather than an intellectual in the specific sense of the word; while to the more radically minded the intellectual pursuit is more often than not a means rather than an end, a path to exactly that kind of wide influence which the professional intellectual exercises. It is therefore probably the fact, not that the more intelligent people are generally socialists, but that a much higher proportion of socialists among the best minds devote themselves to those intellectual pursuits which in modern society give them a decisive influence on public opinion.[5]

The selection of the personnel of the intellectuals is also closely connected with the predominant interest which they show in general and abstract ideas. Speculations about the possible entire reconstruction of society give the intellectual a fare much more to his taste than the more practical and short-run considerations of those who aim at a piecemeal improvement of the existing order. In particular, socialist thought owes its appeal to the young largely to its visionary character; the very courage to indulge in Utopian thought is in this respect a source of strength to the socialists which traditional liberalism sadly lacks. This difference operates in favour of socialism, not only because speculation about general principles provides an opportunity for the play of the imagination of those who are unencumbered by much knowledge of the facts of present-day life, but also because it satisfies a legitimate desire for the understanding of the rational basis of any social order and gives scope for the exercise of that constructive urge for which liberalism, after it had won its great victories, left few outlets. The intellectual, by his whole disposition, is uninterested in technical details or practical difficulties. What appeal to him are the broad visions, the specious comprehension of the social order as a whole which a planned system promises.

This fact that the tastes of the intellectual were better satisfied by the speculations of the socialists proved fatal to the influence of the liberal tradition. Once the basic demands of the liberal programs seemed satisfied, the liberal thinkers turned to problems of detail and tended to neglect the development of the general philosophy of liberalism, which in consequence ceased to be a live issue offering scope for general speculation. Thus for something over half a century it has been only the socialists who have offered anything like an explicit program of social development, a picture of the future society at which they were aiming, and a set of general principles to guide decisions on particular issues. Even though, if I am right, their ideals suffer from inherent contradictions, and any attempt to put them into practice must produce something ut-

[5]Related to this is another familiar phenomenon: There is little reason to believe that really first class intellectual ability for original work is any rarer among Gentiles than among Jews. Yet there can be little doubt that men of Jewish stock almost everywhere constitute a disproportionately large number of the intellectuals in our sense, that is of the ranks of the professional interpreters of ideas. This may be their special gift and certainly is their main opportunity in countries where prejudice puts obstacles in their way in other fields. It is probably more because they constitute so large a proportion of the intellectuals than for any other reason that they seem to be so much more receptive of socialist ideas than people of different stocks.

terly different from what they expect, this does not alter the fact that their program for change is the only one which has actually influenced the development of social institutions. It is because theirs has become the only explicit general philosophy of social policy held by a large group, the only system or theory which raises new problems and opens new horizons, that they have succeeded in inspiring the imagination of the intellectuals.

The actual developments of society during this period were determined, not by a battle of conflicting ideals, but by the contrast between an existing state of affairs and that one ideal of a possible future society which the socialists alone held up before the public. Very few of the other programs which offered themselves provided genuine alternatives. Most of them were mere compromises or halfway houses between the more extreme types of socialism and the existing order. All that was needed to make almost any socialist proposal appear reasonable to these 'judicious' minds which were constitutionally convinced that the truth must always lie in the middle between the extremes was for someone to advocate a sufficiently more extreme proposal. There seemed to exist only one direction in which we could move and the only question seemed to be how fast and how far the movement should proceed.

VI

The significance of the special appeal to the intellectuals which socialism derives from its speculative character will become clearer if we further contrast the position of the socialist theorist with that of his counterpart who is a liberal in the old sense of the word. This comparison will also lead us to whatever lesson we can draw from an adequate appreciation of the intellectual forces which are undermining the foundations of a free society.

Paradoxically enough, one of the main handicaps which deprives the liberal thinker of popular influence is closely connected with the fact that until socialism has actually arrived he has more opportunity of directly influencing decisions on current policy and that in consequence he is not only not tempted into that long-run speculation which is the strength of the socialists, but actually discouraged from it, because any effort of this kind is likely to reduce the immediate good he can do. Whatever power he has to influence practical decisions he owes to his standing with the representatives of the existing order, and this standing he would endanger if he devoted himself to the kind of speculation which would appeal to the intellectuals and which through them could influence developments over longer periods. In order to carry weight with the powers that be he has to be 'practical', 'sensible', and 'realistic'. So long as he concerns himself with immediate issues he is rewarded with influence, material success, and popularity with those who up to a point share his general outlook. But these men have little respect for those speculations on general principles which shape the intellectual climate. Indeed, if he seriously indulges in such long-run speculation he is apt to acquire the reputation of being 'unsound' or even half a socialist, because he is unwilling to identify the existing order with the free system at which he aims.[6]

If, in spite of this, his efforts continue in the direction of general speculation, he soon discovers that it is unsafe to associate too closely with those who seem to share most of his convictions and he is soon driven into isolation. Indeed there can be few more thankless tasks at present than the essential one of developing the philosophical foundation on which the further development of a free society must be based. Since the man who undertakes it must accept much of the framework of the existing order, he will appear to many of the more speculatively minded intellectuals merely as a timid apologist of things as they are; at the same time he will be dismissed by the men of affairs as an impractical theorist. He is not radical enough for those who know only the world where "with ease together dwell the thoughts" and much too radical for those who see only how "hard in space together clash the things". If he takes advantage of such support as he can get from the men of affairs, he will almost certainly discredit himself with those on whom he depends for the spreading of his ideas. At the same time he will need most carefully to avoid anything resembling extravagance or overstatement. While no socialist theorist has ever been known to discredit himself with his fellows even by the silliest of proposals, the old-fashioned liberal will damn himself by an impracticable suggestion. Yet for the intellectuals he will still not be speculative or adventurous enough and the changes and improvements in the social structure he will have to offer will seem limited in comparison with what their less restrained imagination conceives.

---

[6]The most glaring recent example of such condemnation of a somewhat unorthodox liberal work as 'socialist' has been provided by some comments on the late Henry Simons's *Economic Policy for a Free Society* (Chicago: University of Chicago Press, 1948). One need not agree with the whole of this work and one may even regard some of the suggestions made in it as incompatible with a free society, and yet recognize it as one of the most important contributions made in recent times to our problem and as just the kind of work which is required to get discussion started on the fundamental issues. Even those who violently disagree with some of its suggestions should welcome it as a contribution which clearly and courageously raises the central problems of our time. [The book is a collection of essays by Henry C. Simons (1899–1946), Professor of Economics at the University of Chicago, who argued that government should provide a framework in which "effective" competition could exist (this included a recommendation for state ownership of utilities and railroads) and in which monetary disturbances would be minimized by the "ultimate establishment of a simple, mechanical rule of monetary policy" (p. 170).—Ed.]

At least in a society in which the main requisites of freedom have already been won and further improvements must concern points of comparative detail, the liberal program can have none of the glamour of a new invention. The appreciation of the improvements it has to offer requires more knowledge of the working of the existing society than the average intellectual possesses. The discussion of these improvements must proceed on a more practical level than that of the more revolutionary programs, thus giving a complexion which has little appeal for the intellectual and tending to bring in elements to whom he feels directly antagonistic. Those who are most familiar with the working of the present society are also usually interested in the preservation of particular features of that society which may not be defensible on general principles. Unlike the person who looks for an entirely new future order and who naturally turns for guidance to the theorist, the men who believe in the existing order also usually think that they understand it much better than any theorist and in consequence are likely to reject whatever is unfamiliar and theoretical.

The difficulty of finding genuine and disinterested support for a systematic policy for freedom is not new. In a passage of which the reception of a recent book of mine[7] has often reminded me, Lord Acton long ago described how "[a]t all times sincere friends of freedom have been rare, and its triumphs have been due to minorities, that have prevailed by associating themselves with auxiliaries whose objects differed from their own; and this association, which is always dangerous, has been sometimes disastrous, by giving to opponents just grounds of opposition . . . ".[8] More recently, one of the most distinguished living American economists[9] has complained in a similar vein that the main task of those who believe in the basic principles of the capitalist system must frequently be to defend this system against the capitalists—indeed the great liberal economists, from Adam Smith to the present, have always known this.

The most serious obstacle which separates the practical men who have the cause of freedom genuinely at heart from those forces which in the realm of ideas decide the course of development is their deep distrust of theoretical speculation and their tendency to orthodoxy; this, more than

---

[7][Hayek refers here to *The Road to Serfdom*, op. cit.—Ed.]

[8]Lord Acton, "The History of Freedom in Antiquity", *The History of Freedom and Other Essays* (London: Macmillan, 1907; reprinted, Freeport, N. Y.: Books for Libraries, 1967), p. 1. [The English historian John Emerich Edward Dalberg-Acton, Baron Acton (1834–1902), was a Liberal MP from 1859 to 1864, leader of the Liberal Roman Catholics in England, and founder-editor of the *Cambridge Modern History,* to which he contributed the first two volumes.—Ed.]

[9][Hayek is probably referring to Frank Knight (1885–1962) of the University of Chicago, whose "Reply" followed Hayek's article.—Ed.]

anything else, creates an almost impassable barrier between them and those intellectuals who are devoted to the same cause and whose assistance is indispensable if the cause is to prevail. Although this tendency is perhaps natural among men who defend a system because it has justified itself in practice, and to whom its intellectual justification seems immaterial, it is fatal to its survival because it deprives it of the support it most needs. Orthodoxy of any kind, any pretense that a system of ideas is final and must be unquestioningly accepted as a whole, is the one view which of necessity antagonizes all intellectuals, whatever their views on particular issues. Any system which judges men by the completeness of their conformity to a fixed set of opinions, by their 'soundness' or the extent to which they can be relied upon to hold approved views on all points, deprives itself of a support without which no set of ideas can maintain its influence in modern society. The ability to criticize accepted views, to explore new vistas and to experiment with new conceptions, provides the atmosphere without which the intellectual cannot breathe. A cause which offers no scope for these traits can have no support from him and is thereby doomed in any society which, like ours, rests on his services.

VII

It may be that a free society as we have known it carries in itself the forces of its own destruction, that once freedom has been achieved it is taken for granted and ceases to be valued, and that the free growth of ideas which is the essence of a free society will bring about the destruction of the foundations on which it depends. There can be little doubt that in countries like the United States the ideal of freedom has today less real appeal for the young than it has in countries where they have learnt what its loss means. On the other hand, there is every sign that in Germany and elsewhere, to the young men who have never known a free society, the task of constructing one can become as exciting and fascinating as any socialist scheme which has appeared during the last hundred years. It is an extraordinary fact, though one which many visitors have experienced, that in speaking to German students about the principles of a liberal society one finds a more responsive and even enthusiastic audience than one can hope to find in any of the Western democracies. In Britain also there is already appearing among the young a new interest in the principles of true liberalism which certainly did not exist a few years ago.

Does this mean that freedom is valued only when it is lost, that the world must everywhere go through a dark phase of socialist totalitarianism before the forces of freedom can gather strength anew? It may be so, but I hope it need not be. Yet so long as the people who over longer

236

periods determine public opinion continue to be attracted by the ideals of socialism, the trend will continue. If we are to avoid such a development we must be able to offer a new liberal program which appeals to the imagination. We must make the building of a free society once more an intellectual adventure, a deed of courage. What we lack is a liberal Utopia, a program which seems neither a mere defense of things as they are nor a diluted kind of socialism, but truly liberal radicalism which does not spare the susceptibilities of the mighty (including the trade unions), which is not too severely practical and which does not confine itself to what appears today as politically possible. We need intellectual leaders who are prepared to resist the blandishments of power and influence and who are willing to work for an ideal, however small may be the prospects of its early realization. They must be men who are willing to stick to principles and to fight for their full realization, however remote. The practical compromises they must leave to the politicians. Free trade or the freedom of opportunity are ideals which still may arouse the imaginations of large numbers, but a mere 'reasonable freedom of trade' or a mere 'relaxation of controls' are neither intellectually respectable nor likely to inspire any enthusiasm.

The main lesson which the true liberal must learn from the success of the socialists is that it was their courage to be Utopian which gained them the support of the intellectuals and therefore an influence on public opinion which is daily making possible what only recently seemed utterly remote. Those who have concerned themselves exclusively with what seemed practicable in the existing state of opinion have constantly found that even this has rapidly become politically impossible as the result of changes in a public opinion which they have done nothing to guide. Unless we can make the philosophic foundations of a free society once more a living intellectual issue, and its implementation a task which challenges the ingenuity and imagination of our liveliest minds, the prospects of freedom are indeed dark. But if we can regain that belief in the power of ideas which was the mark of liberalism at its greatest, the battle is not lost. The intellectual revival of liberalism is already under way in many parts of the world. Will it be in time?

HAYEK'S REVIEWS OF THE LITERATURE

1. Review of S. and B. Webb, Soviet Communism: A New Civilization[1]

"An attractive world, and you visited it and did not notice this."[2] It is with this reproach that the Communist hero of a new Russian novel quoted in *Soviet Communism* defends his planned world against the foreign critic. No such complaint can be made against the two well-known authors to whom we owe this, the latest and by far the most thorough study of modern Russia. Apart from their undisputed mastery of the technique of investigating the structure of government, they bring to their task a strong sympathy with the aims and ideas of this 'new civilization'. Indeed, they seem to regard it, with much justice, as the realization of many of the ideals for which they have striven and worked for almost half a century. It is indeed probably true that Soviet Communism approaches more closely than anything we have yet seen to that synthetic, scientific civilization which appealed to the peculiar brand of late nineteenth-century rationalism of which the authors are among the most distinguished exponents.

The Whole Structure

The first volume gives a vivid and extraordinarily instructive description of the new machine of government and the whole social structure. As such it is incomparably more comprehensive and more detailed than any of the works which have so far been available, and it will inevitably supersede them all as the first and most complete source of information available. Extraordinary as it is that we have had to wait so long for a really satisfactory exposition, we should be grateful for the delay since from

---

[1][F. A. Hayek, "A 'Scientific' Civilization: The Webbs on Soviet Communism", Review of Sidney and Beatrice Webb, *Soviet Communism: A New Civilization?* (London: Longmans, Green, 1935; second ed., London and New York: Longmans, Green, 1937). The question mark was dropped from the title of the second edition. Hayek's review appeared in *The Times* (London), Sunday, January 5, 1936, p. 11. For more on the Webbs, see chapter 3, note 18.—Ed.]

[2][Sidney and Beatrice Webb, *Soviet Communism*, vol. 2, p. 791.—Ed.]

no other hands could we have hoped for the same combination of real competence and a labour of love.

It is, however, volume two, which deals with the functioning of the new system, which is at the same time the more interesting and the more controversial. It is the central question of the results of economic planning which, as the authors tell us, induced them "despite the disqualification of old age to try to understand what is happening in the USSR".[3] They have no doubt that "this new system of economic relationships, and this new motivation of wealth production" will prove permanently successful and that "it will afford the prospect of increase beyond all computation, alike of national wealth and individual well- being".[4] They heartily concur with the Communists that the employment of wage-labour for the making of profit, and the purchase of commodities in order to resell them at a profit, is an unmixed evil, and rejoice that, although the Communists are willing to make use of all other forms of self-interest as incentives to stimulate production, the profit motive is to be permanently excluded. But, like the Communists themselves, the authors have a curious blind spot which makes them unable to see either the function which profits serve in a capitalist society or the need for an alternative in a society differently organized.

Price System Success

It is, indeed, very clear from their exposition that in so far as the Communists have reintroduced the price mechanism they have been extraordinarily successful. This is particularly true in the labour market, where they have succeeded in making the price system work with an efficiency which, on account of the trade unions, exists nowhere in capitalistic countries.

But while with piecework and a competitive labour market there is no lack of sufficient incentives to efficient labour, and in consequence "the industrial shortcomings of the Soviet Union are to be seen less in the work of the individual operative", it is altogether different with "the manner in which his labour is coordinated and directed in mass production".[5] The authors are rather surprised that, "with so potent a set of incentives to efficiency" as that which they describe in great detail, "the industrial enterprises in the USSR, in comparison with those of Western Europe and the United States, still presented so general a picture of inefficiency".[6]

[3][*Ibid.*, p. 602.—Ed.]
[4][*Ibid.*—Ed.]
[5][*Ibid.*, p. 786.—Ed.]
[6][*Ibid.*, p. 785.—Ed.]

With the Russians they are inclined to put the blame on the lack of enthusiasm and loyalty of the intermediate class between the intellectual leaders and the manual workers, "the clerical workers in the national and municipal offices".[7] But although they themselves point to the difficulty arising out of the fact that the work of this class cannot be accurately measured, it does not seem to occur to them that these evils, which Lenin summarized as "bureaucracy", are here, as elsewhere, closely and inseparably bound up with the impossibility of applying the test of profitability.

They do, indeed, make much of the efforts to apply stringent methods of cost accounting and auditing in order to overcome these difficulties. But what does all this mean if it is not necessary "to worry about possible changes in the price that the customers. . .will pay for their commodities and services, because these prices are, for the most part, fixed, as part of the plan, by the Government itself".[8] For cost accounting, and bookkeeping generally, serves as a test of efficiency only because it is based on prices which reflect the relative scarcity of the different materials and productive factors, and thereby indicate to what extent it is necessary to economize them. If the planning authorities have discovered a method of determining and adjusting from day to day the relative 'social value' of the innumerable commodities, the authors do not at least tell us about it.

A Task Unsolved

Much more might be said about the way in which, prepossessed like their Russian friends with purely technical problems, the authors completely lose sight of the economic problems involved. The real problem of maximizing production does not consist, as they seem to believe, in using all existing resources *somehow,* but in using existing resources in the most effective manner. The Communists have not even attempted to solve this task, which is the function of the price mechanism in the capitalist society, save in so far as they have reintroduced the price system or just imitated the methods which were found profitable in capitalist countries.

It would be interesting to show, if space permitted, how all these shortcomings, and nearly all the peculiarities of the Communist civilization, can be traced to a mistaken belief in the exclusive value of those methods of thought which proved so eminently successful in the natural sciences and engineering in the second half of the nineteenth century of which the authors and the Russian leaders alike are true representatives.

Reason, 'dizzy with success' in these fields, seems to have presumed not only to lay down the methods of thought which alone should be followed

[7][*Ibid.*, p. 796.—Ed.]
[8][*Ibid.*, p. 661.—Ed.]

in the future, but also to stake out the path of its further development. Whether this 'scientific' civilization will really provide the best environment for the progress of mind and thereby ultimately also of material progress is a question on which considerable doubt is possible.

Will It Endure?

Mr. and Mrs. Webb fervently hope and believe that it will, and that it will spread and endure. Whatever the reader's opinion may be, he can only be grateful for their enthusiastic account of the "cult of science"[9] (always meaning pure science and technology) and the closely connected "disease of orthodoxy" which will be invaluable for the interpretation of the whole phenomenon by the future historian. One reader at least found himself rarely so much in agreement with the appraisal by the authors as with a passage quoted from a diary of Mrs. Webb of fifteen years ago in which she confesses that:

> One is tempted to wonder whether this creed does not consist almost entirely in an insistent demand for the subordination of each individual to the 'working plan' of the scientifically trained mind; though, of course, the plan is assumed to be devised in the interest of the community as a whole. . . .[10]

2. *Review of MacKenzie,* Planned Society: Yesterday, Today, Tomorrow[11]

This imposing tome, described on the title page as a "Symposium" by thirty-five authors, consists, to the extent of almost exactly one half of the separate articles contained in it, of reprints from other publications, while the other half appear to have been written specially for the occasion. The authors of the first group range from Stalin and Mussolini to Professors

---

[9][The "Cult of Science" is described in *ibid.*, pp. 1132–1134. According to the Webbs, " . . . the administrators in the Moscow Kremlin genuinely believe in their professed faith. And their professed faith is in science. No vested interests hinder them from basing their decisions and their policy upon the best science they can obtain. . . . The whole community is eager for new knowledge" (p. 1133). They compare this with conditions in the West, where "even the United States has shut down much of its scientific activity" (*ibid.*), a contrast that they do not find surprising.—Ed.]

[10][*Ibid.*, p. 617.—Ed.]

[11][F. A. Hayek, Review of Findlay MacKenzie, ed., *Planned Society: Yesterday, Today, Tomorrow. A Symposium by Thirty-Five Economists, Sociologists, and Statesmen* (New York: Prentice Hall, 1937). Hayek's review appeared in *Economica, N.S.*, vol. 5, August 1938, pp. 362–363. Findlay MacKenzie taught economics at Brooklyn College.—Ed.]

Gustav Cassel[12] and Sidney Hook,[13] while the original contributions also come from authors holding as diametrically opposed views as do Professor H. Gideonse[14] and Mr. George Soule.[15] The only sort of homogeneity one can expect from a volume of this kind is that the individual contributions make consistently interesting reading, and this has on the whole been achieved, although the omission of a few articles might have saved the reader who only dips into the volume from drawing one of the few blanks.

The work deals less with the technique than with the tasks and consequences of economic planning. The greater part of it, after two historical sections, is divided into a group of articles dealing with planning in particular areas of economic activity and a group discussing the planning of all economic activity. The contributions in the first group are highly informative, but particularly varied in character and quality, ranging from highly expert discussions of the general principles of monetary policy to discussions of the details of town planning and the regulation of particular industries. In the second group the discussion of the economics of planning is probably the least satisfactory part. Considerable space is devoted to a survey of the cultural effects of planning, and it is interesting to observe how much all the authors are concerned about the compatibility of planning with freedom and democracy. Whether this finds expression in outright scepticism on this point, or whether it leads the authors to reassert again and again that the two things are compatible without any attempt to show how this is to be achieved, it is at any rate clear that this begins to be recognized as the central problem. One cannot help wondering, however, whether Dr. Mitrany is not somewhat too optimistic when he warns us "that, within a generation, the 'planners' and all their works will be swept away by a violent revulsion of feeling if the material stability they promise has to be bought at the price of intellectual and spiritual oppression".[16]

The Editor has not taken his task easily and, in addition to a general introduction and short introductory notes to every essay, he has provided

[12][For more on Swedish economist Gustav Cassell (1866–1944), see this volume, chapter 1, note 13.—Ed.]

[13][For more on Hook, see this volume, chapter 9, note 5.—Ed.]

[14][Henry (Harry) Gideonse (1902–1985) was an associate professor of economics at the University of Chicago from 1930 to 1938. He served as President of Brooklyn College of the City University of New York from 1939 to 1966, and afterwards as Chancellor of the New School for Social Research.—Ed.]

[15][George Henry Soule (1887–1970) was from 1922 onwards a director-at-large of the National Bureau of Economic Research, and from 1924 to 1947 the Editor of *The New Republic*.—Ed.]

[16][Mitrany, in "Political Consequences of Economic Planning", op. cit., p. 662. For more on Mitrany, see this volume, chapter 9, note 5.—Ed.]

the reader with an ample and useful bibliography and short biographies of the individual contributors. It was evidently a labour of love, but one wonders whether the faith in planning which led him to undertake it has not been somewhat shaken in the course of his work. At any rate, it is hardly consistent with much faith in planning that he predicts that "War would disrupt a planned society even more completely than a society in which free enterprise would make immediate and continuous adjustments to the needs of war".[17]

This admission might well serve as a warning to those who seek to make the necessity of preparation for defense a new argument for further extending the planned sector of economic life.

3. Review of Snyder, Capitalism the Creator[18]

This book is likely to arouse a host of prejudices. Its theme, well described by the title, in itself will probably put off many of the readers who would profit most from its contents. The methodological axe which the author has to grind is likely to make another class of readers suspicious. And certain tricks of style—there are sometimes rows of sentences without a verb—will probably irritate many more. Yet it would be most regrettable if these facts deprived the book of the deserved success. It deals with problems of profound importance. It does so lucidly and effectively. And the author shows in consistently maintaining a highly unpopular attitude towards the great problems of our day an intellectual courage which is rarely found.

Mr. Snyder is a rare and almost unique figure in that, although by training and sympathy a pure scientist, an enthusiast for the application of the methods of the natural sciences to social phenomena, and full of the contempt for "theoretical speculation" which usually accompanies this view, he has not by this been led to advocate "planning", "conscious control", and still less to any heretical views on currency, as is the case with so many, if not most, of the scientists and engineers who have turned their minds to social problems. On the contrary, as will be known to most of the readers of this journal, Mr. Snyder thoroughly believes in the freedom of enterprise, and, though in so far as currency matters are con-

---

[17][MacKenzie, "Introduction", op. cit., p. xx.—Ed.]

[18][F. A. Hayek, Review of Carl Snyder, *Capitalism the Creator: The Economic Foundations of Modern Industrial Society* (New York: Macmillan, 1940). Hayek's review appeared in *Economica*, N.S., vol. 7, November 1940, pp. 437–439. Statistician and author Carl Snyder (1869–1946), President of the American Statistical Association in 1928, wrote frequently on economics.—Ed.]

cerned he believes in control, his views there are much closer to those of the great liberal writers of the nineteenth century, and particularly of the Currency School,[19] than to the fashionable views of our day.

In support of these views Mr. Snyder marshalls a most impressive body of evidence on the rate of progress which capitalism has made possible during the last two or three generations, drawing from an unusually wide and varied stock of knowledge. And as we would expect from an acknowledged master in the field of the statistical study of economic phenomena, the present attempt to make the gist of his more specialized studies accessible to a wider public throws much new light on interesting aspects of economic evolution.

But Mr. Snyder aims at more. He hopes to refute by his array of facts the views now prevalent on the dangers of over-saving, the necessity of planning, and the desirability of abolishing capitalism in general. Yet, although I happen entirely to agree with him on almost all these points, I fear that his facts will convince few who hold contrary opinions. His argument moves throughout on the level of sound, I believe very sound, common sense. But this is scarcely sufficient to refute the current, highly complicated theories—Mr. Snyder would probably say sophistries—by which these facts can be given an entirely different interpretation. While the 'modern' economists who no longer believe in the crucial importance of a sufficient supply of savings for industrial progress, or in the prevention of credit expansion as the only feasible prevention of depression, would do well carefully to study and to ponder over Mr. Snyder's facts, I am afraid the issue will have to be settled in that sphere of abstract reasoning for which Mr. Snyder has so little patience. Although he would probably not admit it, his own interpretation of facts is everywhere, and inevitably, based on theories which differ from those of the theoreticians only by not being stated explicity. In fact the absence of those precise definitions which constitute so large a part of all theoretical work in places considerably weakens his argument. To give a single, but characteristic instance, the author leaves it rather obscure, whether by 'capitalism' he merely means production with the help of large quantities of capital, or the system of free enterprise and private ownership of the means of production to which it is commonly applied. The reference to Böhm-Bawerk when the author undertakes to "show what capitalism is by considering what cap-

---

[19][Debates between members of the Currency School, Banking School, and Free Banking School took place in Britain from the late 1820s through the 1840s. The Currency School wanted the monetary authorities to regulate the quantity of paper currency so that its behaviour would mimic that of gold. For Hayek's account of the debates, see chapter 12, *The Trend of Economic Thinking*, op. cit.—Ed.]

italism does"[20] and the use of the term "state-capitalism" for the present Russian system suggest the former interpretation, but much of the argument of the book would lose its point if it were really meant in this sense.

There is much incidental useful information in the book which cannot be mentioned in a brief review. But special attention may perhaps be drawn to the short but illuminating account of the circumstances which determined the policy of the Federal Reserve System in the crucial period 1927–1928 that has puzzled many writers.[21] The 44 statistical charts which the book contains deserve close separate study, but they have unfortunately not been sufficiently related to the text.

4. Review of Polanyi, Contempt of Freedom: The Russian Experiment and After, *and Clark,* A Critique of Russian Statistics[22]

The four essays which Professor Polanyi has collected in the first of these volumes were, as the preface explains, written during the five years between 1935 and 1940 when the ideas of liberty "were left almost uncultivated" and "the progressive minds were so fascinated by the prospects of the revolution in Russia that they had little interest left for the fate of the traditional liberties".[23] In the first and the last of these essays the author deals, *suaviter in modo, fortiter in re,* with two instances of (although he is too polite to describe them so) that *trahison de clercs* which threatens liberty in this country: Professor J. D. Bernal's book on *The Social Function of Science*[24] and Mr. and Mrs. Sidney Webb's *Soviet Communism.*[25] The third essay, on "Soviet Economics—Fact and Theory", already deservedly well known, gives a most careful and, at the time of its first publication (1935), unrivalled statistical analysis of economic development in Soviet Russia.

---

[20][Snyder, *Capitalism the Creator,* op. cit., pp. 120, 436. For more on Böhm-Bawerk, see chapter 1, note 12.—Ed.]

[21][*Ibid.,* pp. 227–228.—Ed.]

[22][F. A. Hayek, Review of Michael Polanyi, *The Contempt of Freedom: The Russian Experiment and After* (London: Watts, 1940; reprinted, New York: Arno Press, 1975), and Colin Clark, *A Critique of Russian Statistics* (London: Macmillan, 1939). Hayek's review appeared in *Economica,* N.S., vol. 8, May 1941, pp. 211–214. See chapter 10, note 8, for more on Polanyi. Colin Clark (1905–), who graduated in chemistry from Oxford in 1924, went on to teach and hold government posts in England, the United States, and Australia. He was a pioneer in the estimation of national income statistics.—Ed.]

[23][Polanyi, *Contempt of Freedom,* op. cit., p. v.—Ed.]

[24][Hayek refers to J. D. Bernal, *The Social Function of Science,* op. cit. The physicist John Desmond Bernal (1901–1971) was an advocate of the 'rational' reorganization and planning of science. He was instrumental in the postwar era in re-establishing contacts with scientists in Communist countries.—Ed.]

[25][Hayek refers to Sidney and Beatrice Webb, *Soviet Communism,* op cit. For Hayek's review of their book, see this chapter, section 1.—Ed.]

The second essay in the book, finally, on "Collectivist Planning", deals with some of the more general problems raised in particular contexts by the others. It has not been previously published.

The analysis of Professor Bernal's book in the essay on the "Rights and Duties of Science" is perhaps the most illuminating discussion yet attempted of the psychological propensities which so frequently turn the man of science into an ardent advocate of central planning, and of the inconsistencies which this attitude involves. While Professor Polanyi has no doubt that "the major force behind this attitude is the passionate desire to put science into the consciously organized service of human welfare",[26] he is convinced that a consistent policy of "organizing" all scientific research on the lines advocated by Professor Bernal "would actually stop the development of science altogether".[27] And he points out that, characteristically, "all the brilliant and instructive pages of the book have no answer to the question: How should the progress of science be directed in order that it may benefit human welfare?"[28] The picture of the reality of controlled science in Russia, for which, apart from his own direct experience, Professor Polanyi can draw extensively on the Webbs, tends to confirm his worst apprehensions.

The new essay on "Collectivist Planning" is in many ways a further development on the same theme. As a contribution by an eminent scientist to the much discussed question, it deserves full attention, and there is much in it from which the economist can profit. Particularly interesting is the emphasis that "the term 'decentralized planning' is . . . contradictory. The essence of planning is unity achieved by control from a centre".[29] But: "as in the case of science, the comprehensive view is not an essential view but a superficial view and an ignorant view. From it not a single business proposition could be made which would not be rejected out of hand by any businessman of special experience as grossly unprofitable, and which hence—in nine cases out of ten—would not also be grossly wasteful from the point of view of society as a whole."[30] And Professor Polanyi's conclusion is that "general planning is wholesale destruction of freedom; cultural planning would be the end of all inspired inquiry, of every creative effort, and planned economy would make life into something between a universal monastery and a forced labour camp."[31]

[26][Polanyi, *Contempt of Freedom*, op. cit., p. 17.—Ed.]
[27][*Ibid.*, p. 8.—Ed.]
[28][*Ibid.*, p. 18.—Ed.]
[29][*Ibid.*, p. 45.—Ed.]
[30][*Ibid.*, pp. 51–52.—Ed.]
[31][*Ibid.*, p. 60.—Ed.]

Although the essay on "Soviet Economics" is now largely superseded by the second book to be reviewed here, it is remarkable how well its main conclusions have been confirmed by the more detailed and extensive investigations of Mr. Colin Clark, for which Professor Polanyi's study seems indeed to have served as a starting point. Although Mr. Colin Clark is able to point out several errors of detail and has of course been able to draw, not only on more comprehensive material, but also on much later information, the picture which emerges for the period up to 1934 is essentially unchanged—although Mr. Clark is able to report some substantial improvement since. But such conclusions as that food consumption per head in Russia in 1934 was much reduced as compared with 1913 and was 30 per cent below that found by Sir John Orr for the worst fed 10 per cent of the British population[32] (and according to Mr. Clark this has only slightly improved up to 1937, which is the last year on record), and that "the housing of the workers, which, according to a Soviet writer, was in 1928 'more terrible than those described by Engels during the Industrial Revolution in England',[33] suffered a drastic deterioration during the following four years", still stand.

Mr. Clark's *Critique of Russian Statistics* is not so much a direct critique of official Russian figures as an attempt to arrive, from whatever figures are available, at reliable information about the development of the national income of Russia and its distribution. If the closely packed 69 pages of the text are not precisely easy reading, they ought nevertheless to be carefully studied by anybody seriously interested in Russia. Quite apart from the general problem of the success of the socialist experiment, the analysis of the available figures throws extremely interesting sidelights on a number of important and even highly topical questions. That Russia's main problem is still the Malthusian Devil, which Mr. Clark thinks she is only just beginning to corner by absorbing the whole of her population increase in industry, is distinctly interesting; and those who hope for some sort of international socialist regime might well ponder over Mr. Clark's comment on what he calls "the irony of almost cosmic grandeur ... Soviet Russia struggling with huge and uncontrollable increases of population at a time when the economic and political structure of the West is beginning to tremble before the approaching blast of depopulation":[34] indeed, "American and British statesmen who celebrated their

[32][The Scottish biologist Sir John Orr (1880–1971) was for thirty years Director of the Rowett Research Institute. His studies in the mid–1930s on the relation of income to food supply and health found that 10 per cent of Britons were badly undernourished, and only 50 per cent had enough income to afford the sufficiently varied diet that was deemed necessary for normal health.—Ed.]

[33][Polanyi, *Contempt of Freedom*, op. cit., p. 71.—Ed.]

[34][Clark, *Critique of Russian Statistics*, op. cit., pp. 53–54.—Ed.]

victory in the war by complacently blocking up these channels of migration, little knew what their countries would later have to answer for".[35] Of the points of information of special immediate interest one may be mentioned here: the density and congestion of traffic on the Russian Railways, which (measured in million ton kms per km per annum) even in 1913 with 1.13 was higher than in any other country, had by 1936 risen to 3.80, or 3-1/2 times the former figure!

That Mr. Clark handles all the difficult problems which any utilization of Russian statistics raises with the virtuosity we have learnt to expect from him, the readers of this journal will hardly need to be told. As a specimen of his main results, the following figures, combined from two of his tables,[36] may be of general interest:

	Sterling value of output per head			
	1913	1928	1934	1937
Agriculture	51.5	45.3	37.5	42.5
Non-Agriculture ..	76.1	84.8	85.5	122.2
Weighted Average ..	58.5	55.5	51.0	72.3

The significance of these figures must be judged with reference to the following numbers of persons occupied in Agricultural and Non- Agricultural production respectively:

	Numbers engaged (millions)			
	1913	1928	1934	1937
Agriculture	34.1	38.2	39.8	40.1
Non-Agriculture ..	13.85	13.1	21.1	24.0
Total	47.95	51.3	60.9	64.1

5. Review of Burnham, The Managerial Revolution[37]

What in the title of this interesting book is described as the "managerial revolution" is to all intents and purposes the phenomenon of the totalitarian transformation of society which the author's "historical theory" makes him regard as the inevitable sequence of capitalism. If one grants the author's initial premises, that under "capitalism" large-scale unemploy-

[35][*Ibid.*, p. 54.—Ed.]

[36][The charts are found in *ibid.*, pp. 49 and 68.—Ed.]

[37][F. A. Hayek, Review of James Burnham, *The Managerial Revolution, or What Is Happening in the World Right Now* (New York: John Day, 1942; London: Putnam, 1942). Hayek's review appeared in *Economica, N. S.,* vol. 9, November 1942, pp. 401–402. James Burnham (1905–1987) was a professor of philosophy at Washington Square College of New York University from 1929 to 1953, and from 1955 to 1987 a member of the editorial board of *The National Review.*—Ed.]

ment is inevitable and that therefore the tendency towards complete central direction of all economic activity must continue, his conclusions are probably inescapable. The picture of the "managerial society" is realistically and skillfully drawn and deserves careful study, particularly by those who by their desire for such a system make its eventual establishment by no means unlikely. It is made specially interesting by the evidently Marxist background of the author's argument which leads him to the very un-Marxist conclusions, and by the fact that his exposition is so largely based on experiences in the United States during and since the New Deal.

While the author attempts to paint a strictly detached and scientific picture of what he regards as the inevitable developments, and while the picture which he paints of this future is certainly not attractive, his sympathies are yet clearly with the 'new' as against the 'old' system. It is "the Germany of 1933 and of now" which is "the nuclear first stage in the development of that super-state of the future"[38] which he sees coming, and the "social systems of England and France at the outset of the Second World War were remnants of the past, Germany's a start towards the future".[39] But Russia is "the nation most advanced towards the managerial structure",[40] though she is likely ultimately to be absorbed by the German-dominated European block. The author seems to have little doubt that Germany will ultimately emerge victorious from the present conflict (the book was first published in America in 1941!) and in his opinion "Germany had, of course, to accept the challenge"[41] of the backward Western powers, while the war still continues only because "the English capitalists weighed the costs and decided to keep on fighting".[42]

One of the most illuminating passages in the book is a pen- picture of the type of men who run the New Deal and in whom the author sees the type of the future managers of society. Since this passage seems also well to describe the background against which the doctrines of the book ought to be seen, it will bear quoting at some length: "The firmest representatives of the New Deal are not Roosevelt or other conspicuous 'New Deal Politicians', but the younger group of administrators, technicians, bureaucrats, who have been finding places through the state apparatus: not merely those who specialize in political technique, in writing up laws with concealed 'jokers', in handing Roosevelt a dramatic new idea, but also those who are doing the actual running of the extending government enterprises: in short, managers. These men include some of the clearest-

[38][Burnham, *The Managerial Revolution*, op. cit., p. 251.—Ed.]
[39][*Ibid.*, p. 235.—Ed.]
[40][*Ibid.*, p. 159.—Ed.]
[41][*Ibid.*, p. 246.—Ed.]
[42][*Ibid.*, p. 247.—Ed.]

headed of all managers to be found in any country. They are confident and aggressive. Though many of them have some background in Marxism, they have no faith in the masses of such a sort as to lead them to believe in the ideal of a free, classless society. At the same time they are, sometimes openly, scornful of capitalists and capitalist ideas. They are ready to work with anyone and are not so squeamish as to insist that their words should coincide with their actions and aims. They believe that they can run things, and they like to run things."[43]

There are several points in the detail of the argument, such as the presentation of the rise of the managerial class as a cause rather than as an effect of the transformation of society, or the treatment of competitive capitalism as a short phase rather than the greater part of the known history of Western civilization, with which one might quarrel. But as, if one accepts the initial premises, these minor points are not likely to affect the conclusions, they are hardly worth dwelling upon. However much one may disagree with the asserted inevitability of the developments the author sketches, its possibility and even likelihood cannot be gainsaid. The book is one which one hopes will be widely read by intelligent and thoughtful people, though there is every reason to fear its effects on those who are likely to be swayed by a plausible exposition of supposedly "inevitable tendencies". And though the true part of the author's thesis is probably little more than the contention, advanced by Hilaire Belloc thirty years ago, that "the effect of Socialist doctrine on Capitalist society is to produce a third thing different from either of its begetters—to wit, the Servile State"[44], its exposition in the frightening realism of the author's setting may nevertheless prove to be of considerable importance.

6. Review of Carr, Nationalism and After[45]

This brief survey of the changing character of nationalism shows Professor Carr's views in a state of transition, but does not make it quite clear

[43][*Ibid*., pp. 254–255.—Ed.]

[44][French-born British writer and poet Hilaire Belloc (1870–1953), friend to G. K. Chesterton and writer of children's verse, was also the author of the *The Servile State* [1912] (2nd ed., London and Edinburgh: T. N. Foulis, 1913; reprinted, Indianapolis: Liberty*Classics*, 1977), from which Hayek drew this quote (p. 32). Hayek repeated the quotation in *The Road to Serfdom*, op. cit., p. 13, note 2, adding that Belloc's book "explains more of what has happened since in Germany than most works written after the event".—Ed.]

[45][F. A. Hayek, "The End of Nationalism?", Review of Edward Hallett Carr, *Nationalism and After* (London: Macmillan, 1945). Hayek's review appeared in *The Spectator*, March 16, 1945, p. 248. The historian and author Edward Hallett Carr (1892–1982) was Wilson Professor of International Politics at the University College of Wales from 1936 to 1947, a tutor in politics at Balliol College, Oxford, from 1935 to 1955, and from 1955 to 1982 a Fellow of Trinity College, Cambridge.—Ed.]

where he is moving. If for that reason he appears sure of himself, the book also shows that he has learnt to see dangers of which before he seemed oblivious. Some of his statements clearly strike a new note: "'Planned economy' is a Janus with a nationalist as well as a socialist face; if its doctrine seems socialist, its pedigree is unimpeachably nationalist."[46] Or: "In the national community the concentration of all authority in a single central organ means an intolerable and unmitigated totalitarianism."[47] For this progress Professor Carr seems indebted mainly to Dr. F. Borkenau's valuable *Socialism, National or International*,[48] and perhaps to a delayed-action effect of his study of Lord Acton.[49] At the same time, the influence of Karl Mannheim and his doctrine of the "collective freedom of the group"[50] has receded to the extent that he now emphasizes that "it is only by a conventional metaphor, which easily becomes a cliche, and is sometimes barely distinguishable from the Hitlerian exaltation of the nation as an object of worship and an end in itself, that freedom is attributed to nations".[51]

The rapid sketch of the three main phases in the past development of nationalism, with which the book opens, is well drawn, but so compressed that Professor Carr hardly does himself justice. He feels evidently more at home in the periods which preceded and followed the liberal age, and betrays a curious inability to understand the working of a free economic system when he represents the Bank of England, in no merely metaphorical sense, as "the seat of the Government in the laissez-faire age".[52] This suggests an approach significantly like that of the Germans, who, it is said, were so surprised by the efficiency of the black market in Belgium that all their countermeasures were concentrated on an illusory search

[46][Carr, *Nationalism and After*, op. cit., p. 24.—Ed.]

[47][*Ibid.*, p. 51.—Ed.]

[48][Hayek refers to the Austrian Franz Borkenau (1900–1957), whose book *Socialism, National or International* (London: Routledge, 1942) Carr cites on p. 20.—Ed.]

[49][Carr's book begins with the following quotation from Lord Acton: "Nationality does not aim either at liberty or prosperity, both of which it sacrifices to the imperative necessity of making the nation the mould and measure of the state. Its course will be marked with material as well as moral ruin. . . ." The quotation was taken from Acton's article "Nationality" [1862], reprinted in *The History of Freedom and Other Essays*, op. cit., p. 299. For more on Acton, see chapter 11, note 8.—Ed.]

[50][Hungarian-born sociologist Karl Mannheim (1893–1947) taught at Heidelberg and Frankfurt before fleeing to the London School of Economics in 1933. Remembered today principally for his work in the sociology of knowledge, he used the term "collective freedom of the group" in his book *Man and Society in an Age of Reconstruction: Studies in Modern Social Structure*, translated by Edward Shils (London: Kegan Paul, 1940), p. 377 passim.—Ed.]

[51][Carr, *Nationalism and After*, op. cit., pp. 42–43.—Ed.]

[52][*Ibid.*, p. 16.—Ed.]

for the master-brain which they imagined must be responsible for that perfection!

Professor Carr thinks it probable that we may now be entering a fourth phase, during which the importance of nationalism will decline before the obvious need for the integration into larger economic units. The old hankering after an organized *Grossraumwirtschaft*[53] is still there, but it is no longer, as in his earlier books, to be "of the kind that Hitler has undertaken".[54] Professor Carr has come to see many of the objections to, and difficulties of, such a scheme. Most important of all, he has ceased to believe "in the possibility of achieving a community of nations; it now seems to me that this belief must be abandoned".[55] In its place the hope of the future is to lie in regional agreements and a progressive intermingling of national affairs "through an indefinite number of organizations cutting across national divisions and exercising authority for specific and limited purposes over individuals and functional groups".[56]

The picture which emerges is a little blurred and indistinct. If there are no such sweeping generalizations as those which in Professor Carr's earlier books were the source of inspiration or irritation to different groups of readers, it is at the price of leaving his conception somewhat vague, and most of the difficulties unresolved. This may be inevitable in so small a book, but even a sense of urgency is scarcely a justification for treating such a big subject on so small a canvas. Professor Carr is probably right in believing that the nationalism of the smaller states will, in fact, be given less scope than in the past, and that for some time at least the aggressive nationalism of the younger nations will disappear. But his argument provides hardly adequate grounds for his more far-reaching optimism about a gradual disappearance of nationalism. It may well be that for some time to come it will be the old national states of Western Europe where nationalism, not of an aggressive, but of an obstructionist kind, and closely allied to socialism, will form the main obstacle to a sensible solution of the great problems of international order.

---

[53][*Grossraumwirtschaft* translates as "extensive area economy", and refers to the integration of other economies into an expanding German economy.—Ed.]

[54][Carr, *Nationalism and After*, op. cit. This passage does not appear in Carr's book, but the discussion on pp. 35–36 seems to correspond to Hayek's point.—Ed.]

[55][*Ibid.*, p. 44, note 1.—Ed.]

[56][*Ibid.*, p. 52.—Ed.]

EDITOR'S ACKNOWLEDGEMENTS

I would like to thank Jack Birner, Homer Erekson, Andreas Lixl-Purcell, and Karl Milford for their assistance in tracking down information for some particularly obscure footnote citations. Jack Birner, Stephan Boehm, Pete Boettke, Stephen Kresge, and two referees gave my introduction a careful reading and saved me from many errors of fact and infelicities of style. Research assistance was dutifully provided by Shelly Pratt, Faye Newton, and Ian Petta. Finally, General Editor Stephen Kresge has provided his help on innumerable occasions and in innumerable ways. To all of them, thanks.

Bruce Caldwell
Greensboro, North Carolina
March 1996

NAME INDEX

SUBJECT INDEX